Sport and the Emancipation of European Women: The Struggle for Self-Fulfilment

Sport and the Emancipation of European Women: The Struggle for Self-Fulfilment explores the contribution of women in various parts of Europe. It expands understanding of the need for their attitudes and actions but also celebrates their achievements in freeing the female body from unwarranted political, cultural and social restraint in the brave pursuit of the Enlightenment's secular values of 'the unity of mankind and basic personal freedoms and the world of tolerance, knowledge, education and opportunity' (Roy Porter, *Enlightenment: Britain and the Creation of the Modern World*, 2004).

The collection records the pulling down of European barriers via the medium of sport to the realisation of ability and the release of talent, and the pushing aside of crushing inhibitions, inexcusable irrationality, intolerable prejudice and denial of opportunity. No barriers came down without a struggle.

The struggle to overturn them, set for the *first* time in the context of recent European history and the recent evolution of European sport, is described in this pioneering collection – the first publication to focus specifically on European women and their struggle for emancipation via sport.

This collection was published as a special issue of the *International Journal of the History of Sport*.

Gigliola Gori, doctoral degree from Göttingen, Germany, is Professor at the "Carlo Bo" University of Urbino, Italy. Her recent publications focus on the history of Physical Education and Sport in connection with politics, medicine, literature, education, dance and gender in the 19th and 20th centuries. Author of numerous articles and several books, she is co-founder and fellow of CESH, and Honorary Member and Vice-President of ISHPES.

J.A. Mangan, Emeritus Professor, University of Strathclyde, Ph.D., D. Litt., FRHS, FRAI is Founding Editor of the *International Journal of the History of Sport* and the series *Sport in the Global Society*, author of the globally acclaimed *Athleticism in the Victorian and Edwardian Public School, The Games Ethic and Imperialism* and '*Manufactured' Masculinity: Making Imperial Manliness, Morality and Militarism* and author or editor of some fifty publications on politics, culture, and sport.

Sport and the Emancipation of European Women

The Struggle for Self-Fulfilment

Edited by
Gigliola Gori and J. A. Mangan

Routledge
Taylor & Francis Group
LONDON AND NEW YORK

First published 2014
by Routledge
2 Park Square, Milton Park, Abingdon, Oxon, OX14 4RN

Simultaneously published in the USA and Canada
by Routledge
711 Third Avenue, New York, NY 10017

Routledge is an imprint of the Taylor & Francis Group, an informa business

© 2014 Taylor & Francis

British Library Cataloguing in Publication Data
A catalogue record for this book is available from the British Library

ISBN13: 978-0-415-86984-3

Typeset in Times New Roman
by Taylor & Francis Books

Publisher's Note
The publisher accepts responsibility for any inconsistencies that may have arisen during the conversion of this book from journal articles to book chapters, namely the possible inclusion of journal terminology.

Disclaimer
Every effort has been made to contact copyright holders for their permission to reprint material in this book. The publishers would be grateful to hear from any copyright holder who is not here acknowledged and will undertake to rectify any errors or omissions in future editions of this book.

Contents

CONTENTS

SERIES EDITORS' FOREWORD

On January 1 2010, *Sport in the Global Society*, created by Professor J.A. Mangan in 1997, was divided into two parts: *Historical Perspectives* and *Contemporary Perspectives*. These new categories involve predominant rather than exclusive emphases. The past is part of the present and the present is part of the past. The Editors of *Historical Perspectives* are Mark Dyreson and Thierry Terret.

The reasons for the division are straightforward. SGS has expanded rapidly since its creation with over one hundred publications in some twelve years. Its editorial teams will now benefit from sectional specialist interests and expertise. *Historical Perspectives* draws on *International Journal of the History of Sport* monograph reviews, themed collections and conference/workshop collections. It is, of course, international in content.

Historical Perspectives continues the tradition established by the original incarnation of *Sport in the Global Society* by promoting the academic study of one of the most significant and dynamic forces in shaping the historical landscapes of human cultures. Sport spans the contemporary globe. It captivates vast audiences. It defines, alters, and reinforces identities for individuals, communities, nations, empires, and the world. Sport organises memories and perceptions, arouses passions and tensions, and reveals harmonies and cleavages. It builds and blurs social boundaries, animating discourses about class, gender, race, and ethnicity. Sport opens new vistas on the history of human cultures, intersecting with politics and economics, ideologies and theologies. It reveals aesthetic tastes and energises consumer markets.

By the end of the twentieth century a critical mass of scholars recognised the importance of sport in their analyses of human experiences and *Sport in the Global Society* emerged to provide an international outlet for the world's leading investigators of the subject. As Professor Mangan contended in the original series foreword: "The story of modern sport is the story of the modern world—in microcosm; a modern global tapestry permanently being woven. Furthermore, nationalist and imperialist, philosopher and politician, radical and conservative have all sought in sport a manifestation of national identity, status and superiority. Finally for countless millions sport is the personal pursuit of ambition, assertion, well-being and enjoyment."

Sport in the Global Society: Historical Perspectives continues the project, building on previous work in the series and excavating new terrain. It remains a consistent and coherent response to the attention the academic community demands for the serious study of sport.

Mark Dyreson
Thierry Terret

SPORT IN THE GLOBAL SOCIETY – HISTORICAL PERSPECTIVES

Series Editors: Mark Dyreson and Thierry Terret

SPORT AND THE EMANCIPATION OF EUROPEAN WOMEN

The Struggle for Self-Fulfilment

Sport in the Global Society: Historical Perspectives
Series Editors: Mark Dyreson and Thierry Terret

As Robert Hands in *The Times* recently observed, the growth of sports studies in recent years has been considerable. This unique series with over one hundred volumes in the last decade has played its part. Politically, culturally, emotionally and aesthetically, sport is a major force in the modern world. Its impact will grow as the world embraces ever more tightly the contemporary secular trinity: the English language, technology and sport. *Sport in the Global Society* will continue to record sport's phenomenal progress across the world stage.

Sport in the Cultures of the Ancient World
New Perspectives
Edited by Zinon Papakonstantinou

Sport in the Pacific
Colonial and Postcolonial Consequences
Edited by C. Richard King

Sport, Literature, Society
Cultural Historical Studies
*Edited by Alexis Tadié, J. A. Mangan
and Supriya Chaudhuri*

Sport, Militarism and the Great War
Martial Manliness and Armageddon
*Edited by Thierry Terret and
J.A. Mangan*

Sport Past and Present in South Africa
(Trans)forming the Nation
*Edited by Scarlet Cornelissen and
Albert Grundlingh*

**The Balkan Games and Balkan Politics
in the Interwar Years 1929-1939**
Politicians in Pursuit of Peace
Penelope Kissoudi

The Beijing Olympics: Promoting China
Soft and Hard Power in Global Politics
Edited by Kevin Caffrey

The History of Motor Sport
A Case Study Analysis
Edited by David Hassan

**The Politicisation of Sport in Modern
China**
Communists and Champions
Fan Hong and Lu Zhouxiang

The Politics of the Male Body in Sport
The Danish Involvement
Hans Bonde

**The Rise of Stadiums in the Modern
United States**
Cathedrals of Sport
*Edited by Mark Dyreson and
Robert Trumpbour*

The Triple Asian Olympics
Asia Rising - the Pursuit of National
Identity, International Recognition
and Global Esteem
*Edited by J.A. Mangan, Sandra Collins
and Gwang Ok*

**The Triple Asian Olympics – Asia
Ascendant**
Media, Politics and Geopolitics
*Edited by J. A. Mangan, Luo Qing and
Sandra Collins*

The Visual in Sport
*Edited by Mike Huggins and Mike
O'Mahony*

Women, Sport, Society
Further Reflections, Reaffirming Mary
Wollstonecraft
*Edited by Roberta Park and
Patricia Vertinsky*

Sport in the Global Society
Past SGS publications prior to 2010

Sport in Australasian Society
Past and Present
Edited by J.A. Mangan and
John Nauright

Sport in Europe
Politics, Class, Gender
Edited by J.A. Mangan

Sport in Films
Edited by Emma Poulton and
Martin Roderick

Sport in Latin American Society
Past and Present
Edited by Lamartine DaCosta and
J.A. Mangan

Sport in South Asian Society
Past and Present
Edited by Boria Majumdar and
J.A. Mangan

Sport in the Cultures of the Ancient
World
New Perspectives
Edited by Zinon Papakonstantinou

Sport, Media, Culture
Global and Local Dimensions
Edited by Alina Bernstein and Neil Blain

Sport, Nationalism and Orientalism
The Asian Games
Edited by Fan Hong

Sport Tourism
Edited by Heather J. Gibson

Sporting Cultures
Hispanic Perspectives on Sport, Text
and the Body
Edited by David Wood and
P. Louise Johnson

Sporting Nationalisms
Identity, Ethnicity, Immigration and
Assimilation
Edited by Mike Cronin and
David Mayall

Superman Supreme
Fascist Body as Political Icon –
Global Fascism
Edited by J.A. Mangan

Terrace Heroes
The Life and Times of the 1930s
Professional Footballer
Graham Kelly

The Balkan Games and Balkan Politics
in the Interwar Years 1929-1939
Politicians in Pursuit of Peace
Penelope Kissoudi

The Changing Face of the Football
Business
Supporters Direct
Edited by Sean Hamil, Jonathan Michie,
Christine Oughton and Steven Warby

The Commercialisation of Sport
Edited by Trevor Slack

The Cultural Bond
Sport, Empire, Society
Edited by J.A. Mangan

The First Black Footballer
Arthur Wharton 1865–1930: An
Absence of Memory
Phil Vasili

The Football Manager
A History
Neil Carter

The Future of Football
Challenges for the Twenty-First Century
Edited by Jon Garland, Dominic
Malcolm and Mike Rowe

Citation Information

The chapters in this book were originally published in the *International Journal of the History of Sport*, volume 29, issue 2 (February 2012). When citing this material, please use the original page numbering for each article, as follows:

CITATION INFORMATION

J.A. Mangan
International Journal of the History of Sport, volume 29, issue 2 (February 2012) pp. 374-384

Please direct any queries you may have about the citations to clsuk.permissions@cengage.com

Foreword

Roberta J. Park

University of California, Berkeley, USA

The last half century has witnessed remarkable progress by women in many aspects of life. Advances have not been uniform throughout the world but they have been remarkable. Sport has been of major importance in achieving this advance.

Over 200 years ago Mary Wollstonecraft (often referred to as 'the first great feminist') stated in her treatise *A Vindication of the Rights of Woman* (1792) that girls should be allowed to take 'the same exercises as boys'. Her contemporary la Duchesse de Genlis set out exercises for girls and as well as for boys in *Leçons d'une Gouvernante à ses Élèves* (1791) and similar works. More than a century later in 1850 Elizabeth Cady Stanton, the major architect of the nineteenth-century American 'woman's rights' movement, declared: 'We cannot say what the woman might be physically, if the girl were allowed all the freedom of the boy in romping, swimming, climbing, and playing hoop and ball.'[1] In the early-twentieth–century, the Chinese feminist Qui Jin, who 'blamed women themselves for their traditionally subservient position', became proficient in archery and sword fencing.[2] Each of these women was 'ahead of her time'. But time has caught up with them!

Stanton also stated that women had the inalienable right to vote in national elections. New Zealand, Australia, Finland and Norway granted this 'inalienable right' before the United States did in 1920 – the beginning of a decade that ushered in increasing opportunities for females to participate in major sporting events. In spite of Pierre de Coubertin's insistence that they never be part of the Olympic Games, 277 of the athletes at the 1928 Amsterdam Olympics were women. However, this was only slightly less than 10%. Eight decades later 42% of the 11,196 participating athletes at the 2008 Beijing Olympics were women!

The Second World War resulted in large numbers of women in many countries entering into occupations that previously had been considered to be largely, if not exclusively, the province of males. When the war ended many were reluctant to be confined solely to routine customary 'women's duties'. The 'door to new freedoms' having been opened, when the war ended many were reluctant to be confined to customary 'women's duties'.

In the 1960s Betty Friedan, among others, in *The Feminine Mystique* (1963)[3] took up the feminist cause and within a short time what has been referred to as the 'Second Wave' of feminism was on the rise in a number of countries. One of its many consequences was an increase in the number of women engaging in major sporting events. In countries where traditional values remained powerful, of course, advances were considerably slower, as evidenced in the essay 'Women's Sport in Portugal From 1974 to 2000' in *Sport and the Physical Emancipation of European Women*.

During the 1980s Carroll Smith-Rosenberg's *Disorderly Conduct: Visions of Gender in Victorian America* (1985)[4] discussed the growing refusal to accept gender-role divisions as natural, and the rising interest in 'gender studies' offered new dimensions to studies of the history of women and sport. By way of illustration, the final section of *Disorderly Conduct* is entitled 'The New Woman as Androgyne: Social Disorder and Gender Crisis, 1870–1930'. *From 'Fair Sex' to Feminism: Sport and the Socialization of Women in the Industrial and Post-Industrial Eras* (1987) and *Playing the Game: Sport and the Physical Emancipation of English Women, 1870–1914* (1988) offered further novel investigatory dimensions to the history of women and sport. Other historical accounts followed. One was Allen Guttmann's *Women's Sports: A History* (1991), which offered a valuable historical overview of developments from the classical world to the 1970s.

This volume, *Sports and the Emancipation of European Women: the Struggle for Self-fulfilment* is an important contribution to a now quite substantial but not complete volume of studies spanning a good part of the globe. By including chapters dealing with sport in a variety of European countries – and written by individuals who have extensive personal familiarity with a particular culture – the collection obliges the reader to reconsider, and hopefully re-evaluate, much of the simplistically scripted reporting in which the media continues to revel.

Sport and the Emancipation of European Women also helps shed important light upon a significant point that sociologist John O'Neill made in his *Five Bodies: The Human Shape of Modern Society* (1995) when he cautioned readers that two major orientations regarding 'the body' dominated contemporary thought. Whereas the 'physical body' might remain pre-eminent in fields such as physiology and medicine, it was the 'communicative body' (a concept that had been brought forth by postmodernism, semiotics and similar thought) that had become of dominating interest to individuals in the humanities and social sciences. Given the salience of 'the body' in constructions of gender and power, it is not surprising that so many recent writers have included athletics and other physical activities in their analyses. In *Sport and the Emancipation of European Women* how the two approaches may differ, intersect and even meld may be seen clearly in the essay 'Projection of Male Fantasies: The Creation of "Scientific" Female Gymnastics'.

Notes on Contributor

Roberta J. Park is Professor Emeritus at the Department of Integrative Biology, University of California, Berkeley. Between 1982 and 1992 she was Chair of the Department of Physical Education and has written articles dealing with the history of 'sports medicine' and 'exercise science' for numerous years.

Notes

1. Elizabeth Cady Stanton writing in the feminist newspaper in *The Una*, 1 April 1850.
2. Hong, *Footbinding and Freedom*, 91.
3. Friedan, *The Feminine Mystique*.
4. Smith-Rosenberg, *Disorderly Conduct*.

References

Friedan, Betty. *The Feminine Mystique*. New York: W.W. Norton, 1963.

Guttmann, Allen. *Women's Sports: A History*. New York: Columbia University Press, 1991.

Hong, Fan. *Footbinding, Feminism and Freedom: The Liberation of Women's Bodies in Modern China*. London: Frank Cass, 1997.

Mangan, James A. and Park, Roberta J., eds. *From 'Fair Sex' to Feminism: Sport and the Socialization of Women in the Industrial and Post-Industrial Eras*. London: Frank Cass, 1987.

McCrone, Kathleen E. *Playing the Game: Sport and the Physical Emancipation of English Women, 1870–1914*. Lexington, KY; The University Press of Kentucky, 1988.

O'Neill, John. *Five Bodies: The Human Shape of Modern Society*. Ithaca, NY: Cornell University Press, 1985.

Smith-Rosenberg, Carroll. *Disorderly Conduct: Visions of Gender in Victorian America*. New York: A.A. Knopf, 1985.

Prologue: Atalanta as Symbol of European Sportswomen

Gigliola Gori

'Carlo Bo' University of Urbino, Italy

Greek mythology has passed down the story of a young and beautiful girl named Atalanta who challenged, competed with and defeated male athletes in disciplines such as running, wrestling and hunting. The fame of her invincibility eventually reached the ears of her father. Since he had wanted a son, he had cruelly abandoned the girl since her birth. Atalanta's father was proud of his daughter's successes, and he accepted her back into his home once more as his child. He decided to find her a husband, but the indomitable and independent girl set as a condition that her numerous admirers must defeat her in a foot race, and if they lost, they would be killed without mercy. However, one young suitor who was protected by Aphrodite, the goddess of love, had succeeded at last in touching Atalanta's heart and feelings. He devised a clever ruse thanks to which he slowed the girl down three times during the race and thereby won the contest. Was this merely an effective trick, or was it rather a free and conscious choice by Atalanta who had decided to renounce victory because she was willing to surrender to the young man?

In a world that is still dominated by men, modern woman's emancipation is intimately bound up with her athletic ability – and certainly with her physicality.[1] But a number of women choose (or rather are forced to choose) to conceal their own strength and abilities in order to support man's role in society. They therefore adapt themselves to social convention, to family pressures and – to be frank – sometimes to their partner's egotism. The collection of essays presented here offers reflections on these and other related matters.

Most of these essays have been written by young scholars from a number of European countries and published for the first time. They are products of the first Italian *International Journal of the History of Sport* (*IJHS*) conference/workshop that was hosted in 2010 by the University of Urbino. The collection aims to advance academic reflection on the cultural phenomenon of European women and modern sport from its appearance at the end of the nineteenth century to its present consolidation The essays use a wide range of sources and investigate a variety of activities in different nations and historical periods, but they all stress women's long struggle to achieve acceptance and to win equality in modern sport: their battle for self-fulfilment.

The essays lay bare the undeniable links between the practice of sport and the transient concepts of gender identity. The pairing of sport and gender can provide an unusual and innovative means for interpreting ideological, historical, economic and social dynamics throughout Europe. Like tiny pieces of a large mosaic, this collection provides novel patterns of and new perspectives on the evolution of the social emancipation of European sportswomen in terms of power, visibility, personal achievement and self-fulfilment.

In recent years research on the subject of the female body, female sport and female gender has increased steadily, not only in my own country but in other countries and continents. This includes the work of several renowned male and female scholars; among the women are Susan Bandy, Jennifer Hargreaves, Fan Hong, Dong Jinxia, Leena Laine, Gerd von der Lippe, Roberta Park, Gertrud Pfister and Patricia Vertinsky, whose important works I can recommend to the reader without hesitation. But, first of all, I should cite the detailed historical analysis presented by the outstanding male scholar Allen Guttmann, entitled 'Historiographical Vicissitudes'.[2] This work is valuable for the extensive perspective on the most significant publications issued in the last 30 years in which the author quotes for example the pioneering work of Kathleen McCrone,[3] *Playing the Game* (1988), which stresses the emancipatory potential of female sport rather than sport's complicity in patriarchal oppression. According to Guttmann, McCrone was squarely in the liberal tradition, but a few years later an innovative voice came from Jennifer Hargreaves's book *Sporting Females*,[4] and then in her *Heroines in Sports*,[5] published in 1994 and 2000 respectively, where she advocated a radical feminism and the treatment of the female body as subject rather than object.

I would be remiss if I did not mention James A. Mangan and his commissioning of collections dealing specifically with the issue of the international emancipation of women through the phenomenon of modern sport; his own edited sequence of collections on the subject published in his journals such as the journal in which this collection appears, and including *Freeing the Female Body: Inspirational Icons*; his encouragement of his Asian students such as Fan Hong and Dong Jinxia to both pursue doctorates on women and emancipation in Asia at his research centre and then to seek publication in his journals and his series *Sport in the Global Society*; and last but not least his seminal association with Roberta Park which resulted in the much praised groundbreaking *From 'Fair Sex' to Feminism: Sport and the Socialization of Women in the Industrial and Post-industrial Eras*.

As far as European feminism is concerned, I believe it is fitting to remember that since the last decades of the nineteenth century a number of early feminist movements were active in Denmark, England, Finland, France, Ireland and Norway; their leaders reached Washington in 1888 and took part in the congress organised by the International Council of Women (ICW). This was the first women's organisation to work across national boundaries for the common cause of advocating human rights for women, independent of any political party or religious denomination. It was at the ICW that the first steps were also taken in the direction of promoting gender consciousness. In the following years new national feminist movements arose in Europe, one example of which was the CNDI (Italian Women's National Council), founded in 1903 as a branch of the ICW; in 1907 this body participated in the European feminist congress held in Berlin, where the basis for the development of an international collective identity was established. One year later Italian women succeeded in holding the first CNDI conference which involved about 30 different associations.[6]

To return to Atalanta's modern sisters in sport and their feminist supporters, in the last few years a number of articles, essays and books have been devoted to explaining the phenomenon of women's sport worldwide; however, only few of them have investigated the European cultural environment. Among them I must mention the collections entitled *International Perspectives on Sporting Women in Past and Present* (2005), *Gender, Body and Sport in Historical and Transnational Perspectives* (2008) and *Sport and Gender Matters in Western Countries: Old Borders and New Challenges.* (2008).[7] These books all demonstrate that the barriers to divergent interpretations of femininity relate more or less incisively to the patterns, customs, politics, religion and degree of modernisation achieved in each country.

The same defining thread is woven through the collection of articles presented here, where European women's bodies seem to act as both subjects and objects of the constant goal of self-fulfilment. As Patricia Vertinsky wisely notes, contemporary feminist theory has finally underscored the notion that the body has always been of central importance to understanding difference, domination and subversion: 'These are critical starting points for understanding the conditions and experiences of embodiment in society and are implicated in any comparative analyses of embodied practices and the construction of the gendered body in different cultures, social contexts and historical epochs.'[8]

In his essay, Anssi Halmesvirta asserts that at the start of the twentieth century Finnish male physicians who were especially expert in human physiology and training maintained total control over both the bodies and minds of female gymnasts. Gradually, those doctors began a dialogue with female sport instructors and organisers, clashing or compromising with the female self-perception of the body which they believed they knew more than women! Arguing that the female body was much more fragile than the male, these doctors recommended that sportswomen should present themselves as composed and graceful, in other words as pure feminine examples of the Finnish 'race'.

At about the same time in Denmark, Dr Johannes Lindhard played a decisive role in the gendering of the body, as Hans Bonde clearly explains. He chose to give his support to the traditional 'difference-feminism' embodied in graceful and healthy gymnastics for girls, and consequently opposed the modern 'resemblance feminism' represented by female athleticism and sport. Inspired by his principles, Lindhard's former female student Agnete Bertran created a new method of gymnastics accompanied by classic music. This soft gymnastics was addressed to bourgeois girls and was greatly influenced by ancient Greek arts and clothes.

In her consideration of a recent case of gender discrimination against female ski jumping, Annette Hofmann asks how early ski jumpers such as Paula Lamberg and Johanne Kolstad could receive recognition and achieve recognition in a male-dominated sport system. Was it the result of the emancipatory spur occurring in the 1920s, the so-called Golden Years? What is certain is that both these women became successful in their sport, achieving fame and even becoming role models for women, as well as men. However, success and personal power did not suffice to open up this sport to girls and women in general, as moral reasons and medical arguments were, and still are, used to inhibit their participation.

The aim of Roberta Vescovi's essay is to analyse the history of female involvement in the Italian scouting movement, which contributed to women's self-fulfilment and to their struggle for cultural and political equality in the twentieth century. After pointing out that initially the female scouting movement had only a few members due to traditional preconceptions about femininity, the author argues that during and after the Second World War women entered a period of general 'female self-promotion' and thus were able to achieve important goals also within the women's scouting associations. Thus, although they were brought back to more traditional female models of behaviour by the Catholic Church and moderate conformists, the new progressive ambitions and achievements survived.

Sport remains an area where gender bi-categorisation (meaning the logical basis of rules defining the official status of citizens) is institutionalised from both a legal and organisational point of view. In his essay Sylvain Ferez examines various strategies of masculinisation or feminisation utilised to create gender bi-categorisation; in particular, homophobic abuse among sportsmen and suspicions of lesbianism among sportswomen. His analysis focus on the debates resulting from the introduction of 'femininity testing' for sportswomen from the late 1960s. It reveals how these debates testify to a determination to establish gender bi-categorisation biologically, despite the difficulties and dead-ends in the way.

The different stages of recognising female fencers by sports institutions are the concern of the research jointly presented by Thierry Terret and Cécile Ottogalli-Mazzacavallo. The analysis of the process, based on the archives of the FIE as well as on the specialised press, reveals the influence of three successive time contexts: the 1920s, the 1960s and the 1990s. The long resistance of the male fencing community to any challenge to gender order has been very relevant as is clearly illustrated. The authors argue that despite the explicit defence of women's sport by the leading sports institutions, women until recently have been the victims of the lengthy negotiations between the IOC and the FIE.

Helena Tolvhed's essay examines the reaction of the Swedish popular press to both the summer and winter Olympic Games during the 1950s and 1960s, as part of a process of affirmation of national and gender identity. Media representation focusing on the good looks and attractiveness of Swedish female athletes is read as cultural negotiations of the challenges facing women's sport, as these women were visually and textually represented as women rather than as athletes. This is related to the historical context of Sweden, where the female body was a crucial site and symbol for the separation of gendered spheres. Female athletes from Communist states, in contrast, were presented by the press as athletes first and foremost.

In her essay, Sandra Heck deals with women's striving for equal participation in the discipline of modern pentathlon. Whereas the development of men's modern pentathlon remained exclusively within the Olympic domain for the first 37 years, the female developments in favour of this sport gained ground through regional and national activities, and Germany was among the most active countries. The creation of female modern pentathlon World Championships in 1981 was not only a result of women's enthusiasm, tenacity and patience but also of men's concession to a female competency which could no longer be denied.

In Portugal, the political, legal and social changes that occurred during the transition to the democratic period contributed to a faster increase in the numbers of women attending university, entering the labour market and undertaking professional careers. According to Maria Claudia Pinheiro they also became more involved in women's groups fighting for changes in relation to sports policies that followed after the revolution, taking part in sport in general, and in traditionally male-appropriate sport. However, this did not mean that women did not have to face resistance.

Ivana Matteucci's writing on Italian women's soccer shows that stereotypes and social prejudices associated with gender still dominate the game. At the same time, she states that the dynamics of communication and consumption, closely related to one another in the sphere of sport over the last ten years, reproduce and subsequently reinforce the separation of men and women in social relationships that can also be found in society. Even today, Italian sport is characterised by deep gender differences: in comparison to women, men participate more in sport in general and at the same time male sport is more relevant economically and culturally.

A few concluding remarks: this collection should offer further understanding of the process whereby the female body becomes sexualised, controlled and oppressed. It also shows how sport plays a dynamic but paradoxical role in both reinforcing the male's hegemonic status while emancipating women from traditional repression. This is still the trend!

Should the modern sporting sisters of Atalanta eschew their bodily strength and capacity to renounce victories for a 'cause'? In my view, women should not deny the qualities of their womanhood, nor conceal their hard-earned physical and moral achievements; rather, they should try to work at gender relations, using intelligence and sensitivity. They should always retain the right to chose freely not only in sport but in any other matter.

In such a politically and socially changed arena, the authors of this collection resisted the temptation to simply read the past into the present without first evaluating the ideas and events in terms of the times in which they occurred. Mangan affirmed: '[N]othing could be more unwise than to tightlace past men and women into today's sometimes inflexible and constraining conceptual corsets; ... we must be sensitive to chiaroscuro so as to read political, social and cultural contours correctly; ... and should embrace complexity.'[9]

This is quite a magisterial lesson.

Acknowledgements

My sincerest gratitude goes to David Chapman for translating this writing from Italian, and to James Mangan for reviewing it.

Notes on Contributor

Gigliola Gori is professor of History of Education and Sport History at the 'Carlo Bo' University of Urbino, Italy. She serves as vice-president of the International Society of the History of Physical Education and Sport (ISHPES). Her most recent publications focus on Italian sports history in connection with politics, medicine, literature, education, dance and gender, in the nineteenth and twentieth centuries.

Notes

1. Park, 'Embodied Selves', 5.
2. Guttmann, "Historiographical Vicissitudes', 14.
3. McCrone, *Playing the Game*.
4. Hargreaves, *Sporting Females*.
5. Hargreaves, *Heroines in Sports*.
6. Among recent contributes on the Italian history of feminism these should be quoted at least: Taricone, *L'associazionismo femminile in Italia dall'unità al fascismo*; Pironi, *Femminismo ed educazione in età giolittiana*.

7.   Hofmann and Trangbæk, *International Perspectives on Sporting Women*; Bandy et al., *Gender, Body and Sport*; Gori, *Sport and Gender Matters*.
8.   Vertinsky, 'Gender Relations, Physical Education and Sport History', 25.
9.   Mangan, 'Series Editor Foreword', x.

References

Bandy, S.J., A.R.Hofmann and A. Krüger, eds. *Gender, Body and Sport in Historical and Transnational Perspectives*. Hamburg: Verlag Dr. Kovač, 2008.

Hofmann, A. and E. Trangbæk, eds. *International Perspectives on Sporting Women in Past and Present*. Copenhagen: Institute of Exercise and Sport Sciences, 2005.

Gori, G. 'Sport and Gender', in *'Serious Sport'. J. A. Mangan's Contribution to the History of Sport*, ed. Scott A.G.M. Crawford. London and Portland, OR: Frank Cass, 2004.

Gori, G., ed. *Sport and Gender Matters in Western Countries: Old Borders and New Challenges*. Sankt Augustin: Academia Verlag, 2008.

Guttmann, A. 'Historiographycal Vicissitudes', in *International Perspectives on Sporting Women in Past and Present*, eds A.R. Hofmann and E. Trangbæk. Copenhagen: Institute of Exercise and Sport Sciences, 2005.

Mangan, J.A. and Park, R., eds. *From 'Fair Sex' to Feminism: Sport and the Socialization of Women in the Industrial and Post-Industrial Eras*. London: Frank Cass, 1987.

Mangan J.A. and Fan Hong, eds. *Freeing the Female Body: Inspirational Icons*. London and Portland, OR: Frank Cass, 2001.

Mangan J.A. 'Series Editor Foreword', in *Freeing the Female Body: Inspirational Icons*, eds. J.A. Mangan and Fan Hong. London and Portland, OR: Frank Cass, 2001.

Park, R. 'Embodied Selves: The Rise and Development of Concerns for Physical Education, Active Games and Recreation for American Women, 1776–1865'. *Journal of Sport History*, no. 5 (1978).

Park, R. 'Searching for a Middle Ground. Women and Professional Physical Education in the United States 1885–1930', in *International Perspectives on Sporting Women in Past and Present*, eds A.R. Hofmann and E. Trangbæk. Copenhagen: Institute of Exercise and Sport Sciences, 2005.

Pfister, G. *Frauen und Sport in der DDR*. Cologne: Sport + Buch Strauss, 2002.

Pironi, T., *Femminismo ed educazione in età giolittiana. Conflitti e sfide della modernità*. Pisa: Edizioni ETS, 2010.

Taricone, F., *L'associazionismo femminile in Italia dall'unità al fascismo*. Milan: Unicopli, 1996.

Trangbæk, E. and A. Krüger, eds. *Gender & Sport from European Perspectives*. Copenhagen: CESH, 1999.

Vertinsky, P. *The Eternally Wounded Woman: Women, Doctors and Exercise in the Late Nineteenth Century*. Manchester: Manchester University Press, 1990.

Vertinsky, P. 'Gender Relations, Physical Education and Sport History: Is It Time for a Collaborative Research Agenda?', in *Gender & Sport from European Perspectives*, eds E. Trangbæk and A. Krüger. Copenhagen: CESH, 1999.

Vertinsky, P. 'Foreword', in *Sport and Gender Matters in Western Countries: Old Borders and New Challenges*, ed. G. Gori. Sankt Augustin: Academia Verlag, 2008.

Emancipation Through Sports: Doctors and the Rise of the Female Body in Finland *c*.1900–1920

Anssi Halmesvirta

University of Jyväskyla, Finland

While the cultural history of body and sports have become well-established fields of historical studies since the 1980s, it has been demonstrated that medical practice has functioned as a moral discourse which produces a regulation of the female body. It has been realised that theories (e.g. of 'degeneration') concerning the functioning of the human body bore a great significance to planning and defining the programmes of physical education, gymnastics and sports in the spirit of muscular nationalism. Doctors studying human physiology and training were eager to control not only the female body but also the mind of a gymnast or a sportswoman. This is what happened also in Finland from the late nineteenth century, when the emancipation of women started there. In pace with the demands of educational opportunities and suffrage – gained in 1906 with the establishment of the Finnish one-chamber Parliament – women started to yearn for their own kind of physical exercise, to organise in gymnastic clubs and finally in the 1900s–1910s to argue for a respectable role in the Finnish sports movement. My contribution analyses the dialogue between doctors and influential female organisers of gymnastics and sports over what and how the female body could perform in sports. It should throw light on the ways expert knowledge of medical authorities clashed or compromised with women's self-definition of their body and its functions, which they thought they knew better.

Introduction

The cultural history of the body and the history of sports have become well-established fields of historical study since the 1980s. They soon joined hands to explore how the roles of men and women had defined their physical education and sport, and it was demonstrated that medical practice has functioned as a moral discourse that produced regulation of the female body.[1] Since the middle of the nineteenth century medical experts assumed the role of 'public moralists'[2] in mediating largely gloomy messages of medicine and hygiene to the increasingly body- and sex-oriented reading public. They realised that new evolutionary theories concerning the growth and functioning of the human body had great significance for the planning and defining of programmes of physical education, gymnastics and sport. Medicine operating at local level in Finland was not only interacting with the state, law and charities but supported sport and gymnastics, which became to be seen as important factors in improving the hygiene and public health of the nation.[3] Finnish health care was in the process of modernisation and its advisory role was enhanced with the rise of Finnish gymnastics and sports movement which saw the nation 'on the move' on a large scale. In the spirit of muscular nationalism, the message was that small nations like that of the Finns had to be saved from the throes of decline and 'degeneration' so that they could survive in the age of imperialism.[4] Doctors and medical researchers were ready to apply the results of their studies into human physiology to physical education and training and were keen to give instruction and advice on how to develop the human body, build character and educate the mind of a gymnast or a sportsman/woman.

The projects aiming to translate the language of medicine in Finland from Swedish into Finnish ('finnicisation') and regenerating the Finnish 'race' coincided with the gradual emancipation of the (Finnish-speaking) female body into gymnastics and sports in the country from the 1880s. In keeping with the demands that grew out of broadening educational and occupational opportunities, as well as of suffrage[5] – gained in 1906 with the establishment of the Finnish one-chamber Parliament under Russian rule – women began to yearn for their own kind of physical education, to organize gymnastic clubs and finally, in the 1910s, to argue for representation in the Finnish sports movement.[6] For them the future function of physical education was to prepare women for participation in the public sphere and sports politics: with other women's movements, such as gymnastics and sports associations being involved in educating women to be 'fit for citizenry' (in Finnish: *kansalaiskunto*), without which they thought they did not deserve to have the right to vote.[7] The Finnish sports (and gymnastics) movement was to become the most popular mass movement in Finland, its ultimate goal being to democratise Finnish society.[8] Educated women, eager to join the movement, did not want to remain onlookers while men prepared themselves to gain 'power' and finally independence for the nation.

What follows includes an analysis[9] of the debate – never really a hard-fought controversy – between doctors and influential female organisers of women's gymnastics and sport over what and how the female body could/should perform in those spheres. It should throw light on the ways in which medical authority, harnessed with expert knowledge, negotiated with women's new, outward-seeking definitions of themselves and their bodies and of their growing awareness of the potential of the female body. New meanings were attached to old notions and wholly new ones were invented in women's sports language. The aim here is also to show how important the role of doctors, especially those specialising in health care and hygiene and who popularised medical advice to the wider public, really was in estimating the value of gymnastics and sport for the physical regeneration of women, and consequently Finnish national health in general. In this process the role of women was also re-assessed as being physically more active Finnish citizens than before. This seems to have been motivated not only by the urge to regenerate the Finnish nation or 'race' but also to some extent by the threat to the autonomy of the Grand Duchy of Finland posed by the integration policies of the Russian imperial authorities. It was as if the contribution of the 'weaker' sex was also needed in its defence. It can be elicited from the relatively scarce sources of the female sports debate that although there was some disagreement between women as to what extent sport was suitable for their 'weaker' bodies, active female leaders of the gymnastics movement and sports quite readily accepted and pursued their new 'progressive' role for the sake of the Finnish nation. It is important to remember that this new role involved working-class women in a rather different way, since they organised in their own workers' gymnastics and sports associations and developed a socialist version of physical education.[10] Much of the above refers only to women of educated, bourgeois classes.

The Doctors' Gloomy Message

Initially it was the doctors as medical experts who were given the major say in the Finnish health care and sport reviews (*Suomen Terveydenhoitolehti*, est. 1889; *Suomen Urheilulehti*, est. 1898; *Kisakenttä*, est. 1911) to evaluate the benefits and dangers of physical exercise and sport for men and women alike. The value of gymnastics and sport as a means to 'make the nation move' was emphasised to reinforce the message that they could heal the declining nation and help it to regain its vital forces (*élan vital*).[11] The doctors' point of view was largely determined by what they discovered, in the light of current medical theories, about the state of health and physical abilities of the Finnish nation. In the 1870s, when military conscription was instituted, doctors – to their great embarrassment – had realised how 'weakly' and 'sickly' the younger generation of male Finns really was. Signs and symptoms of impaired physical efficiency and fitness to defend the country in comparison to the previous hardy peasant generations were detected – among town-dwellers in particular. These alarming results made the doctors impatient to reconsider their 'progressive' theories of evolution and turn instead to reflect upon looming 'degeneration'. Yet only rarely after the turn of the century did they recommend positive eugenics or other forms of racial hygiene.[12] The Finnish nation was so small – just over three million – it was thought that even the weak and infirm should have been strengthened by exercise and the sick, handicapped or mentally retarded should be helped back into society as they might be capable of some contribution to the national cause. As one doctor-cum-moral educator explained, in the era of 'armed peace and electricity' it did not suffice to gather wealth and riches, but everybody had the duty to take care of his/her health and shy away from all forms of modern 'vice' (free love, prostitution, alcoholism etc.); otherwise Finland would be ruined in the same way as ancient Greece and Rome.[13]

One of the gravest causes of the 'degeneration' of male bodies was that young men frequented prostitutes and thereby disseminated venereal diseases among women.[14] As to 'women's tasks', their 'holy duty' was to breastfeed their babies for at least six months in order to combat the high infant mortality rate (over 16% in 1872–86).[15] This was the period when women should not exhaust themselves in heavy work or regular gymnastics. However, as soon as the babies could eat normal food, women should resume work or other physical exercise: for example, chopping wood or going to gymnastics or a sports club, because it was the law of nature that if an organ or muscle like the breast was not exercised it would shrink and become dysfunctional.[16] A modern woman should listen to the scientific advice of the medical authorities, not 'old women's' idle talk which exhorted them to stay in bed and out of sight as long as possible before and after giving birth.[17]

In two articles for *Suomen Terveydenhoitolehti* ('Health Care Review') entitled 'Women's Task in Elevating the General Level of Health of the Nation', one district practitioner and popular health authority, sympathetic to gymnastics and sports movements, proclaimed that it was high time – before the end of the century of 'progress' – for women to rise and free their bodies and souls from the shackles of prejudice and ignorance. A too refined or luxurious lifestyle tended to spoil (especially upper-class) women who, it was believed, passed their habits of comfort, flabbiness and weakness on to their offspring, thus increasing the impact of 'degeneration' in the nation. Referring to the biblical dictum that God had created also the female body as 'his temple and holy residence', the doctor warned women not to let it lie unexercised and combined the then current scare of 'racial suicide' with warnings of doom familiar to the general public: if women would not pay heed to family hygiene, God's revenge would fall on them. While state bureaucracy already controlled official institutions of health care, hygienic and health care conditions in average homes were still deleterious to health, and it was the housewives who were blamed. It was their task to ensure that their progeny grew into bodily and mentally able adults who could work for and also defend the nation in possible war, not allowing them to become 'parasites' of society. Following the example of Spartan women, they should have hardened themselves and their children with physical exercise and work outdoors.[18] This was the first public diatribe of an expert in health care in Finland that was aimed at awakening the female sex to an understanding of the value of rational health care and physical exercise to the entire nation.

Since there was not a gymnastics club or a sports field in every town and village in Finland at that time, it was suggested that some form of physical exercise be performed by housewives during and after their household work. This was all the more important since they became more degenerate than countryside women, who gained physical strength from their everyday agricultural toil. In contrast, because bourgeois and upper-class townswomen did not have such a hardening struggle for life, they had to learn to perform voluntary but regular bodily exercises. In case of hysterical women or women who suffered from neurasthenia (nervous exhaustion), physical exercise in the form of gardening, lugging or sawing wood and cooling off with cold water was highly recommended.[19] Certainly this piece of advice was not in line with that normally given at the time in Finland, since it opposed the use of any kind of medication. It was as if physical exercise, gymnastics or 'light sports' could become the panacea for every disease that did not need a scalpel.[20] The shibboleth of so-called folk medicine, which had become deemed to be deleterious to national health, was to be jettisoned and replaced by modern, scientifically corroborated and publicly elucidated prescriptions of rational hygiene. Gymnastics and sports were destined to become the best allies to this grass-roots modernisation of both Finnish national health and the Finnish way of life in general.[21]

As was to become customary, in order to make their message more persuasive the doctors cited invented life-stories of young women saved by some kind of physical effort or sport. There was 'Mary Steelstump', who had been in good health until her 14th birthday but had, thanks to natural causes – menstruation and its mentally disturbing effects – soon become 'nervous and somnolent'. These symptoms had made her neglect school work and brood on suicide. During the Christmas holidays she had taken to skiing but in the spring had again become 'listless but occasionally overjoyed'. The only cure that had helped was that she had been sent to the countryside for the summer holidays, where she had started swimming, rowing, running barefoot and taking part in agricultural work. That autumn she returned to school as 'flourishing as a rose'.[22] This story was composed as an object-lesson on how a girl should grow from adolescence to womanhood. Between reading schoolbooks, every girl should in particular peruse the Danish gymnast ideologue J.P. Müller's *My System for Women* (translated into Finnish in 1912) and the German social hygienist Fr. W. Foerster's guidebooks in sexual hygiene. In the Finnish context, their message of bodily and mental hygiene was directed against the teachings of 'free love' associated with revolutionary socialism that was infiltrating into the country from Germany and Russia. In this way the idea of 'racial regeneration' by exercise of the female body was reborn in Finnish hygiene, not only as an argument to be scientifically corroborated but also as a persuasion for women to be active in physical exercise and education and not to participate in any anti-social movements.

The theories and images of doctors concerning the workings of the female body found their way to *Suomen Urheilulehti* (the Finnish Journal of Sport), in the first issue of which it was declared that the ultimate goal of sport was simply to increase the 'physical and mental strength' of the Finnish nation. This idea was collectivist, and opposed to individualism, athleticism and professionalism from the very start. Toying with Charles Darwin's doctrine of evolution, the editor supposed that acquired characteristics were hereditary, and as a corollary to this, stated that it was a 'law of nature' that 'flabby nations' would be 'trampled on' by nations fortified by gymnastics and sport. History was called upon to prove that sport greatly helped the rise of civilisation, the model nation in this respect being England.[23] Further progress also presupposed that women should leave their 'embroidery, piano-playing and novel reading' and take to 'light' outdoor sports so that they would gain beauty and harmony in their bodies and thus add value to the nation in their own ways.[24] The differences in sex did not count and were not so significant that women should be left out of this 'mass movement of the nation' since many lighter forms of sport could be performed by them. According to a leading medical specialist, writing for the *Kisakenttä* (*Women's Sports Journal*), the main difference was that if men would gradually go for more difficult and demanding movements, such as in wrestling and athletics, women were made for lighter exercises, for instance, performing movements in gymnastics and suitable sports 'more perfectly and uniformly'. Behind this differentiation lay the notion that if women performed drastic and powerful jumps or dives, their intestines and reproductive organs might be damaged.[25] Women had to be careful to abstain from any exercise when tired because overstrained muscles needed more nervous energy to contract, which in the long run might lead to neurasthenia, already diagnosed among upper-class ladies but also among some athletes in Finland.[26] It was generally believed that gymnastics and 'lighter' sports would also help to resist the temptation to onanism by diverting the attention of adolescents to physical exercise and directing blood away from the genitals.[27] In the 'danger zone' were, for instance, schoolgirls who were more or less forced to perform tiring gymnastics or sports programmes and soon afterwards taught theoretical lessons. When the freshness and perkiness gained in physical education was consumed, learning became increasingly difficult. Tests among schoolchildren had shown that all the running and playing during breaks did not actually make them more fresh or frisky but, on the contrary, tired and exhausted. Thus the highest authority in hygiene in Finland, Professor Max Oker-Blom (1863–1917), who was the first holder of the chair of hygiene at Helsinki University from 1914 to 1917, advised teachers to allow children a brief period of rest after gymnastics and physical education.[28] He also recommended sport and gymnastics to unmarried working women, among whom degenerative nervous disorders were usual. In this way they could compensate for their 'unnatural' stressful way of life and not become a burden to their family and/or the nation.[29]

Women Come Forward

The special journal for female gymnasts and sportswomen *Kisakenttä* ('Playground') was edited by Anni Collán (1876–1962), the pioneer of the second generation of the Finnish female gymnastic movement. She worked as the female teacher at the Helsinki University Gymnastics Department from 1909 until 1919, when she became Inspector of Women's Physical Education, a post she held until 1945. Collán exemplified commitment to the cause of female gymnastics in her own life and articulated this in trying to change the conservative attitudes towards female bodily emancipation in Finnish society. In her diaries she shows a relentless preoccupation with matters of female physical education, ranging from managing courses in play for girls and women and travelling around Finland lecturing and teaching to drawing plans of playgrounds and gymnastics equipment for schools.[30] She and her other active colleagues working in gymnastics and sports largely accepted the model of physical education suggested by the doctors, but they also enthusiastically defended their own, independent standpoints against male-dominated sports leadership and its programme to develop a sports movement in Finland. Collán also tried to base her arguments on available physiological knowledge. Referring to the then current medical theory of degeneration, Collán stated that in the same way as male bodies female ones and their organs would also be atrophied if not used or exercised constantly (in Finnish, *liikunto*). Actually, all life was dependent on physical exercise. In order to avoid premature death or becoming physically unfit (a shameful condition), women should perform any possible regenerative movement. The proof of regeneration lay in the causal chain: 'exercise increases energy – energy invigorates the nervous system making the brain-cells vibrate [*väreily*]'. 'Energy' itself was transported to the brains by 'fresh blood' – best aired in the outdoor exercises of gymnastics or sport – making the brains-cells more 'receptive to the impulses of the mind's movement'. Without its influence, the 'grooves carved by thoughts' in the brain would fade away and all mental effort would be stupefied, possibly leading to serious nervous ailments. The cure to female neurasthenia was to 'unload' nervous stress in light sports and gymnastics (physiotherapy of a kind), which made 'the brain-grooves increase'. Couched in more generalised terms, if women were to take physical education seriously and make it their regular regimen, they should soon gain 'more intellect' and realise what new, active womanhood was awaiting them in the future.[31] The pre-condition to female emancipation through physical education for Collán was the ability of women to comprehend the workings of their body and make it more energetic.

The most concrete manifestation of the new notion of female bodily movement was to pinpoint its capabilities by means of a prominent outward sign. What both medical experts and leaders of women's gymnastics and sports movement recommended in 1914, instead of demanding competitive sport for women, was that they should strive for a sports badge especially designed for women. Women could achieve this badge by performing a series of gymnastic and 'light' sports tasks. It was agreed that they should be moderate but exacting enough to arouse enthusiasm for sport in women and save them from exhaustion and such grave accidents as occurred, for instance, in long-distance running (cf. Dorando Pietri's case in London Olympics).[32] The tasks included the following:

gymnastic programme in ten phases (mostly harmonious, bending movements of hands and legs, dancing steps, light jumping or climbing);

high jump over 90 cm high crossbar, long jump of 5.5 metres with both legs;

javelin (500g) throw 14 metres, ball-throwing at target (30 cm diameter) 5 metres away, Finnish baseball hitting (10 metres);

100 metre run in 17 seconds and 1,500 metre run in 10 minutes;

5 km walk in 50 minutes, swimming of 200 metres plus one deep dive;

5 km cross-country skiing and 10km cycling.

All this to be completed within a period of one year and certified by a standing committee. Performing the above once earned a bronze badge; performing the sequence three times earned a silver, and performing it six times a gold badge.[33] Although some argued that the 'badge-earning' sports were only gymnastics moved from indoors to outdoors and concluded that the change was quite easy and smooth for women,[34] it is clear that some of the tasks, such as 10 km cycling and the 1,500 metre run were neither familiar nor easy for many women to perform without preparation. Difficulty was increased when in 1919 Collán added a 15 km row and a 2 km run (the latter in 10 minutes) to the list.[35] At that time, there was usually some shame in a girl trying any 'manly' sports. One woman who had already earned the badge remembered being reproached by her mother for hill jumping with the boys. It was felt that girls and young women should stay within home boundaries and attend to household tasks.[36] Changes of attitude were evidently needed, and in one sentimental play written about female gymnastics and sports associations the reform was acted out: we come across a doctor who, as an expert in hygiene, assumes the role of a saviour rescuing a country girl eager to participate in sport from her home, where all bodily exercise was deemed 'sinful torture of oneself'.[37] These objections to female sport became the object of public ridicule and it was advertised that every woman should adopt the 'badge-system' since more than 1,400 had already done so between 1914 and 1917. In the year 1920 the number stood at about 5,000.[38] Further boost was given to the rise in women's emancipation from domestic prejudice and manly sports in 1916–17, when women's associations drafted plans to establish a separate, nationwide sports federation. Their efforts were rewarded in 1917 when the Finnish Parliament voted 60,000 Finnish marks to finance gymnastics and sports, out of which women's associations were allocated 9,000 marks, a sum which greatly helped them to launch advisory work, sports teaching programmes and especially to train female teachers for gymnastics and sport. Money was also allotted to the promotion of children's play, the principal aim being that children would gradually take up gymnastics and sport under the guidance of female teachers.[39]

Encouraged by the growth of the 'badge sports' among women in Finland, Collán wrote the first guide to sport for women in the Nordic countries, entitled *Naisten urheiluopas* ('Women's Guide to Sports, 1917; second edition 1921). In it she leaned towards the radical position that who could participate in what depended on the level of development of the *individual* rather than on gender. Even for women who had been assessed as 'weak', there would always be the teacher or other expert present who could ensure that she would not overstress herself while performing. Collán enumerated five main points in her defence of sports for women:

(1) Women (also) need healthy bodies;

(2) Health gained in sports turned into beauty since in performance the female body was under the control of the will which made it 'more beautiful than slack recklessness or raw power' of men;

(3) A healthy body is more 'practical', i.e. more fit to work than 'undeveloped or slow' one;

(4) Sports helped women to retain their female respectability or chastity in the sense J.J. Rousseau had put it when he had said 'the sicker and weaker the body, the more it commands, the healthier and stronger it is, the better it obeys';

(5) Sport calls forth sociability which manifests itself in 'friendliness and kindliness' which enhances the coherence of the society and nation.[40]

In addition to gymnastics and lighter sports, one attractive form of physical exercise for women was play. Collán was so fascinated by it that she wanted to launch a playground movement with which to overcome the problem of upper-class women not wanting women from the lower classes to join them.[41] The real obstacle, however, was the lack of special, separate playgrounds for women where they could play independently from men. From the point of view of national health this lack was reprehensible, since overstressed female factory workers, clerks and teachers in particular needed refreshing and joyful exercise.[42] Collán brought the model for play from the United States (Dayton playgrounds in Ohio), where the playground movement flourished, and exhorted women's associations to occupy empty plots or wasteland owned by states or townships and then demand free lease of them from the authorities. Unused private plots could be rented. The plan for such a playground containing all possible equipment from carousels, swings, slides, climbing trees, swimming pools, volleyball nets and a separate sports ground with all its paraphernalia in Finland was rather ambitious. On this ground women could perform almost all sports and even compete, for instance, in jumping, running and the horizontal bar. It was also proposed that, not to make it too serious, women should also sing and dance there. Again, the final goal was not to have only fun but to 'educate' girls and women into the 'discipline of citizenship' (*kansalaiskuri*).[43] Collán's plan was in line with the principle that gymnastics and sports for women should train not only the strongest and best developed for competition but also to strengthen those who were weaker and less developed for sufficient performance in daily work. In this way it was possible, for example, to correct deformation and posture in young girls' bodies. In spite of considerable pressure from the female associations, petitions to municipal and state authorities (the Senate) to build such playgrounds were regularly rejected. Obviously Collán's plan was too ambitious and untimely in the face of male opposition.

Collán, who was the spearhead in promoting physical exercises for women in the 1910s and also the founder of the Finnish Girl Scout movement, was not, after all, very revolutionary in her demands for the emancipation of women. She did not pursue any changes in the male-dominated Finnish social system as drastic as some of the so-called 'new women'. Gymnastics was for Collán a more regulated form of physical education than sport and her ideal was the performance of demonstration gymnastics in front of larger audiences so that the overall affect would be harmony, mirroring the unity of women in collective movement. For instance, in the women's section of *Suomen Urheilulehti* she explained to her students at the university

17

gymnastic department why it was important to obey leaders in social life and in sport. On the one hand, it kept both society and voluntary associations working together, and on the other, it pacified the mind and eased the tension of the nerves as the performer 'let her will relax from continuous strain, and abandon her own will to be led by another person'. Such rigid regimen which was not so different in men's or women's exercises – the same bodily movements suited them both[44] – was typical of the Swedish (Lingian) system adopted and revised for the 'slower moving' Finnish woman. Collán referred also to English gentlemen who had learned strict discipline through the games ethic during their public-school education. It was only after the Civil War (1918) that Collán pursued her campaign for sport at elementary schools, but gymnastics retained its role as the prevalent form of bodily exercise for girls and women in the first decade of the twentieth century.[45] It was all about making the female will control the body by 'command, orders and absolute obedience'; otherwise the formations adopted by the gymnasts in public would collapse. Analogically, the entire Finnish nation would fall if its citizens did not conform to the national ideal of self-controlled, healthy life and, more to the point, gymnastics supplemented with 'light' sports was the road from adolescent 'unruly behaviour to [the] self-conscious social freedom' of adulthood in which the body would also enjoy freely chosen regular movements. Thus physical education served the purpose of developing women's 'ability to self-determination' which enabled them finally to reach the level already achieved by men: to be able both to obey and command. Reminding her readers of the importance of 'detachment', Collán formulated a rule: all work and physical exercise was to be performed as if one were an approving outside observer of one's own actions.[46] Her preferred example of the 'perfected' form of socially respectable exercise for such self-conscious women was (gymnastic) dance refined from the 'animal condition of intoxication' of the ecstatic dancers seen in dance-halls and clubs of the capital to the controlled 'burst of joy in life' – preferably outdoors.

This kind of dancing was to keep 'bad' habits and 'dangerous' sensuality, a menace to selfhood by hidden impulses, at bay. It was men who evidently stood in the way of this reform of dance since their sexual impulses and other needs, such as seeking women and smoking during dance, dominated the scene.[47] Dancing in groups according to rules and performing gymnastic movements or sport presupposed lighter dress for female bodies so that they could move more freely. This was liberation from uncomfortably tight skirts to light trousers, and it was intended that corsets would be replaced by looser garments.[48] In the same vein, Collán advised girls to practise play and games which could enliven the shy and melancholy Finnish female type: in play she could 'gather power and skill and accumulate courage and self-confidence'.[49] She had published a handbook of Finnish play containing over 200 task examples, some of which demanded considerable physical strength to perform.[50] She borrowed lessons from German sources, for instance, from Karl Groos's *Die Spiele der Menschen*, and had visited the University of Ghent in Belgium and criticised its Catholic severity, proposing singing play and playful sports instead.[51]

In 1909–10 Collán clearly opened a new perspective for female physical education by adding to gymnastics such forms of movement as dancing, playing and some lighter sports that gave women opportunities to express themselves more freely through their bodies. This was to counteract the double standard of morality in relations with men, since play for adults would purify female minds by eradicating 'bad feelings' (cheating, soliciting etc.) and in preparing young women for love in marriage.[52] With a view to modernising working relationships and situations, Collán wanted to combine physical education and play with sociology lessons, since work in factories and offices also demanded from women new skills and the energy to cooperate with others which had not been the case in their traditional way of life.[53] All this meant that women should become more open-minded towards the wider society so that they could adapt with it as it changed from agricultural to industrial and professional.

Having read Henrik Ibsen's radical novels, Collán took her notion of emancipating the female body one step further. She had discovered that women could expect and seek more from life than fulfilling a duty in work or sacrificing themselves to husband and children. Even gymnastics for women did not seem to suffice any longer, and Collán started to develop the idea of 'exposing or risking one's life' in order to give more freedom of movement to innate femininity – which was by definition sexually differentiated from masculinity by its separate social tasks and functions.[54] This sudden reorientation towards new womanhood seemed even more accentuated than before in the face of the renewed 'russification' measures launched from St Petersburg in the early 1910s. Women also had to assume a more active (activist) role in defending the Finnish nation. A 'scandalous scene' was enacted at the Stockholm Olympics in 1912 when the Finnish athletes and gymnasts, men and women together, highlighted their national identity and protested against imperial legislation by boldly carrying the forbidden Finnish flag in the opening ceremony.

Considering the success of Finnish athletes and gymnasts in international sport and the ensuing expansion of the badge sports movement, Collán revised her system of physical education in favour of sport. She was bending to the view that 'without competition there was no progress' also applied to women. Having compared the purposes of both male and female sports, she reached the conclusion that for females it was 'the ability to perform' (*osaaminen*) while for males it was to produce 'the best performance' (*paras osaaminen*). Pure 'performance' was to maintain female fitness and health; 'best' was to win in competitions. For women the advantage of sport in comparison to gymnastics was that it brought female bodies more often into the open air, such as in cycling and rowing in summer and skiing and skating in winter.[55] The ideal form of sport for women was, however, javelin, because as a physical effort it also carried with it a metaphoric meaning by connecting hand and mind in a goal-oriented activity. At first a female thrower thinks 'I cannot do this', then she says to herself 'I want to try' and concludes by deciding 'I can now throw longer than before'.[56] The message was not coming from brain to hand but conversely from hand to brain, thus making the female body – rather paradoxically – the 'commander' of the mind.

An Opinion Poll

The ideas and attitudes of Finnish women concerning the physical limits of their sporting performance can be best illustrated by analysing the results of a survey conducted in 1911 by *Kisakenttä*, the first journal dedicated to women's gymnastics and sport. It was intended to investigate how women felt about the widespread 'sports madness' that was prevalent in Finnish society before the Stockholm Olympics. It put to women the questions 'What is your opinion concerning sport and competition and would you wish women to take part in them, and which sports would be suitable for them?' In three consecutive issues 28 answers, mostly from gymnastics teachers from the biggest towns in Finland, were reprinted. Most of the answers were strictly against any form of competitive sport for women; some were ambivalent as to the value of sport to women in general; and some were tentatively in favour of lighter sports such as promoted by the sports badge system.

As for the first part of the question, women's opinions were divided. In the first letter received by the editor (Collán) the writer, Elli Björksten (1870–1947)[57] gave her objections to competitive sports since she found trophies and medals 'repulsive'. She understood that the well-meaning purpose of medical science in promoting sport had been to awaken and heal a 'flabby and physically degenerated' generation through physical exercise and realised that competition had been thus far the best way to do it. However, she had serious qualms about the health benefits of hard training and looked forward to hearing that scientific congresses dealing with topics of physical education could corroborate the argument that it was harmful. From the vantage point of morality competition was also harmful since – in contrast with the Hellenes who had competed only for glory – it aroused egoistic ambitions which hampered the development of a pure and altruistic mind. Competitive sports also spoiled the spectators who did not see 'harmonious and beautiful bodies' on the field but muscle-men with their overreached performances. Sport had degraded into circus-like popular entertainment and women should not have anything to do with this. Happily for the critic, women's competitions in Finland had so far been so 'worthless' that they did not really count – they were organised by men and women had found them to be against their 'nature'. For Björksten, who advocated rhythmic gymnastics, it was a recognised fact that women were 'too fragile and weak' to bear the risks which the systematic training indispensable for competition brought with it. What was fitting for women was 'general and simple but respectable' gymnastics that would not harm their bodies. In principle, women also had to be 'strong and healthy', but the physical education of the times – still in its infancy according to Björksten – had not yet been able to envisage a new and 'more sensible' ideal of woman suited to sport. If women were captivated by the 'spirit of competition', it may not be harnessed and could lead to most harmful consequences. What they might be Björksten did not want to say, but insinuated that there would be possible damage to sexual morality. Of all sports only lawn tennis and other ball games were acceptable. Remarkably no mention was made by medical authorities of any specific female bodily limitations in relation to sports, only vague references to 'general weaknesses'.[58] It was evidently taken for granted that everybody knew just what they were.

A more positive and authoritative response came from Elin Kallio (1859–1927),[59] the founder of the women's gymnastics movement in Finland and the organiser of the first gymnastics jubilee there in 1887. Her letter was originally a lecture given in 1904 when she had attended a gymnastics show in Viborg, in Karelia County. Collán reprinted it in the *Kisakenttä* because she regarded it as a persuasaive statement from a pioneer. Kallio had also been delighted that women had joined the sports movement since Finnish women always been accustomed to demanding physical effort both inside and outside their homes, particularly in walking and skiing long distances. More recently, inspired by the British skater Jackson Haynes, who had visited Helsinki in the 1870s, some women had taken to skating and many belonged to rowing, skating and skiing clubs and had taken part in competitions organised by them. To the amazement of elderly ladies, some women had also won many trophies.

Kallio realised that opinion over the issue was sharply divided: sporting enthusiasts emphasised that sport was the mother of all progress whereas medical authorities had sounded grave warnings over the 'overstrain and exhaustion' of physical exercise and competition. Kallio herself was hesitant to take a definite scientific stand, although she endorsed the view that competition might 'have an unhealthy effect' on the female body. The problem was the old Jewish one: 'Was it better to let a few die than allow the whole race to be exterminated?' – a telling comment on what women should expect if they followed men into serious sport.[60]

The solution lay in the national character of the Finnish woman. Kallio conceded that majority of them were 'slow and comfort-loving' and that they were not very 'enterprising'. From this it followed that all sports had to be adapted to accommodate this and the sports movement had to be supported and directed into 'healthy' pursuits. When it came to competition for women it was the responsibility of female teachers of women's gymnastics rather than men to control them. On this point Kallio agreed with Collán. Although no accidents had happened to women in the care of male teachers, it was difficult for them to gauge the physical strength of women – Kallio had seen so many examples of mistakes in this respect. If sports should become fashionable and be performed by both men and women, only female self-control could restrict the rise of women's ambitions and prevent their 'over-exertion'. Kallio was, however, of the opinion that women were usually 'too lazy' to train themselves, although it would be necessary in order to stay fit before competition. Importantly, women did not, in Kallio's opinion, like to be inspected by male doctors. It was, however, necessary during practice and before performance so that 'weak and sickly' women would be disqualified. Competing was in any case strictly forbidden during menstruation. In order to be able to supervise female sport, the female gymnastics teachers should carefully study the medical aspects of women in sport and try to join sports clubs in order to further their 'inside' knowledge. Subject to these preconditions being met, Kallio did not have any further objections to female participation in competitive sport.[61] Her opinion was not mirrored among the female teachers who answered the poll. The majority of them opposed sport and criticised Kallio for being so open to 'manly' sports.

Conclusion

In conclusion it is fair to point out that generally, medical authorities, female gymnasts and sportswomen agreed on what women could and should physically perform. They saw the female body as more fragile than its male counterpart, which was also reflected in the way women expressed themselves during sporting or gymnastic performance. This mirrored the subtle and contained ways of female performing artists of the theatres or dance halls of the early years of the twentieth century. Compared to male actors, who would burst into violent passion in any moment, it was felt that women should present themselves as composed beautiful and morally pure examples of the Finnish 'race'. The same contrast applied to sexual politics: as women were encouraged to become more active partners in sexual intercourse rather than simply attempting to pacify men's dominance, through sport they could learn to politicise and challenge men in the public sphere. Women no longer had to complain to doctors of their fear of sexual energy, and they were encouraged to enjoy both sexual satisfaction and take pleasure from sport, which could become an escape route from the day-to-day routines of the household or workplace. Usually sportswomen were not married and so did not have to comply with the old roles and rules and social expectations. Although there remained some uncertainty and ambiguity in women's statements concerning sport, they had begun to use their own rhetoric, make their own choices and occupy their own spaces in seeking and finding alternative physical activities with their 'sisters' or 'comrades', as they usually called each other.

As J.A. Mangan has suggested, women interested in sport were not only victims living in a fantasy world but performers and protagonists. This also held true of Finnish women promoting sport who obtained a platform in the Finnish media and made their own voices heard.[62] Nevertheless, their perceived 'weakness' and aesthetic sensibilities demanded slower, more harmonious and collective movements than performed by men. They would also be more beautiful while producing joy and happiness in the minds of other performers and spectators. The approach in creating sportswomen was holistic; the dualism of body and mind was overcome by their working in cooperation: *mens sana in corpore sano*, as the motto engraved in the Finnish women's sports badge read.

Women were seen as being ready to enter most sports, starting with lawn tennis, swimming, rowing, sailing, skiing and skating, and other so called 'lighter sports' mentioned in the badge list. Hard sports, over-exertion and athletic performance were as yet deemed too much for their bodies and nervous systems. Exhaustion of the female body would lead to the inability to fulfil the female biological duty to reproduce healthy and fit children for Finland, a country for which independence from the Russian Empire was the dream of many a female activist since the end of the nineteenth century. In this sense, the emancipation of (sports)women had to conform to the ideals of Finnish nationalism, rather than become sisters of the rare breed of 'new women' who since the 1902–3 feminist debate had threatened men's cultural hegemony.[63] Women involved in physical education wanted to work with men in order to strengthen the entire nation. Sportswomen were not like the female 'artists' who were seen by anthropologists and psychologists of the time as degenerate or decadent, neurotic or hysteric beings. Sportswomen despised and pitied such creatures who had betrayed nature's intention to make women beautiful and supple.

Thus the dictum of J.F. Stephen, 'Nations grow like men, by exercise', could be rephrased to read 'Nations grow like men and *women*, by exercise', irrespective of the fact that male sport was also seen as preparation for the battles of a war.

Notes on Contributor

Anssi Halmesvirta is a professor of general history and the Jean Monnet teacher of the history of European integration at the University of Jyväskylä, Finland. He has studied the interplay of scientific and political ideas of the late nineteenth and early twentieth century, also with reference to history of sports and physical education.

Notes

1. Cf. Turner, *Regulating Bodies*, I; Porter, 'History of the Body Reconsidered', 236; Mangan and Park, 'Introduction', *passim*.
2. Coined by Stefan Collini in his *Public Moralists*.
3. Cf. Jordanova, 'Social Construction of Medical Knowledge', 352.
4. Pick, *Faces of Degeneration*. For Finnish ideas of degeneration, see, Halmesvirta, 'Ideology and Argument', part II.

5. In Finland women's emancipation was from the 1840s preached by the 'ladies' associations' which were charity organisations of the upper classes. John Stuart Mill's *The Subjection of Women* was introduced to Finnish public in 1869 by Mrs Adelaide Ehrnrooth, who was the first female journalist in the country. Later, from the 1880s the women's movement organised on the model of other mass movements but did not especially attract Finnish women and remained politically dispersed and internally quarrelsome. The main targets of reform were equality of men and women (in 1887 they gained the right to choose their employer and govern their own property), abolition of prostitution and double standards and general chastity and temperance. See Ramsay, 'Rouvasväen yhdistykset', 313; Ramsay, 'Naisasialiike – itsevarmuuden pitkä taival', 252–9.

6. In 1900 there were 108 gymnastics and sports associations with 3300 members. In Denmark their number was about 10,000 and in Germany 600,000. In 1907 their numbers stood at 301 associations and 10,600 members. Out of them 14 were women's associations. The Association of Women's Gymnastic Clubs was established in 1897.

7. Cf. Ollila, 'Naisliike, nationalismi ja kansanvalistus'.

8. The rise of the Finnish sports is well told in Pyykkönen, *Suomi uskoi urheiluun*.

9. Halmesvirta, 'Ideology and Argument', Introduction.

10. This issue has been studied by Laine, 'Käsi kädessä siskot veikot?'.

11. Halmesvirta, 'Sports as Medicine'.

12. Aro, 'Muutamia mietteitä urheilusta'; Pihkala, *Nykyhetki ja urheiluväen velvollisuudet*, 4.

13. Relander, 'Vuoden vaihteessa'. 1.

14. Relander, 'Siveellisyyskysymyksestä sananen'.

15. Relander, 'Vuotta nuorempain lasten kuolevaisuus Suomessa'.

16. Relander, 'Työn siunaus', 34.

17. Relander's remark in *THL* [*Terveydenhoitolehti*] 11 (1895), 174.

18. Relander, 'Naisen tehtävästä kansan yleisen terveyskannan kohottamiseksi'.

19. Relander, 'Hysteriia eli luulotauti sekä keinoja taudin voittamiseksi'.

20. See Halmesvirta, 'Sports as Medicine', 173–6.

21. For a theoretical and methodological overview, see Stark, 'Empowering Practises'.

22. ReijoWaara, 'Tytöstä naiseksi kehittyessä', 4–6; ReijoWaara, 'Hoida sydäntäsi, keuhkojasi', 115.

23. *Suomen Urheilulehti* 1 (1898), 2; Hällberg, 'Sananen urheilusta arvosteltuna lääkärin-urheilijan kannalta', 144.

24. Ivar Wilskman in *Suomen Urheilulehti* 1 (1898), 177.

25. 'C.S.', 'Mikä erotus tulee olla tyttöjen ja poikien voimisteluliikkeiden välillä', 100.

26. Oker-Blom, 'Ruumiinharjoitukset ja henkinen työ'', 231.

27. Halmesvirta, 'Sukupuolihygienia ja nuorisopolitiikka', 73.

28. Oker-Blom, 'Ruumiinharjoitukset ja henkinen työ', 234.

29. Oker-Blom, 'Heikkohermoisuus ja kasvatus', 53–4, 68–70.

30. E.g. Collán's diary from the year 1913: Collán's Collection, Central Archives of Finnish Sports, Sports Museum, Olympic Stadium, Helsinki (hereafter Collán's Collection), box no. 9.

31. Collán, 'Elämä ja liikunto', 65–6; Collán, 'Voimistelu kasvatuskeinona', 94–5.

32. Oker-Blom, 'Urheilumerkkijärjestelmästä sananen'.

33. Anon., 'Urheilumerkki'.

34. 'K.K.', 'Suomen Naisten Voimisteluliitto', 71.

35. Collán's notes from the year 1919, Collán's Collection, box 9.

36. Anon., 'Naisten urheiluvastuksia', 212.

37. 'O.K.', 'Maijan huolet', 154.

38. Collán, *Naisten urheiluopas*, 24; Collán's notes from the year 1920, Collán's Collection, box 9.

39. (Collán), '60.000 markkaa voimistelun'; 'A.C.', 'Voimistelunopettajan tehtävä maaseudulla'.

40. Collán, *Naisten urheiluopas*, 26.

41. This did not in the 1910s context mean children's play but young women's own alternative 'play' including e.g. joyful running, dancing and singing, or it could be, in sports-like fashion, basketball 'play'. Also competitions in 'play' were organised but they aroused confusion and resentment among people who had been accustomed to competitive sports. See, for details, Laine, 'Voimistelu, leikki urheilu', 156–64.

42. Collán's remark in *Suomen Urheilulehti* (1906), 392–3.

43. Collán, 'Leikkikenttätoiminnan järjestely'.
44. 'C.S.', 'Mikä erotus tulee olla tyttöjen ja poikien voimisteluliikkeiden välillä', 98.
45. Collán, *Urheilun järjestely kansakouluissa, passim.*
46. 'A.C.' (Women's Section), 1356.
47. Collán's remark in *Suomen Urheilulehti* (1909), 326; Collán, 'Kansallispukuja ja kansantansseja', 626.
48. 'A.C.', 'Voimistelupuku', 353.
49. 'Tyttö', 'Leikin merkitys', 497.
50. Collán, *Suomen kansan leikkejä.*
51. Collán's report, 614–16.
52. Collán, *Kansan laululeikkejä*, 30–34.
53. Collán's lecture at Varala (women's summer school), 21 July 1916, Collán's speeches, lectures and occasional writings 1905–1918, Collán's Collection, box 9.
54. 'A.C.', 'Tovereille'.
55. Collán, 'Vastakohtia urheilusta ja voimistelusta', 167.
56. Ibid., 171–2.
57. For a short biography, see Laine, 'Björksten, Elli, 1870–1947'.
58. Elli Björksten's letter to *Kisakenttä* 1 (1911), 6–9.
59. For a short biography, see Laine, 'Kallio, Elin (1859–1927)'.
60. Elin Kallio's lecture in *Kisakenttä* 2 (1911), 21.
61. Ibid., 21–2.
62. Mangan, 'Prospects for the New Millennium'.
63. Of the new woman in Finland, see Rojala, 'Modernia minuutta rakentamassa'.

References

'A.C.' [Anni Collán]. 'Voimistelupuku'. *Suomen Urheilulehti* (1909): 353.
'A.C.' (Women's Section). *Suomen Urheilulehti* (1909): 1356.
'A.C.' 'Tovereille'. *Suomen Urheilulehti* (1910): 27–8.
'A.C.' 'Voimistelunopettajan tehtävä maaseudulla'. *Kisakenttä* 10 (1917): 218.
Anon. 'Urheilumerkki'. *Kisakenttä 6* (1912): 114–15.
Anon. 'Naisten urheiluvastuksia'. *Kisakenttä* 10 (1915): 212.
Aro, Toivo. 'Muutamia mietteitä urheilusta'. *Suomen urheilulehti* (1908): 574–5.
Björksten, Elli. 'Kirje' [letter to the editor]. *Kisakenttä* 1 (1911): 6–9.
Collán, Anni. *Kansan laululeikkejä.* Helsinki: Helsingin sentraalikirjapaino, 1907.
Collán, Anni. 'Elämä ja liikunto'. *Opettajain lehti* 6 (1909): 64–7.
Collán, Anni. 'Kansallispukuja ja kansantansseja'. *Suomen Urheilulehti* (1909): 626.
Collán, Anni. 'Voimistelu kasvatuskeinona. Helsingin suomalainen tyttökoulu ja suomalainen jatko-opisto', in *Kertomus lukuvuodesta 1911–1912.* Helsinki: SKS, 1912, 91–103.
Collán, Anni. 'Leikkikenttätoiminnan järjestely'. *Valvoja* (1916): 172–84.
Collán, Anni. *Naisten urheiluopas.* Porvoo: *Urheilukustannus Oy*, 2nd edn. Helsinki: Otava, 1921 [orig. pub. 1917].
Collán, Anni. 'Vastakohtia urheilusta ja voimistelusta'. *Kisakenttä* 9–10 (1918): 167–72.
Collán, Anni. *Urheilun järjestely kansakouluissa.* Helsinki: Otava, 1920.
(Collán, Anni). '60.000 markkaa voimistelun, urheilun ja leikin hyväksi'. *Kisakenttä* 7–8 (1917): 157–9.
Collán, Anni. *Suomen kansan leikkejä.* Porvoo: WSOY, 1904.
Collini, Stefan. *Public Moralists. Political Thought and Intellectual Life in Britain 1850–1950.* Cambridge: Cambridge University Press, 1991.
'C.S.' 'Mikä erotus tulee olla tyttöjen ja poikien voimisteluliikkeiden välillä'. *Kisakenttä* 7–8 (1911): 100.
Halmesvirta, Anssi. 'Sukupuolihygienia ja nuorisopolitiikka', in *Politiikkaa lastenkirjoissa*, eds Anssi Halmesvirta, Kari Pöntinen and Sulevi Riukulehto, Tietolipas 178. Pieksämäki: SKS:, 2001, 67–78.
Halmesvirta, Anssi. 'Sports as Medicine: Public Health, Hygiene and the Rise of the Sports Movement in Finland, 1880–1920, in *Proceedings of the 6th Congress of the International Society for the History of Physical Education and Sport.* Budapest: Platin-Print, 2002, 171–9.

Halmesvirta, Anssi. *Ideology and Argument. Studies in British, Finnish and Hungarian Thought.* Studia Historica 73. Helsinki: Gummerus, 2006.
Hällberg, Karl V. 'Sananen urheilusta arvosteltuna lääkärin-urheilijan kannalta'. *Suomen Urheilulehti* (1899): 144.
Jordanova, Ludmilla. 'Social Construction of Medical Knowledge', in *Locating Medical History. The Stories and Their Meanings*, eds Frank Huisman and John Harley Warner. Baltimore, MD, and London: The Johns Hopkins University Press, 2006.
Kallio, Elin. 'Luento' [lecture reprinted]. *Kisakenttä* 2 (1911): 19–22.
'K.K.' 'Suomen Naisten Voimisteluliitto'. *Kisakenttä* 4 (1915): 65–71.
Laine, Leena. 'Björksten, Elli, 1870–1947, Finnish Educator and Gymnastics Theorist', in *International Encyclopedia of Women and Sports*, vol. 1 ed. Karen Christensen, 139–40. US: Macmillan, 2001.
Laine, Leena. 'Kallio, Elin (1859–1927). Finnish Teacher and Founder of Gymnastics Movement', in *International Encyclopedia of Women and Sports*, vol. 2 ed. Karen Christensen, 617–18. US: Macmillan, 2001.
Laine, Leena. 'Voimistelu, leikki urheilu. Naisliikunnan ohjelmanrakennusta 1910.luvulla'. *Suomen Urheiluhistoriallisen Seuran vuosikirja* (2005): 155–72.
Laine, Leena. 'Käsi kädessä siskot veikot? Naiset ja työväen urheiluliike', in *Tuntematon työläisnainen*, eds Leena Laine and Pirjo Markkola. Tampere: Vastapaino, 1989, 186–209.
Mangan, J.A. and Roberta J. Park 'Introduction', in *From 'Fair Sex' to Feminism. Sport and the Socialization of Women in the Industrial and Post-Industrial Economy*, eds J.A. Mangan and Roberta J. Park. London: Frank Cass, 1987, 1–8.
Mangan, J.A. 'Prospects for the New Millennium: Women, Emancipation and the Body', in *Freeing the Female Body. Inspirational Icons*, eds J.A. Mangan and Fan Hong. London and Portland OR: Frank Cass, 2001, 238–9.
'O.K.' 'Maijan huolet'. *Kisakenttä* 7–8 (1916): 147–60.
Oker-Blom, Max. 'Heikkohermoisuus ja kasvatus'. *Tieteen työmailta* 3. Helsinki: Otava, 1903.
Oker-Blom, Max. 'Urheilumerkkijärjestelmästä sananen'. *Kisakenttä* 6 (1912): 113–4.
Oker-Blom, Max. 'Ruumiinharjoitukset ja henkinen työ'. *Kisakenttä* 11 (1914): 230–4.
Ollila, Anne. 'Naisliike, nationalismi ja kansanvalistus', in *Naisten hyvinvointivaltio*, eds Anneli Anttonen, Lea Henriksson and Ritva Nätkin. Tampere: Vastapaino, 1994, 63–5.
Pick, Daniel. *Faces of Degeneration: A European Disorder, c.1848 – c.1918.* Cambridge: Cambridge University Press, 1989.
Pihkala, Lauri. *Nykyhetki ja urheiluväen velvollisuudet.* Lahti, 1917.
Porter, Roy. 'History of the Body Reconsidered', in *New Perspectives on Historical Writing*, 2nd edn, ed. Peter Burke. Cambridge: Polity, 2005, 233–60.
Pyykkönen, Teijo, ed. *Suomi uskoi urheiluun.* Helsinki: VAPK-kustannus, 1992.
Ramsay, Alexandra. 'Rouvasväen yhdistykset – naisasialiikkeen orastava alku', in *Suomen kulttuurihistoria 2*, eds Rainer Knapas and Nils Erik Forsgård. Helsinki: Tammi, 2003, 311–13.
Ramsay, Alexandra. 'Naisasialiike – itsevarmuuden pitkä taival', in *Suomen kulttuurihistoria 3*, eds Anja Kervanto Nevanlinna and Laura Kolbe. Helsinki: Tammi, 2003, 252–9.
ReijoWaara, Konrad. 'Tytöstä naiseksi kehittyessä'. *THL* [Terveydenhoitolei] 1 (1907): 4–6.
ReijoWaara, Konrad. 'Hoida sydäntäsi, keuhkojasi'. *THL* 7–8 (1907): 115.
Relander, Konrad. 'Vuoden vaihteessa'. *Terveydenhoitolehti* 1 (1890).
Relander, Konrad. 'Siveellisyyskysymyksestä sananen'. *THL* 1 (1891): 1–2.
Relander, Konrad. 'Vuotta nuorempain lasten kuolevaisuus Suomessa'. *THL* 1 (1890): 9–11.
Relander, Konrad. 'Työn siunaus'. *THL* 3 (1892): 34.
Relander, Konrad. 'Naisen tehtävästä kansan yleisen terveyskannan kohottamiseksi'. *THL* 6–7 (1896): 81–7.
Relander, Konrad. 'Hysteriia eli luulotauti sekä keinoja taudin voittamiseksi'. *THL* 2 (1906): 24–6.
Rojala, Lea. 'Modernia minuutta rakentamassa', in *Suomen kirjallisuushistoria 2. Järkiuskosta vaistojen kapinaan*, ed. Lea Rojala. Helsinki: SKS, 1999, 155–64.
Stark, Laura. 'Empowering Practises: Perspectives on Modernization in Finland'. *Ethnologica Fennica* 36 (2009): 4–17.
Turner, Bryan S. *Regulating Bodies: Essays in Medical Sociology.* London and New York: Routledge, 1992.
'Tyttö.' 'Leikin merkitys'. *Suomen Urheilulehti* (1909): 497.

Projection of Male Fantasies: The Creation of 'Scientific' Female Gymnastics

Hans Bonde

Institut for Idræt, Copenhagen, Denmark

About 100 years ago, in 1909, the Danish medical doctor Johannes Lindhard (1870–1947) became associate professor, and in 1917 professor, of the theory of gymnastics at the University of Copenhagen. Lindhard's collaboration with the physiologist and 1920 Nobel Prize winner August Krogh (1874–1949) laid the foundation for the birth of exercise physiology in Scandinavia. In addition to his basic-level studies of physiology, Lindhard also became deeply involved in developing a theory of gymnastics that would bring a wide range of Danish gymnastics traditions onto a surer theoretical footing. Lindhard's importance in the history of gymnastics is mainly attributable to the fact that he had a huge influence in the 'gendering' of the behavioural codes of conduct and the formulation of a gender-specific movement programme aimed at the socialisation of boys and girls as well as men and women in accordance with the new gender roles of the emerging capitalist society with its strict division of education and labour between the two sexes. Lindhard clearly supported 'difference-feminism' in contrast to 'resemblance-feminism'.

These two concepts of femininity clashed in a fierce struggle in the inter-war period. Advocates of women's athletics interpreted competitive sports as perfect tools for women's conquest of male territory, whereas supporters of female gymnastics considered athletics to be an antidote to the health-promoting and graceful essence of femininity. Agnete Bertram was one of Lindhard's first students at the Laboratory for the Physiology of Gymnastics and in the 1920 she created a new graceful women's gymnastics system based on Lindhard's principles. Besides taking its inspiration from Lindhard's notions of psycho-aesthetics, Bertram's system was immersed in ancient Greek influences and was sometimes performed in Greek robes in the neo-classic building of the Carlsberg foundation to the accompaniment of classical music such as Mozart's sonata in A-major. This was well suited to the bourgeois women in their roles as aesthetic domestic angels.

Boys must be brought up to be men, girls to be women.[1]

(J. Lindhard, *The Theory of Gymnastics*)

Introduction

About 100 years ago, in 1909, the Danish medical doctor Johannes Lindhard (1870–1947) became associate professor and in 1917 professor of the theory of gymnastics at the University of Copenhagen. Lindhard's collaboration with the physiologist and in 1920 Nobel Prize winner August Krogh (1874–1949) laid the foundation for the birth of exercise physiology in Scandinavia.[2] In addition to his basis-level studies of physiology, Lindhard also became deeply involved in developing a theory of gymnastics that would bring a wide range of Danish gymnastics traditions onto a surer theoretical footing. The current article will focus on sides to Lindhard that were beyond the scientific and reveal how the scientist in person can exert a forceful influence quite outside the realm of his scientific inquiry.

The main question of this article is the following: How did Lindhard contribute to gender and not least femininity constructions with the body as a medium? My main theses can be expressed in this way:

(1) Lindhard's importance for the history of gymnastics is mainly attributable to the fact that he had a huge influence in the 'gendering' of the behavioural codes of conduct and the formulation of a gender-specific movement programme aimed at the socialisation of boys and girls as well as men and women in accordance with the new gender roles in the emerging capitalist society with its strict division of education and labour between the two sexes.

(2) The trend within parts of women's studies to enlarge the research approach from women to gender in general, including men and the interplay between the two genders, has now become a scientific must. The article demonstrates how not only women but also men to a high extent are exposed to normative socialisation which limits their possibilities to express themselves freely. Comparable to women's problems in elite sport, men are met with barriers and prejudices in relation to dance, rhythm and non-aggressive body contact.

(3) Until now academic publications have mainly focused on Johannes Lindhard's conflicts with so-called Ling, or Swedish, gymnastics, but though Lindhard was a main contributor in this struggle, he also moved with the times. It was a much more uphill struggle against the emerging and highly gendered system of Niels Bukh's gymnastics that evolved from Ling gymnastics from 1916–17.

In order to understand the personal and cultural driving forces behind Lindhard's scientific endeavours I take inspiration from what is labelled *symptomatic reading*, which is 'used in literary criticism as a means of analysing the presence of ideology in literary texts'.[3] In his book *The Political Unconscious* Frederic Jameson defines the object of academic analysis as a 'diagnostic revelation of terms or nodal points implicit in the ideological system which have, however, remained unrealized in the surface of the text'. Therefore 'it would make sense to seek a latent meaning behind a manifest one, or to rewrite the surface categories of a text in the stronger language of a more fundamental interpretive code'.[4] In *Mapping Ideology* the Slovenian sociologist and psychoanalyst Slavoj Žižek, with inspiration from George Lacan, defines this form of text analysis as follows: 'The aim of the critique is to discern the unavowed bias of the official text via its ruptures, blanks and slips.' [5] More plainly, the text is understood not only for what it says directly but also for what it implies and suggests indirectly about the author and his world view. Not only what is in the lines but also what is between the lines is of analytical interest. More concretely, Lindhard can be said to operate in a field of activity onto which he projects his own masculine imagery. As will be shown, his outline of a theory of gymnastics is to a large extent an expression of his own cultural taste as a male academic. And his masculine imagery of virile conquest, power and bodily charisma, inspired partly by medieval times and the Viking age, can be seen as a projection of his own masculine fantasies which he, as a small and somewhat inhibited white-coated scientist, in no way could live up to himself but dreamed out in his gymnastics theory.

It is the ambition of this article to demonstrate that science, however 'pure' it might be imagined, cannot necessarily be characterised as a lofty endeavour beyond society but in effect can be undertaken by individuals strongly motivated by their own personal experience and life history who take part in the everyday social conflicts about power and prestige and with the aim of changing human social life. In this regard the article is inspired by studies in the genre of scientific biography, defined as the analysis of the life of scientists at the personal, the social and the academic level. The Scandinavian expert in scientific biography, Thomas Söderqvist, has described how originally a 'cold war generation of historians of science' tried to 'professionalize their craft by weeding out the personal aspects of science'. However, during the last two decades we have witnessed a 'return of biography as an *ancilla historiae*, that is, as a tool for contextualizing the history of science'.[6]

The main source of inspiration of this article derives from the French sociologist Pierre Bourdieu, who is one of the few social scientists to have elaborated on the importance of the body in culture.[7] By *habitus* Bourdieu highlights the – as a rule unconscious – attitudes to the world of a group such as a social class. According to Bourdieu these attitudes result in a number of *practices*, namely, bodily actions which signal class identity both inwardly in relation to the social group's own self-perception and outwardly in relation to other social classes. In the following, Lindhard's attempt to create a new gymnastics theory will be interpreted as an expression of his upper-class, academic *habitus*. By expressing the bodily norms and values of his own social class in gymnastics, Lindhard makes use of his *cultural capital* – the power of his scientific knowledge and vocabulary – in order to *distinguish* himself from and *dominate* other agents or social groups in the field who compete for authority and respect in gymnastic matters. He does this by attributing value to his own educated and well-bred *taste* based on bourgeois elite culture with its preference for aesthetics, fine arts and scientific knowledge and disapproving of the taste of other social agents in the field. Lindhard can be said to use *symbolic violence* in his categorisation of other social agents as being ignorant or misguided by bad taste. In all societies a strong drive towards gaining honour can be observed. In Bourdieu's terms there is a struggle to acquire *cultural capital*. Lindhard's successful use of his impressive scientific authority in aesthetic and ethical matters demonstrates a great amount of *symbolic capital* that allows him to influence areas outside his immediate physiological expertise.

The *illusio* of the game is defined by the belief of the social agents in the importance of their *social field* to such a degree that they are absorbed by the game and eventually forget that it is a game. Though there might be a fierce struggle between opponents, they 'agree to disagree' on what is felt utterly important to all of them. Without this basic belief in the social field's own logic, the field falls apart.

The main source material of this article consists of all Lindhard's published works with special reference to those related to the theory of gymnastics. Previous research on Lindhard's life and times comprises the biographical sketches by K. Jørgensen and E. Trangbæk,[8] K. Jørgensen[9] and K. Jørgensen and B. Saltin,[10] the gender-specific studies by H. Bonde[11] and E. Trangbæk,[12] the writings on school gymnastics by E. Møller,[13] O. Korsgaard,[14] P. Fibæk[15] and P. Jørgensen,[16] the studies related to Ling gymnastics in Sweden conducted by J. Lindroth and P. Schantz[17] and the Niels Bukh-related research by H. Bonde.[18] On August Krogh some scientific articles[19] and a monograph[20] have been written. Professor Erling Asmussen from Lindhard's old laboratory, the Laboratory for the Physiology of Gymnastics, who became professor there in 1964, has written a detailed and thorough book on his old workplace, of which he has first-hand knowledge from around 1926.[21]

It is important to realise that in the period from the turn of the century until the Second World War, Anglo-Saxon sports and Continental gymnastics were generally opposed to each other, with the outcome of the battle between them being far from certain. In many Continental European countries such as Czechoslovakia, Germany, Denmark and Sweden, gymnastics was looked upon as something more refined, which could foster good, healthy and disciplined citizens, whereas competitive sports were often characterised in a pejorative way as being dangerous for both body and morals. Thus, there was a fierce struggle for supremacy between sports and gymnastics within the pedagogical systems of many continental European countries.

The Epoch of Masculine Heroic Endeavour

Being the son of a grocer, Lindhard's way to science was in no way predictable. However, some important events during his youth and early adulthood seem to have motivated him to enter the world of science. At the age of 18 he had a very negative encounter with the specific Danish 'folk high school romanticism'.[22] Here, he developed a disgust for everything hypocritical and sentimental,[23] which might have led him into the more objective sphere of science.

Furthermore, it seems that during his time as a soldier and as a lieutenant in the Danish artillery in 1891 Lindhard developed a strong sense of self-discipline that might have helped him in his later academic career. We can use the aforementioned method of symptomatic reading to detect his strong passion for discipline. Without in any way intending to describe his own personality, he implicitly does so in an attempt to argue in favour of the benefits of discipline in gymnastics, which he underscores by relating his personal experience.

> I will definitely claim, also based on personal experience, that military drill is capable of creating discipline ... as the basis of self-discipline. It is a widespread misunderstanding that a military education only relies on force and threats ... It is the rule that the discipline of your time as a soldier becomes part of you and later is expressed in all of your actions.[24]

In 1898 Lindhard graduated as a doctor of medicine and from 1902 to 1906 he worked as a medical doctor in the small provincial town of Karise. However, his work as a doctor appeared to him to be rather pointless compared with the strong striving for science that now urged him to join the Mylius-Erichsen polar expedition, the so-called 'Denmark Expedition' in 1906–8, when the young poet and adventurer Mylius-Erichsen explored the entire coastline of the then unknown region of north-east Greenland.[25] Lindhard's objective was both to carry out physiological research of the human body under extreme circumstances and to function as the expedition's doctor. In his diaries – written to his wife – Lindhard states that he could no longer bear the pointless routines of everyday life and that his conscience had urged him to leave her and their three children for two years in order to conduct Arctic scientific studies.[26] The expedition was by no means without its dangers, since Mylius-Erichsen and two other members of the team tragically lost their lives in the icy Greenlandic landscape, adding even further to the mythological fervour surrounding the author and polar hero Mylius-Erichsen.[27]

Though the expedition as a whole can be seen as part of a more general masculine heroic *vitalistic*[28] enterprise of the time around 1900 – which included mountain climbing and other dangerous endeavours – it seems that Lindhard in no way nurtured romantic feelings about the hazardous exploration of the hostile northern environment. In his diary he condemns the many hardships of the expedition, especially the sled dogs that he can't control and that consequently make him extremely frightened. However, Lindhard and his family's great sacrifices and Lindhard's enormous devotion to his research work under the most extreme circumstances points in the direction of another type of masculine heroic striving connected with the endeavours of science. As will be demonstrated, Lindhard developed a very steadfast belief in the powers of science to explain and solve human problems, which can be interpreted as an expression of a general epoch-specific exaltation of male courage and sacrifice in a time of remarkable human exploration and devotion to progress.

In his personal and professional development Lindhard evolved a 'cogent and absolutely inexorable logic that was useful in his work but didn't really make him a family man'.[29] Perhaps this trait mainly arose as an antidote to his time at the Danish folk high school. His grandson, the esteemed Danish historian Søren Mørch, wrote that when 'my grandmother and the six daughters and one son were paying a visit or going for a picnic, he [Lindhard] followed later. "I don't like to walk in procession", he said.' Mørch adds that Lindhard didn't recognise his own children when he passed them in the street.[30] It seems that, not only in respect of his devotion to his occupational life but also in his rather distanced relationship to his family, Lindhard can be seen as a clear-cut prototype of the new male role of early industrial society, when men increasingly had to build their own careers and women of the upper strata were becoming more and more domesticated.

It is somewhat peculiar that Lindhard became associate professor of the theory of gymnastics from 1909. He apparently did not have any prior gymnastics experience except from teaching at Kaare Teilmann's physiotherapeutic course in 1908. In 1917 he became professor and from 1910 to 1920 he worked with August Krogh in his Zoophysiological Laboratory in Copenhagen, a collaboration that came to mark the birth of work physiology in Scandinavia. In 1920 Krogh was awarded the Nobel Prize for his discovery of the regulation mechanisms of the capillaries in skeletal muscles. This finding was a product of Krogh's genuine work, but the road that led to this outstanding scientific level of research was to a large degree attributable to his cooperation with Lindhard on circulatory physiology.[31] As a result of the Nobel Prize the American Rockefeller Foundation donated the so-called Rockefeller Building at Tagensvej to Danish Science, and Krogh made sure that Lindhard could move his laboratory into the new building from 1928.[32]

Homosesexuality and Gender Controversies

None of the existing or emerging gymnastics systems that were not based on Lindhard's own ideas were entirely acceptable to him. With very derogatory and often arrogant arguments he tried to discredit the competing systems of gymnastics. In Bourdieu's terms, he attempted to delegitimise the positions of his opponents in the *social field* in order to establish a monopoly of symbolic capital via his dogma of the supremacy of theory over practice.

In Denmark the Finn Elli Björkstén's women's gymnastics gained great influence after the turn of the twentieth century, which was further boosted by the establishment of Snoghøj Gymnastics Folk High School in 1925. Björkstén's gymnastics was based on original, stylistically pure exercises, a sense of rhythm and relaxation, close contact between gymnasts and an economisation of effort. Though Lindhard in general praised the trend towards women performing gender-specific exercises, his verdict on Elli Björkstén's writings was a scathing criticism – probably additionally motivated by the fact that she had dared to criticise Lindhard: 'Mrs Björksten's book should never have been written.' [33]

Besides criticising the exponents of orthodox Ling gymnastics, Lindhard also paid particular attention to the gymnastics of the emerging international star of gymnastics, Niels Bukh, the charismatic founder of the Danish school of modern gymnastics. He and his team of young elite gymnasts travelled around the world demonstrating his gymnastics in Europe, Africa, South America and Asia. [34]

Lindhard did not join the general chorus of praise after Bukh's display in Copenhagen in 1917. But, surprisingly, Lindhard's criticism was not made on physiological grounds but rooted in a bourgeois *taste* for a correct, traditional male demeanour without too much flamboyance, rhythm and physical contact. In Lindhard's view, Bukh's display lacked any clear direction: 'There was a military-like route march with heel first, there was a swaying march with song and the holding of hands', which Lindhard found 'unmanly'. His overall impression was that in the display there 'was too little masculinity and too much broidery'. And as for primitive gymnastics, Lindhard wrote: 'Now the great Ring Master Bukh appeared with a whistle clenched between his teeth and a whip between his fingers.' [35] We don't know if Lindhard knew about Bukh's homosexuality[36] and consequently tried to signal his disdain for 'homo-erotic' gestures[37] in gymnastics such as holding hands.

'The sweating, naked bodies' of Bukh's gymnasts, 'dressed only in their famous "little black" boxer shorts, the splashes of sweat on the floor that traced the gymnasts' positions during entrance and exit, and the pride of the eager gymnasts, altogether struck Lindhard as un-aesthetic and even disgusting.' [38] Or, in Lindhard's own words in his main popular work that was translated into Spanish and English in 1934: 'Occasionally aesthetic claims are disregarded to such a degree in Bukh's system that the effect is almost repugnant.' [39] As German sociologist Norbert Elias has pointed out in his theory of civilisation, these bodily marks of distinction constitute a fundamental way of creating *distinction* between different class cultures.[40] Lindhard's immediate disgust with the sweat, body contact and rhythm of Bukh's gymnastics shows that not only an intellectual detachment is at play but also a feeling of repulsion deeply rooted in *habitus*. In this context it is ironical that Bukh actually named his basic training gymnastics proudly 'primitive gymnastics' in order to signal a return to the 'natural body' of pre-modern people. According to Lindhard, Bukh's gymnastics was filled everywhere with 'a strange blend of nationalism, grandiloquent ethics and home-grown hygienics, mixed with odds and ends of less well-considered gymnastics theory'. Bukh supposedly championed 'the inflated chest that is not only characteristic of Ling but of his successors'.[41]

Bukh reacted by claiming that Lindhard was trying 'to do away with' him and declared that the support 'we crave and are in need of through science will never come from him'.[42] A mutual hostility developed between Lindhard and Bukh, who both gained international recognition within their respective fields of theory and practice. Throughout his entire life, Bukh found himself in fierce opposition to doctors and sports physiologists. Bukh was contemptuous towards 'the dry professors' who, in his opinion, 'had no contact with practical life'.[43] Erling Asmussen, who was later to become a professor of physiology, recalls the reactions of both Bukh and Anna Krogh, one of the founders of the stronghold of women's gymnastics in Denmark, Snoghøj Gymnastics Academy, after a display of 'academic gymnastics' by grammar school gymnasts: Bukh: 'It's pathetic'; Krogh: 'Where is the spirit?' [44]

It was Bukh's women's gymnastics that Lindhard found especially provocative. He characterised Bukh's method as distinctly masculine. It had nothing to do with female gymnastics. Again, Lindhard was prompted by his bourgeois taste and its view of women, in so far as he opposed Bukh's use of the 'wide-stance position', in which the women would stand with feet wide apart, dubbing it 'the most masculine and least feminine of all gymnastics positions'.[45] Despite his position as a scientist, Lindhard's main criteria for assessing the correctness of gymnastics were clearly founded on an aesthetic judgement. All in all, it seems clear that Lindhard in his criticism of Bukh paid much attention to warning men against giving rise to any suspicions of homosexual leanings through a 'feminised' demeanour.

New Modes of Gender Movement

Lindhard did not just criticise other forms of gymnastics but also began in earnest to develop his own system of gymnastics. His basic starting point was the assumption that physiological gender differences were such important dividing lines that a gymnastics theory should consider these above all else. In this respect he was riding with the tide, not least due to the independent development of a women's gymnastics at the same time as science was beginning to devote attention to the field. With the help of gymnastics Lindhard paved the way for the emerging new upper-middle-class and bourgeois modes of behaviour for the two genders, or to put it in Bourdieu's terms, Lindhard worked on creating, through the body, a new *habitus* that was better suited to the division of gender roles in the emerging industrial society. For the men of these social strata it was becoming increasingly important to be the sole breadwinners and self-made men instead of just following in the footsteps of their fathers. For the women of the upper classes the trend was not just to carry out the household chores but to spend time and energy on making themselves and their homes look aesthetically pleasing. Lindhard's concept of gymnastics reflected this shift in gender roles, which also could be said of the many dance schools in Denmark in the inter-war period.

Lindhard's emphasis on the importance of gender difference[46] should be seen against the backdrop of the joint institutions that modern bourgeois society was setting up for both men and women, which threatened to undermine the traditional accent on fundamental contrast, most clearly marked in the separation of sexes within the space of the church. Now, both boys and girls were being trained in gymnastics together. It was important for Lindhard and other educational pioneers, therefore, that this joint training emphasised gender differentiation so that bourgeois society's twin-sex institutions should not eradicate the difference between the sexes but reinforce it.

The period around 1900 in Denmark was distinguished by women's struggle on behalf of 'the mother project'. The great utopia for many women was to have sufficient time in which to care for, tend and protect their children. Through the creation of housewives' 'leagues' and maternity groups, women fought for the recognition of motherhood as the natural goal of a woman's life; to a great extent with the assistance of the medical profession.[47] In that respect, Lindhard as a doctor fits in well with the overall picture, but he also chose to extend the lines of battle by incorporating gymnastics. Many women were well and truly fed up with the stiff, male-dominated position gymnastics that they found to be far too militaristic.[48]

For Lindhard not only gender but also age was a fundamental category of distinction. Lindhard claimed that 'What sport is to the grown-up man and dance to the woman, play is for the child'.[49] In this he was largely in accordance with the tendency around the turn of the century to promote childhood as an extremely important period in the making of healthy and socially capable human beings. The internationally renowned Swedish author Ellen Key epitomised the idea of nourishing and cultivating the precious child in her two volumes entitled *The Century of the Child* (1900). In one of the very rare instances that Lindhard praised another gymnastics educator, he wrote with reference to the Swede, Elin Falk: 'Miss Falk is the only person in Scandinavia who has done independent work in gymnastics, and she differs from her predecessors ... by really working with children, whereas all others have found it more convenient to play with tin soldiers.'[50]

Lindhard found that

> From an aesthetic point of view there can be no doubt that the aim of gymnastics differs for the two sexes. A form midway between the male and the female type will be repugnant to most people. A pair of strong masculine shoulders is no ornament to the female form, and even an artist of the rank of Praxiteles cannot but excite dislike when he mingles too pronouncedly feminine elements in the figures of youth (The Lizard Killer).[51]

From a theoretical point of view it is important to note that notions of femininity always imply notions of masculinity and vice versa.

Lindhard continues by demonstrating that the position of standing to attention praised by traditional Ling gymnastics[52] 'has nothing in common with antique sculpture, and that it is useless as an expression of the oft-mentioned qualities [bravery, courage, energy, firmness, will-power, a noble mind]'.[53] Lindhard contrasts the stiff posture to his own ideal, on which he comments that

> the position should give the impression of freedom, that it should be straight and erect but not rigid. It must as little as possible have the appearance of a straitjacket. Within the limits that must necessarily be drawn in free-standing gymnastics, it should seem to the spectator to be feely chosen.[54]

According to the American sociologist Erving Goffman, it is the most powerful who can grant themselves permission to break with convention. By doing so, they demonstrate that they are in charge of the situation to such an extent that they can slacken the outward expression of power. The appearance of such a state of relaxed, complete control can only be achieved if no one else is allowed to breach the set standards. Using Goffman's central conceptual couplet, subjects are required to demonstrate 'tightness' towards the 'looseness' of authority.[55] Thus Lindhard's ideal of a more relaxed attitude can be seen as an attempt on the part of the academically educated and privileged members of society to *distinguish* themselves from the less well-to-do, who in their demeanour express obedience and restraint. Whereas the children of ordinary people could be subjected to immediate external control by authoritarian means in a military-like gymnastic style, grammar-school students could be taught to express a 'looser' and more relaxed, flexible and almost invisible self-control that demonstrated a subtle control of the situation.

For traditional school gymnastics, it was claimed that standing to attention with a rigidly straight back was particularly beneficial to respiration, and that it gave the student more energy to work with. As a demonstration of creative, systematic and meticulous science, Lindhard proceeded to examine 'The Effects of Several Gymnastic Postures on the Chest and Lungs' – the title he gave to a dissertation he published in 1924.[56] To achieve his aims, Lindhard used special apparatus, a so-called thoracograph, which could measure the shape of the upper torso by drawing horizontal contours of the chest at various intervals. The experimental subject was Emanuel Hansen, who would become Lindhard's successor as professor of gymnastics theory in 1935. Through this simple method, Lindhard managed to undermine *the* central principle of traditional Ling gymnastics: 'With only one exception to all the gymnastics positions tested, the circumference of the chest in motion, measured in terms of its vital capacity, is significantly reduced with restrictions of up to 33%.'[57]

Lindhard did not, however, agree with the praise heaped on the dynamic, forward-moving and quantitative masculinity of modern competitive sport.[58] In his criticism of the 'record mania', therefore, Lindhard shared the views held by traditional Ling supporters. However, Lindhard also found that games and athletics in a moderate form were just as valuable an educational tool as gymnastics. However, this did not hold true for children because 'the undeveloped or as yet incompletely developed body should not be subjected to the strain of maximum effort'.[59]

Despite Lindhard's severe criticism of the exponents of Ling gymnastics, he nevertheless used Ling's exercises, although sometimes in a modified version. Lindhard clearly attempted to strengthen masculine bourgeois body language in his descriptions of the basic positions. The fundamental position in gymnastics was the position of attention (*retstillingen*) that Lindhard characterised in the following way:

> For a man, the position of attention should be firm and well balanced, should give the impression of unshakable equilibrium. The contours of the position should be well marked, but not angular; the whole figure should bear the stamp of controlled force, of a condensed will, only waiting for some external occasion to blossom into action.[60]

Lindhard elaborated upon his description of the masculine position of attention, noting:

The knights of the straddling type seem to feel as if they embodied the whole world, heaven and earth in their own persons. ... These traits are the very ones which, in a subdued form, should characterise the male position of attention.' [61]

On 'masculine walking' Lindhard wrote:

> A walking man follows a definite course. The masculine walk is purposeful, following straight lines; when a man walks he has the appearance of pursuing a definite plan even if this is not the case, whereas a woman does not convey the impression that she is deliberately walking in a certain direction even if this is the case.[62]

With somewhat militarist metaphors Lindhard continued: 'A man should tread firmly on the ground as if he set his foot on the neck of a vanquished foe.' [63] This militarist form of description was also revealed in the description of the 'masculine march':

> The difference between the masculine and the feminine will perhaps appear most plainly in marching. Marching is a typically masculine form of movement. There is an element of the machine-like in it, something that recalls the modern 'tank' which makes its way across graves and through barbed-wire fences.[64]

From these and many other quotations it becomes clear that Lindhard has many strong fantasies on a revitalisation of masculinity not least based on physical criteria. It remains a paradox that Lindhard, as a white-coated scientist and in some aspects inhibited person, a man who was not very athletic and not at all a polar hero, projected such strong masculine fantasies into gymnastics.

Symptomatic reading aims at uncovering aspects of the text that are unconscious to the author or perhaps even discrepancies between the author's actions and words. In this case, it seems that, despite his collaboration with the anti-military party *Det Radikale Venstre*, Lindhard uses strings of metaphors that praise male chivalry in a militaristic form. According to George Lakoff and Marc Johnson's metaphor theory, outlined for instance in their ground-breaking book *Metaphors We Live By*,[65] metaphors are not merely accidental but reveal something fundamental about the communicator of a message. Originally, the rather martial quotation might have been inspired by its provenance around the beginning of the Great War, but he retained the expression in later editions.

Finally, it is obvious that Lindhard's upper-class taste with regard to notions of masculinity also permeates his gymnastics theory, for example in the passage in which he describes 'male touching':

> Hence it seems unpleasant and confusing to the spectators if men are made to join hands, as it may happen in the gymnasium during walking exercises. If it is desired to make a man cut a comic figure on the stage, one of the meanings of achieving this effect is to let him move with dancing steps. Hence the swaying rhythmic movements that occur in several of the artificial forms of walking seem absurd or repugnant when performed by men in the gymnasium.[66]

From a contemporary point of view, we can be tempted to believe that the sole function of 'patriarchal society' was to suppress women. But from a close reading of Lindhard's writings, for example, we can see that just as many restrictions were directed towards men's as well as women's freedom of movement. Not least for the growing male middle classes of this emergent capitalist era in Danish history, the aim was to maintain strict mental composure to achieve advancement and not to follow in one's father's footsteps but to mould a career of one's own. Any form of aesthetic complacency, passivity, or nonchalance was considered 'un-manly'. Every movement that might signal femininity or even homosexual leanings was absolutely banned.

Lindhard's proposed modes of bodily 'practices' could be used to create *distinction* in relation to other strata of society by means of unconscious corporeal presence. In general, the upper-class notion of touching in sport was much more Victorian than that of the working classes. As a whole, working-class power sports around 1900 should be seen as an expression of an independent class culture. Working-class men were not primarily drawn to the time sports, favouring instead power sports such as weightlifting, wrestling and boxing, in which the ideal was the strong man and where the experience of sweat, close bodily contact and direct physical struggle, man against man, were central.[67]

The Perfect Woman

Lindhard's interest in developing a women's gymnastics dates back to the very beginning of his academic career. In his early writings he demonstrates a positivist belief in basing women's gymnastics on biological characteristics in line with the general tendency around 1900 to use methods from the natural sciences as models for all scientific work. He maintains this conviction long after he has abandoned the idea of a general gymnastics founded on physiology. In 1913–14 he wrote:

> The prior requirement for a rational gymnastics is knowledge of the body's construction and its life-long processes, as well as the mechanisms involved in exercise, to such a degree that the results of every exercise can be calculated both qualitatively and quantitatively in advance. This requires that the human material undertaking the gymnastics be of uniform type, in regards to anatomy and physiology.[68]

It is somewhat paradoxical that Lindhard criticised traditional Ling gymnastics for using physiological arguments to give reasons for individual positions whereas he himself used physiological arguments to back up his theory about the necessity of gender-specific gymnastics. However, precisely on this point traditional gymnastics did not see any fundamental biological difference between the two sexes.

In contrast to the masculine movements, Lindhard commented that female walking should demonstrate that women were less dynamic and goal-oriented than men:

> In a woman's walk there is nothing that recalls marching; this kind of gait is very unsuitable for women. A woman does not set her foot on the neck of the earth, she glides over it. She does not make her way straight though all obstacles, she does not avoid them either; she follows her own path. She does not, like the man, follow straight, continuous or broken lines, she moves in softer curves. She does not, like a man, pursue a definite course. A woman's walk is less balanced, less stable than a man's ... If we find it natural that a woman leans on a man's arm when walking, this is undoubtedly because of our immediate conception of the difference in stability.[69]

On the feminine gait Lindhard wrote that 'A woman's walk is less balanced, less stable than a man's; hence it does not seem inconsistent to the spectator when young girls, as is often the case, link arms and form a chain, or when the female pupils in the gymnasium join hands and move with dancing steps'.

The role of an upper-class woman was not to storm the gates of heaven but to ensure the human race through her role as a mother. Women should

> maintain the special feminine form of movement, i.e. the movements should not be sharp and abrupt but smooth and plastic. The positions should be clean and beautiful, but should not bear that stamp of concentrated energy which distinguishes the positions of men. Movements and positions should be varied as much as possible and can be varied more than in masculine gymnastics. The word of command should not be sharp or rousing, but act more as a guide to the pupils. Women should be taught gymnastics by women.[70]

Lindhard's remark about female instructors for women's gymnastics was the subject of great controversy at the time.[71] Lindhard's standpoint shows that he cannot be characterised merely as a patriarchal type searching for male domination in all spheres of society; on the contrary, he actually supported women in gymnastics who fought for female liberation from the dominance of male authority. At the same time, Lindhard himself, of course, tried to exercise control over female gymnastics teachers by emphasising the importance of his gymnastics theory as the father of all rational gymnastics. Lindhard clearly supported 'difference-feminism' in contrast to 'resemblance-feminism'. These two concepts of femininity clashed in a fierce struggle in the inter-war period. Advocates of women's athletics interpreted competitive sports as perfect tools for women's conquest of male territory, whereas supporters of female gymnastics considered athletics to be an antidote to the health-promoting and graceful essence of femininity.[72]

Lindhard had a very strange view of the female stand-at-ease position (in Danish *hvilestilling*). Was it for moral or physiological reasons that he wrote: 'As will be seen, the free foot is not carried forward but a little to the side, the whole extremity being rotated so much inward that the flexed knee of the free extremity almost touches the stationary extremity'.[73] That Lindhard's ideas of female modes of demeanour could have broad ramifications can be observed in two different captions of the so-called Egtved-Girl at different historical contexts. The Egtved Girl (1370 BCE) lived in the Nordic Bronze Age, and her remains were found at Egtved in Denmark in 1921. Figure 1(a) is a picture from the 1930s and Figure 1(b) a picture taken in 1961. The images illustrate a clear cultural forming of the body. The caption of the later picture reveals an emerging female liberation of attitudes towards the body whereas the picture from the 1930s clearly demonstrates the influence of Lindhard's ideas about the correct female stand-at-ease position.

The young woman shown in Figure 1(a) was a performer of so-called Bertram gymnastics. Agnete Bertram was one of Lindhard's first students at the Laboratory for the Physiology of Gymnastics, and she created a new Lindhard-inspired graceful women's gymnastics system in the 1920s which she showed to audience in different European countries and the US.

Besides taking its inspiration from Lindhard's notions of psycho-aesthetics, Bertram's system[74] was immersed in ancient Greek influences and could be performed in Greek robes in the neo-classical building of the Carlsberg Foundation to the accompaniment of classical music such as Mozart's Sonata in A major, which was well suited to bourgeois women in their roles as aesthetic domestic angels. Lindhard wrote in *The Theory of Gymnastics*:

> The renewal of women's gymnastics only appeared with Agnete Bertram. Mrs. Bertram has introduced the feminine form of motion into gymnastics. Previous reformers have with more or less success tried to adapt men's gymnastics to the necessities of women, none of them has dared to take the step of dispensing entirely with men's gymnastics.[75]

Lindhard also defended Bertram against accusations made by other educators that her gymnastics were too markedly aesthetic and had only superficial influence on the physical form of the body:

> Her gymnastics are pronouncedly kinetic gymnastics. In so far as they resemble Niels Bukh's, but in an aesthetic sense they are as opposite as poles. Mrs Bertram of course has been obliged to lay great stress on aesthetic viewpoints; without this, justice could not be done to the feminine form of motion. But this does not mean, as has been

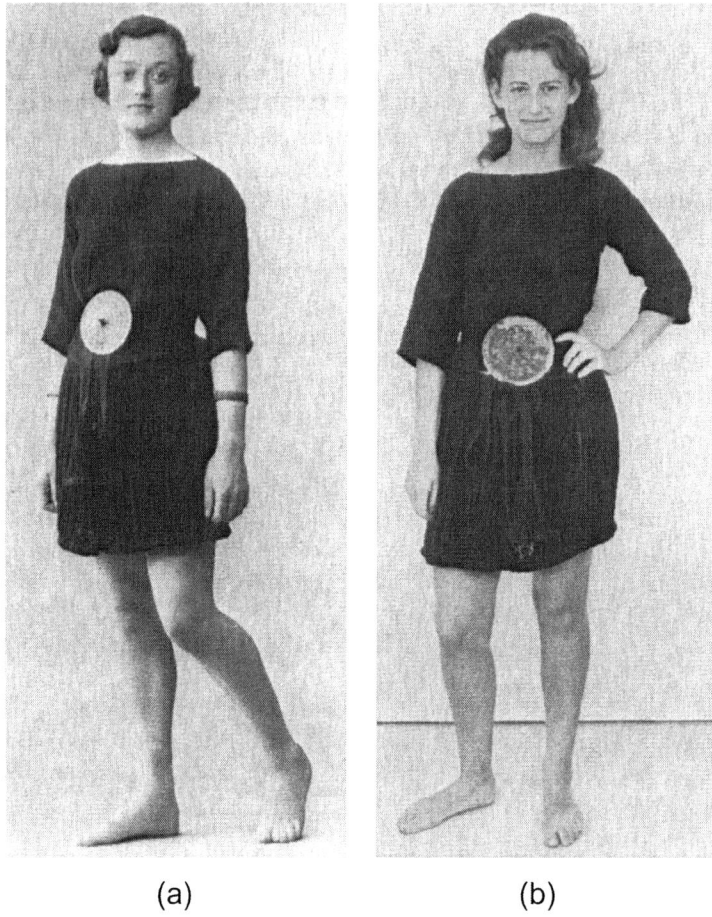

(a)   (b)

Figure 1.   (a, b) Jensen, J. *I begyndelsen – Fra de ældste tider til ca. år 200 f.kr.*, p. 11.

> maintained in several quarters, that Mrs Bertram has abandoned gymnastics to land in
> plastic exercises. ... Mrs Bertram's gymnastics are ... gymnastics according to the
> fundamental principles of Ling.[76]

Lindhard did not explain how Bertram's gymnastics could both dispense entirely with
men's gymnastics and at the same time be in accordance with Ling's theory, which was
created for men as a pronounced male activity. Later on in her career Agnete Bertram
tried to express 'scientific' views on her gymnastics, for example on the meaning of
equilibrium in 'the laws of human movement'.[77] Lindhard evidently found these
attempts rather pseudo-scientific and withdrew his support of Bertram, probably because
he finally realised that it was impossible to establish a scheme of women's gymnastics
on physiological grounds. Eventually Bertram gymnastics died out, apparently because
it was too elitist and exclusive on account of the high costs of participating.[78]

Conclusion

Johannes Lindhard was one of the founding fathers of modern exercise physiology.
However, not least by means of his book *The Theory of Gymnastics*, published in

Spanish and English in 1934, he had important ramifications outside the realm of science. Lindhard's criticism of the rigidity of Ling gymnastics and his introduction of new modes of female carriage, not least through his pupil Agnete Bertram, who with her team gave displays in many European countries and the US, was all part of the general evolution of gymnastics. However, he came to play a key role in the scientific legitimisation of women's gymnastics and the delegitimisation of traditional Ling gymnastics' claim that its health benefits were scientifically proven.

To a large degree Lindhard built on Pehr Henrik Ling's old stock of exercises; however, Lindhard's particular contribution crystallised into the separation of women's and men's gymnastics, which he perceived as being fundamentally rooted in physiological gender differences. Thus he managed to lend the Lingian movements a new meaning according to his perception of movements that could express manly and expansive dynamism and force in contrast to female beauty, ease and curved movements. Lindhard also succeeded in making the positions more supple, thereby demonstrating a more refined self-control of the (academic) bourgeoisie that was fitting for the youth of the grammar schools.

In his attempt to 'gender' the field of gymnastics, Lindhard not only tried to mould female gymnastics and thereby the everyday behaviour of the girls and young women of the upcoming bourgeois society with its praise of motherhood and domestic life. He also incorporated in his theory of gymnastics strict notions of the new expansionist masculinity that above all should not show any sign of homosexual or too feminine rhythm, dance-like behaviour or non-aggressive bodily contact between men. In this sense, the article contains an appeal to enlarge women's studies into a broader interest in gender socialisation, demonstrating that men also have been exposed to and limited by strict social norms.

The article tries to argue that gender history cannot at all be reduced to a power struggle between women and men. During the inter-war period there was a fierce struggle for supremacy between a so-called 'difference-feminism' in contrast to a so-called 'resemblance-feminism'. This struggle was mainly conducted by women who supported female athletics against women who in accordance with essentialist thinking supported female gymnastics. After all, it was a woman (gymnastics inspector Else Thomsen) who in 1932 left the board of the Danish sport federation in protest against female 'masculinising' athletics. And it was a male medical doctor, Knud Secher, who a year later, by means of a medical report based on scarce scientific evidence, paved the way for the acceptance of female competitive sports within the Danish sports federation.[79] The complexities of gender relations also become obvious when it is noticed that the otherwise quite patriarchal Lindhard actually supported female emancipation in his opinion that women should lead women within gymnastics. All in all, we are much in need of sophisticated and open-minded gender analyses.[80]

Seen from a present-day point of view, Lindhard's positions, as well as those of his fierce gymnastics opponents, bear many similarities with regard to the basic acknowledgement of Lingian principles and their eschewal of competitive sport. In his eccentric and conceited belief in his own gymnastics knowledge, Lindhard resembled more the grand old gymnastics educators that he felt contempt for than the clinical white-coated scientist. Thus he himself became one of the influential gymnastics pedagogues of the twentieth century. Coinciding with the fact that Linhard's opponents – supporters of traditional Lingian gymnastics – eventually had to relinquish their lead position to competitive sports (assisted by Lindhard's *coup de grace*), Lindhard's importance, too, depreciated drastically in the wider history of gymnastics, symbolised not least in problems experienced by his former student Agnete Bertram in conducting her exclusive and expensive women's gymnastics in the 1930s.

A quote from the scholar of the scientific biography, Thomas Söderqvist, is fitting here: 'Traditional historical and sociological accounts of science are complemented by narratives that emphasize the importance of the scientific subject in the production of science.' [81] I hope through this article to have provided a contribution to this acknowledgement by pointing to Lindhard's utter dedication to science, aided by his anti-romantic world view. In addition, at the level of the theory of science, the influential sociologist Anthony Giddens has developed a notion of *double hermeneutics*. He points to the fact that 'findings of the social sciences very often enter constitutively into the world they describe'.[82] Taking Lindhard as an example, we might ask: what about the natural sciences?

In Bourdieu's terminology the conclusions can be summarised as follows. Lindhard used his scientific authority to promote his own gender gymnastics, which was actually based on his own upper-class *habitus* with its preference for the ethical and aesthetic aspects of physical culture, thereby poaching on the preserves of the humanities and arousing opposition from the psychological-pedagogical *field*. It seems that until the very end of his life Lindhard kept the belief that the confrontations within the social field of gymnastics were a struggle between pure science and lay superstition – without realising the significance of the *illusio* aspects of the passionate game of power, position, passion and *distinction* by means of the privileged and superior *taste* based on the fine arts and the neoclassicism of the cultural bourgeoisie that Lindhard had come to belong to. When we look, from our present vantage point, at the determination and the amount of energy invested in the struggle for supremacy in the field of gymnastics theory and pedagogy, all this is hard to comprehend at a time when gymnastics internationally has more or less been outmanoeuvred by competitive sport and reduced to just another sub-discipline of sports.

Finally, it should be underlined that Lindhard, besides his attempt to propagate his own class-based interests, was also a devoted scientist who made an important contribution to the early formation of the international field of sport physiology, helped to pave the way for August Krogh's Nobel Prize in 1920 and contributed, with his own clear words, to a much-needed critique of the pseudo-science of Ling gymnastics in the decades after 1900.

Notes on Contributor

Hans Bonde is a professor of Sports History and leader of the Sport, Politics and Welfare research group at the University of Copenhagen. He has extensively published on the history of sport, with a focus on gender, politics and national identity.

Notes

1. Lindhard, *The Theory of Gymnastics*, 47.
2. On Lindhard's scientific biography and his co-work with August Krogh, see Jørgensen and Saltin, 'Træk af Johannes Lindhards videnskabelige bidrag og værk', 64ff.

3. Thurston, 'Symptomatic Reading', 638.
4. Jameson, *The Political Unconscious*, 48ff.
5. Žižek, *Mapping Ideology*, 10.
6. Söderqvist, 'Introduction', 13.
7. The following definitions are extracted from Bourdieu, *Distinction*, and Bourdieu and Wacquant, *An Invitation to Reflexive Sociology*.
8. Jørgensen and Trangbæk, 'Professor Johannes Lindhard'; Trangbæk and Jørgensen, 'Striden mellem Johannes Lindhard og K.A. Knudsen'.
9. Jørgensen, *Fra læge på Danmarks Ekspeditionen til Nordost Grønland*, 3–16.
10. Jørgensen and Saltin, 'Træk af Johannes Lindhards videnskabelige bidrag og værk'.
11. Bonde, 'Kønnet i kroppen'.
12. Trangbæk, *Kvindernes idræt*, 189–11.
13. Møller, *Træk af skoleidrættens historie i Danmark*, 38, 138.
14. Korsgaard, *Kampen om kroppen*, 182–7.
15. Fibæk Lauersen, *Idrætsdidaktikkens modernisering*, 266–79.
16. Jørgensen, 'Ikke at more, men at opdrage', 137–9.
17. Lindroth, *Ling, Från storhet till upplösning*, 115–21; Schantz, 'Om Lindhardskolan och dess betydelse i ett svenskt perspektiv', *passim*.
18. Bonde, *Niels Bukh*. 106f, 110, 119, 375, 429.
19. Brandt Rehberg, 'August Krogh'; Kildebæk Nielsen, 'August Krogh, Første fysiolog ved Det naturvidenskabelige Fakultet'; Kildebæk Nielsen, 'August Krogh (1920), Videnskabsmand forklarer'.
20. Pauck, *Den selviscenesættende videnskabsmand*.
21. Asmussen, *Gymnastikstudiet og Det Gymnastikteoretiske Laboratorium*.
22. The folk high schools, which still constitute a vital force in Danish society today, rebelled against the examination process of Danish pedagogical systems. Instead of learning for specific purposes, the folk high schools aimed at learning for life. There were no grades and the main goal was that the young pupils mainly between 18 and 25 years of age would develop their personality through contact with the great questions in life.
23. Mørch, *Den sidste Danmarkshistorie*, 184.
24. Lindhard, 'De gymnastiske øvelsers inddeling', 306.
25. Andreassen and Medonos, *Danmark-Ekspeditionen til Nordøstgrønland*.
26. Jørgensen, *Fra læge på Danmarks Ekspeditionen til Nordost Grønland (1906–1908) til docent i gymnastikteori på Københavns Universitet. En fortælling om Johannes Lindhards første forsker- og lære(r)år* 4, 6.
27. One of the most recent books on masculine Arctic conquest is Hastrup, *Vinterens Hjerte*, on the Danish polar researcher Knud Rasmussen.
28. On vitalism, see Hvidberg-Hansen and Oeslner, *Livslyst*. The book and museum catalogue on Danish vitalism especially in art, about 450 pages long, is currently being translated into English (Museum Tusculanum Press, Copenhagen).
29. Mørch, *Den sidste Danmarkshistorie*, 184.
30. Ibid., 184.
31. Schmidt-Nielsen, *August and Marie Krogh*, 95–11.
32. Schmidt-Nielsen, *August og Marie Krogh*, 231.
33. Ibid., 61.
34. Bonde, *Gymnastics and Politics*, 103ff.
35. Lindhard, 'Hr. N. Bukhs Opvisning i Koncertpalæet'.
36. On Bukh's homosexuality in connection with his gymnastics, see Bonde, 'The Gymnastics Sexual Revolution'.
37. A general introduction to the theme of 'homoeroticism' in sport is given in Krüger, 'The Homosexual and Homoerotic in Sport'.
38. Asmussen, *Gymnastikstudiet og Det Gymnastikteoretiske Laboratorium*, 15.
39. Lindhard, *The Theory of Gymnastics*, 30.
40. Elias, *The Civilizing Process*.
41. Lindhard, *Den specielle gymnastikteori*, 47ff.
42. Bonde, *Gymnastics and Politics*, 70.
43. Interview with 'Niels Bukh junior'', 26/7, 1995.
44. Asmussen, *Gymnastikstudiet og Det Gymnastikteoretiske Laboratorium*, 17.

45. Lindhard, *Den specielle gymnastikteori*, 48.
46. For some rather patriarchal remarks by Lindhard on women's gymnastics see Lindhard, 'Legemsøvelser for kvinder'.
47. Løkke, 'Forældrebilleder- Skitser til moderskabets og faderskabets historie', 6ff.
48. Lykke Poulsen, *Den kvindelige kvinde*, 84ff.;Trangbæk, *Kvindernes idræt*, 109ff.
49. Lindhard, *Den specielle gymnastikteori*, 5.
50. Lindhard, *The Theory of Gymnastics*, 91.
51. Ibid, 69.
52. Lindhard explicitly refers to K.A. Knudsen's book from 1916.
53. Lindhard, *Den specielle gymnastikteori*, 141.
54. Ibid., 150.
55. Goffmann, *Behavior in Public Places*, 198–216.
56. Lindhard, 'Nogle gymnastiske stillingers indvirkning på brystkassen'. 1924.
57. Ibid.
58. Bonde, 'The Time and Speed Ideology'.
59. Lindhard, *Den specielle gymnastikteori*, 412.
60. Ibid., 115.
61. Ibid., 115.
62. Ibid., 160.
63. Ibid., 160.
64. Lindhard, 'Kvindegymnastik', 64 and Lindhard, *The Theory of Gymnastics*, 159.
65. Lakoff and Johnson, *Metaphors We Live By*.
66. Lindhard, *The Theory of Gymnastics*, 160f.
67. Cf. Bourdieu, *Distinction*, 208–25. See also Bonde, *Mandighed og sport*, 84ff.
68. Lindhard, 'Kvindegymnastik', 2.
69. Lindhard, *The Theory of Gymnastics*, 162.
70. Ibid., 70.
71. Lykke Poulsen, *Den kvindelige kvinde*, 84ff.
72. Bonde, 'Idrættens tabte uskyld', 47ff.
73. Lindhard, *The Theory of Gymnastics*, 150.
74. On Bertram gymnastics, see Trangbæk, *Kvindernes idræt*, 161ff.
75. Lindhard, *The Theory of Gymnastics*, 41.
76. Ibid., 41.
77. Bertram, *Bevægelseslove*.
78. Asmussen, *Gymnastikstudiet og Det Gymnastikteoretiske Laboratorium*, 17f.
79. Bonde, 'Idrættens tabte uskyld', 49.
80. Ibid.
81. Söderqvist, 'No Genre of History Fell Under More Odium', 251.
82. Giddens, *Social Theory and Modern Sociology*, 20.

References

Andreassen, J. and J.C. Medonos. *Danmark-Ekspeditionen til Nordøstgrønland 1906–1908 – i jubilæumsårene 2006–2008*. Copenhagen: Arktisk Institut, 2005.
Asmussen, E. *Gymnastikstudiet og Det Gymnastikteoretiske Laboratorium ved Københavns Universitet*. Copenhagen: Idrættens Forskningsråd, 1988.
Bertram, A. *Bevægelseslove*. Stockholm, 1937.
Bonde, H. *Mandighed og sport*. Odense: Odense Universitetsforlag, 1991.
Bonde, H. 'Kønnet i kroppen – Om historisk køns- og kropssemiotik'. *Den Jyske Historiker* 58/59 (1992): 101–9.
Bonde, H. *Gymnastics and Politics*. Copenhagen: Museum Tusculanum, 2006.
Bonde, H. *Niels Bukh. En politisk-ideologisk biografi (CD-ROM)*. Copenhagen: Museum Tusculanum, 2007.
Bonde, H. 'Idrættens tabte uskyld', in *København i en Jazztid*, ed. Jens Andersen. Copenhagen: Politikens Forlag and Golden Days, 2008, 38–55.
Bonde, H. *Det ekstreme køn [the Gender of Extremes]*. Højbjerg: Forlaget Hovedland, 2008.

Bonde, H. 'The Time and Speed Ideology. 19th Century Industrialisation and Sport'. *The International Journal of the History of Sport* 26, no. 10 (Aug. 2009): 1315–34.

Bonde, H. 'The Gymnastics "Sexual Revolution": Niels Bukh, Male Aesthetics and Homophilia'. *The International Journal of the History of Sport* 26, no. 10 (Aug. 2009): 1396–1413.

Bonde, H. 'From Hygiene to Salvation: I.P. Muller, International Advocate of Gymnastics'. *The International Journal of the History of Sport* 26, no. 10 (Aug. 2009): 1357–75.

Bonde, H. 'Political Assertion: Rural Revolutionary Gymnastics'. *The International Journal of the History of Sport* 26, no. 10 (Aug. 2009): 1335–57.

Bourdieu, P. *Distinction, A Social Critique of the Judgement of Taste*. Cambridge, MA: Harvard University Press, 1979.

Bourdieu, P. and L. Wacquant, *An Invitation to Reflexive Sociology*. Chicago: University of Chicago Press, 1992.

Brandt Rehberg, P. 'August Krogh'. *Dansk Medicinhistorisk Årbog* (1974): 7–28.

Elias, N. *The Civilizing Process, vol. I: The History of Manners*. Oxford: Blackwell, 1969.

Fibæk Lauersen, P. *Idrætsdidaktikkens modernisering*. Copenhagen: DHL, 1995.

Giddens, A. *Social Theory and Modern Sociology*. London: Stanford University Press, 1987.

Goffman, E. *Behavior in Public Places*. New York: Simon & Schuster, 1966.

Grue-Sørensen, K. 'Gymnastik- og karakterudvikling m.m'. *Vor Ungdom* (1930/31): 413–16.

Hastrup, K. *Vinterens Hjerte – Knud Rasmussen og hans tid*. Copenhagen: Gads Forlag, 2010.

Hvidberg-Hansen, G. and G. Oeslner. *Livslyst: Sundhed, Skønhed, styrke i dansk kunst 1890–1940*. Odense: Forlaget Odense Bys Museum & Fuglsang Kunstmuseum, 2008.

Jameson, F. *The Political Unconscious*. Ithaca, NY: Cornell University Press, 1981.

Jensen, J., I begyndelsen – Fra de ældste tider til ca. år 200 f.Kr. (vol. 1). Copenhagen: Gyldendal, 1988.

Jørgensen, K. and E. Trangbæk. 'Professor Johannes Lindhard – om gymnastik, videnskab og kulturel forskellighed', in *Fakultære højdepunkter. Episoder fra Det Naturvidenskabelige Fakultets 150-årige historie*, ed. J. Lützen. Copenhagen: Faculty of Science, University of Copenhagen, 2000, 115–28.

Jørgensen, K. *Fra læge på Danmarks Ekspeditionen til Nordøst Grønland (1906–1908) til docent i gymnastikteori på Københavns Universitet. En fortælling om Johannes Lindhards første forsker- og lære(r)år*. I Copenhagen: Department of Exercise and Sport Sciences, 2007.

Jørgensen, K. and B. Saltin. 'Træk af Johannes Lindhards videnskabelige bidrag og værk'. In *Forskning i Bevægelse: Et nyt forskningsfelt i et 100-årigt perspektiv*, edited by A. Lykke Poulsen. Copenhagen: Museum Tusculanum, 2009, 59–81.

Jørgensen, P. 'Ikke at more, men at opdrage', in *Een time dagligen: Skoleidræt gennem 200 år*, eds I. Berg Sørensen and P. Jørgensen. Odense: Odense Universitetsforlag, 1998.

Kildebæk Nielsen, A. 'August Krogh, Første fysiolog ved Det naturvidenskabelige Fakultet', in *Fakultære højdepunkter. Episoder fra Det Naturvidenskabelige Fakultets 150-årige historie*, ed. J. Lützen. Copenhagen, 2000, 97–114.

Kildebæk Nielsen, A. 'August Krogh (1920), "Videnskabsmand forklarer, hvorfor piger rødmer"', in *Nabo til Nobel – Historien om tretten Nobelpriser*, eds H. Nielsen and K. Nielsen. Aarhus: Aarhus Universitetsforlag, 2001, 345–69.

Knudsen, K.A. *Lærebog i gymnastik for seminarier*. Copenhagen: J. Frimodt, 1916.

Knudsen, K.A. *Lærebog i gymnastik*. Copenhagen: J. Frimodt, 1930.

Knudsen, K.A. *Danmarks Højskole for Legemsøvelser 1898–1948*. Copenhagen: Gyldendal, 1948.

Korsgaard, O. *Kampen om kroppen*. Copenhagen: Gyldendal, 1982.

Korzybski, A. 'A Non-Aristotelian System and its Necessity for Rigour in Mathematics and Physics'. *Science and Sanity* (1933): 747–61.

Krogh, A. 'Visual Thinking'. *Organon – International Review* (Warsaw), 1938.

Krogh, A. 'Johannes Lindhard. 25. april 1870 – 11. oktober 1947: Tale i Videnskabernes Selskabs møde den 23. januar, 1948'. Copenhagen, 1948.

Krüger, A. 'The Homosexual and Homoerotic in Sport', in *The International Politics of Sport in the Twentieth Century*, eds J. Riordan and A. Krüger. London, 1999, 191–216.

Lakoff, G. and M. Johnson, *Metaphors We Live By*. Chicago: University of Chicago Press, 1980.

Lindhard, J. 'Akademiske gymnastiklærere'. Special issue of *Gymnastisk Selskabs Aarsskrift* (1912).

Lindhard, J. 'Kvindegymnastik'. Special issue of *Gymnastisk Selskabs Aarsskrift* (1913/14): 1–29.

Lindhard, J. 'Gymnastikkens ligestilling med andre skolefag'. Special issue of *Gymnastisk Tidsskrift* 2 (1915): 2.

Lindhard, J. 'Hr. N. Bukhs Opvisning i Koncertpalæet'. *Akademisk Gymnastik* (Copenhagen) (1917): 43–9.

Lindhard, J. *Den specielle gymnastikteori*. Copenhagen: C. Larsen, 1918.

Lindhard, J. 'Nogle gymnastiske stillingers indvirkning på brystkassen'. Special issue 270 of *Meddelelser fra universitetets gymnastikteoretiske laboratorium* 1–2 (1924): 1–96.

Lindhard, J. *Den specielle gymnastikteori*, 3rd edn, reworked and enhanced version. Copenhagen: Levin & Munksgaard, 1927.

Lindhard, J. *Legemsøvelser*. Copenhagen: J. Jørgensen og co., 1930, 1–24.

Lindhard, J. 'De gymnastiske øvelsers inddeling'. *Vor Ungdom* (1930/31): 304–8.

Lindhard, J. 'Gymnastik og Sundhed'. *Vor Ungdom* (1931): 20f.

Lindhard, J. 'Muskelvirksomheden'. Special issue of *Bibliotek for læger* (Dec. 1933): 469–97.

Lindhard, J. *The Theory of Gymnastics*. London: Methuen, 1934.

Lindhard, J. 'Legemsøvelser for kvinder'. *Vor Ungdom* 55, no. 8 (1933–4): 363–9.

Lindhard, J. 'Legemsøvelser og legemsøvelser'. Special issue of *Tidsskrift for Legemsøvelser* 1 (1937): 1–9.

Lindroth, J. *Ling, Från storhet till upplösning*. Stockholm: Brutus Östlings bokf Symposion, 2004.

Lützen, J., ed. *Fakultære højdepunkter, Episoder fra Det naturvidenskabelig Fakultets 150-årige historie*. Copenhagen: Faculty of Science, University of Copenhagen, 2000.

Lykke Poulsen, A. *Den kvindelige kvinde*. Copenhagen: Department of Exercise and Sport Sciences, University of Copenhagen, 2005.

Lykke Poulsen, A., Trangbæk, E., Jørgensen, K. and Nordsborg, N., eds. *Forskning i bevægelse: Et nyt forskningsfelt i et 100-årigt perspektiv*. Copenhagen: Museum Tusculanum, 2009.

Løkke, A. 'Forældrebilleder- Skitser til moderskabets og faderskabets historie'. *Social Kritik*, 25–26 (1993): 6–22.

Møller, E. *Træk af skoleidrættens historie i Danmark*. Nyborg: Skoleidrættens Forlag, 1980.

Mørch, S. *Den sidste Danmarkshistorie*. Copenhagen: Gyldendal, 1996.

Pauck, T. *Den selviscenesættende videnskabsmand*. Copenhagen: Forlag1.dk, 2009.

Schantz, P. 'Om Lindhardskolan och dess betydelse i ett svenskt perspektiv', in *Forskning i bevægelse: Et nyt forskningsfelt i et 100-årigt perspektiv*, ed. A. Lykke Poulsen, E. Trangbæk, K. Jørgensen and N. Nordsborg. Copenhagen: Museum Tusculanum, 2009, 137–67.

Schmidt-Nielsen, B. *August og Marie Krogh: Et fælles liv for videnskaben*. Copenhagen: Gyldendal, 1995.

Schmidt-Nielsen, B. *August and Marie Krogh, Lives in Science*. New York: American Physiological Society, Oxford University Press, 1995.

Secher, K. 'Legemsøvelser og sundhed'. *Vor Ungdom* (1931): 195–200.

Söderqvist, T., ed. *The History and Poetics of Scientific Biography*. Aldershot: Ashgate Pub Co, 2007.

Söderqvist, T. 'Introduction: A New Look at the Genre of Scientific Biography', in *The History and Poetics of Scientific Biography*, ed. T. Söderqvist. Aldershot, 2007, 1–16.

Söderqvist, T. 'No Genre of History Fell Under More Odium than that of Biography', in *The History and Poetics of Scientific Biography*, ed. T. Söderqvist. Aldershot, 2007, 241–62.

Thurston, J. 'Symptomatic Reading', in *Encyclopaedia of Contemporary Literary Theory: Approaches, Scholars, Terms*, ed. I.R. Makaryk. Toronto: University of Toronto Press, 1993, 638.

Trangbæk, E. *Kvindernes idræt: Fra rødder til top*. Copenhagen: Gyldendal, 2005.

Trangbæk, E. and K. Jørgensen. 'Striden mellem Johannes Lindhard og K.A. Knudsen', in *Forskning i bevægelse: Et nyt forskningsfelt i et 100-årigt perspektiv*, eds A. Lykke Poulsen, E. Trangbæk, K. Jørgensen and N. Nordsborg. Copenhagen: Museum Tusculanum, 2009, 92–101.

Žižek, S. *Mapping Ideology*. London: Verso, 1994.

The 'Floating Baroness' and the 'Queen of the Skis'

Annette R. Hofmann

University of Ludwigsburg, Germany

Recently women's ski jumping has attracted public attention because a group of female jumpers went to court to fight the IOC decision to exclude them from the 2010 Olympic Winter Games in Vancouver. After almost nine months in court the jumpers lost their case, and maybe their story will disappear into nowhere again.[1] Especially before the Olympics it was a worthwhile story for the media to report about. Thus not only the existence of women's ski jumping but also this case of gender discrimination was spread all over the world. For many people not involved in ski sports it was the first time they heard about women's ski jumping.

However, ski jumping is not a new sport for women. First sources tell us about ski jumping women in nineteenth-century Norway. Not until the twentieth century do we hear about women performing this sport on the European continent and in North America. Throughout the history of this sport, there were always examples of extraordinary women jumpers. Two of them from different European countries, living in different periods, shall be the focus of this paper. The Austrian Baroness Paula Lamberg (1887–1927) from the famous Austrian ski resort Kitzbühel, and the Norwegian Johanne Kolstad (1913–1997), who reached international fame due to her long jumps in the 1930s.

Considering the fact that ski jumping was and still is seen as a male-only sport, the questions arise, who were these women who lived in different parts of the world during different times and managed to receive recognition in a male-dominated sport? What were the social and cultural circumstances that made it possible for them to attain fame at a time in which women's participation in sports was very much restricted? Or were they simply a product of the rising emancipatory currents of the time?

After an introduction to the beginnings of women's ski jumping and the arguments opposed to it, this paper tries to find answers to these questions and build a link to the image of the 'New Women' in the early twentieth century who also had some impact on women's sports participation.

The Early Years of Women's Ski Jumping and the Public View

Skis have existed a few thousand years. Originally they were used for hunting and transportation on snow by men and women.[2] The sport of skiing goes back to nineteenth-century Norway and was performed early on by women. One of the most prominent early examples of a skiing woman was Eva Sars, the wife of the famous explorer and ski pioneer Fridtjof Nansen.[3] Skiing also became popular for women on the continent. It was a physical activity that was seen appropriate by male opinion for the female body. However, competitions were considered immoral. Max Schneider, a ski manufacturer from Berlin and editor of the journal *Tourist*, wrote in his *Katechismus des Wintersports* in 1894 that skiing was a sport very much in favour for women:

> Especially for the female gender there is not enough physical activity in the winter. No prejudices need to be conquered here, as at the end of the last century with ice skating; the Scandinavian ladies have long since stopped it and whoever sees the women bursting with youthfulness, vitality and health on the snowshoe hills close to the Nordic capitals will recommend introducing snowshoeing for the benefit of German women.[4]

Whereas skiing women were accepted, ski jumping was considered to be only for men. One of the first written sources on this sport goes back to 1796 in which the Dutch officer Cornelius de Jong describes the jumping exercises of Norwegian soldiers. The Norwegian Sondre Andersen Nordheim became an early pioneer. He reached fame in 1860 when he jumped 30.5 metres. In 1866 the first official jumping competition took place.[5] At that time there were only combined competitions: cross-country skiing and ski jumping. Not until 1883 did single jumping events exist.[6] In central Europe the first official ski-jumping event was organised in 1893 in Austrian Mürzzuschlag.[7]

Although, the history of ski jumping has clearly been dominated by men, according to Von der Lippe, in the second half of the nineteenth century there were already some Norwegian women who jumped in competitions. In 1863, the Norwegian Ingrid Olsdatter Vestby became the first woman known to participate in a ski-jumping competition. The writer of a local newspaper of the time stressed how unusual it was:[8]

> She pushed off and raced down to jump, took off and flew until she landed, firmly, planted on her skis, past the point where many a brave lad had lost his balance earlier in the competition.The spectators roared their approval – the first 'bravos' of the day. Their relief was great for they had never seen a girl jump on skis and they had been more than a little anxious as she flew over their heads.[9]

In 1896 a first unofficial national competition for women, the *Landesrennet for Damen*, was organised by the Norwegian Asker Ski Club with 20 participants. In 1902 the Norwegian Hilda Stang jumped 14.5 metres, and eight years later 21 metres. In 1914 28 women participated at a jumping event in Trondheim.[10] In Germany, too, ski jumping women can be found: In 1905 a female jumper in the Harz reached 15 metres,[11] and the journal *Der Winter* lists Ilsemarie Feustell in 1909.[12] Ashburner mentions in his *History of Ski Jumping* the English Miss Hocking, who participated in 1911 at the first British Ski Championships; she not only supposedly jumped very nicely, she also landed after 7 metres without falling.[13] Around the same time a Fräulein Engelbrecht from Munich and the Austrian Baroness Paula Lamberg appeared as active jumpers. Especially the latter caused a stir by competing with men. She is the best-known forerunner of female ski jumpers in continental Europe.

Not only European women dared to ski down a *bakken*. North American women also showed some interest in this activity. Sandie Gibson leaped 46 feet and 4 inches in 1904, 'the greatest leap by a woman on skis ever made' according to Wisconsin's *Ashland Daily Press* in March of that year.[14] Looking at various winter carnivals in North America, in some places women were on the jumping programme. Examples are the Steamboat Springs Winter Carnival in the US, the Rossland Winter Carnival and the Revelstoke Winter Carnival in Canada. Isabel Coursies was the great female jumper of Canada's east who in 1922, at the age of 16, jumped 84 feet.[15] She was the first woman allowed to go over the famous Côte des Neiges ski jump in Montreal.[16] On the American East Coast, it was Dorothy Grace, 'the daredevil girl' from New Hampshire, whose father ordered her a pair of skis to strengthen her legs that were weakened by scarlet fever. She made a name for herself in ski jumping in the 1930s and 40s.[17]

This was a time when several Norwegian women jumpers became internationally known and travelled on tours throughout the world, participating in ski-jumping shows. Besides Johanne Kolstad, Hilda Braskerud and Eda Gulbrandsen were big names. At a jumping competition for women in Odnes, 17-year old Johanne and 14-year old Hilde were listed as the top competitors among the 18 participants.[18]

Despite the high praise for these women by the contemporary press, there has always been resistance to women ski jumping from various corners. In the late nineteenth and early twentieth century many reporters – at that time only men – regarded female ski jumping as 'unladylike' and the performing women as 'simply unattractive'. They even classified them as 'immoral'.[19] What was even more important were the medical arguments. Looking at the history of women's sports in general, the medical argument was consistently used by physicians, educators and others to exclude women from physical activities, certain sports and competitions, both in Europe and North America. In 1896 Norwegian Christian Døderlein justified the exclusion of women from ski jumping – 'especially married women who have given birth, and whose reproductive organs have been through a process which all too often reduces them to a morbid state'.[20]

Still in the 1920s and 1930s, doctors and female physical educators, keen to promote the therapeutic benefits of physical activity for female health, encouraged a number of sports, but ski jumping was certainly not among them.[21] The Canadian physical educator Ethel Cartwright, for instance, encouraged young women to skate, snowshoe and ski in the winter months – as long as no jumping was involved.[22] By this time vital energy theory (VET) had largely given way to fears that physical activity was responsible for uterine displacement which was believed to cause sterility.[23] This made jumping – particularly landing – seem very dangerous for women, who were already perceived as fragile. The German physician Gustav Klein-Doppler wrote in 1926 that 'there is no need or reason to organise jumping competitions for ladies. Because of the unanswered medical question as to whether ski jumping agrees with the female organism, this would be a very daring experiment and should be strongly advised against.'[24]

The German ski instructor Henry Hoek advised in the 1930s: 'No jumping for you, girlfriend – it is not for any woman, no matter how brave or powerful or young.'[25] Even Germany's best female skier, Christel Cranz, said in the 1930s (although she herself liked to jump in her youth) that cross-country skiing and ski jumping were 'athletic performances, ... for which a lot of strength and endurance is necessary, more than women can give without harming themselves'. Moreover she mentioned a lack of interest among women in ski jumping: 'Certainly no reasonable sporting girl would think about participating in a marathon or boxing, and that is how it is with us women skiers; there is no interest in running or jumping competitions.'[26]

However, the examples mentioned above show that Christel Cranz's opinion cannot be transferred to every woman. Some were extremely attached and interested in ski jumping.

Paula Lamberg

In many books on the history of women's skiing around the world one can find the famous pictures of the 'Jumping Baroness': a rather stiff-appearing woman dressed in a long black skirt, floating through the air. However, searching in the various archives one does not find too much information on her. One can only rely on written documentation, such as winter sport magazines and newspapers. No personal notes, such as letters, notebooks or diaries, which could have given an inside perspective on her difficulties and also joys in taking up ski jumping, exist.[27]

Comtesse Paula Lamberg, who in most English sources is called 'Baroness', descended from an old aristocratic family that had been in Kitzbühel since the sixteenth century. She was born in 1887 in Kitzbühel as the second child of Reichsgraf Hugo Anton Lamberg and the Italian Comtesse Giulietta Brunetti from Bologna.[28] In the 1890s Kitzbühel's history as an Austrian ski and winter sport resort had just started. Schloss Lebenberg, the home of the Lambergs, became the first hotel, and as such important for the establishment of tourism in the region.

In 1904 the local winter sport club distributed free skis to the local boys who soon discovered the joy of ski jumping.[29] The 20-year-old Comtesse joined these boys. Apparently, later on she was known as a skier as well, but according to a note in the *Kitzbüheler Winterlob*, at the beginning of her jumping years she was not even able to ski a turn. This means that after landing, she was forced to sit down to come to a stop.[30]

The year 1910 was when most of Paula Lamberg's jumping results can be found in official documents. For instance on 6 January a jumping event took place at the new junior hill: 17 adults and a few boys participated. The winner reached 19.5 metres; the baroness 14.5 metres. Only two weeks later Paula Lamberg started at another event in Kitzbühel – outside the official competition. She managed two jumps of 24 and 23 metres, only 7 metres less than the winner.[31] The author of the *Illustrierte Zeitung* praises the performances of the 23-year-old aristocrat highly, but also expresses his reservations about ski-jumping women. He sees the baroness as an exception, and does not give other women much of a chance in this sport. With this he reflects the general opinion that ski jumping was not considered being acceptable for females at that time:

> An excellent female ski jumper is Baroness Lamberg from Kitzbühel. At ski competitions which the winter sports club of Kitzbühel held a short while ago, this lady, who is an avid, enthusiastic skier, was able to perform two jumps without falling, reaching a distance of 24 and 23 metres, in excellent style. Jumps of this length are very good, even for men. It is understandable that ski jumping is performed very rarely by women, and taking a close look, not really a recommendable sport. One prefers to see women with nicely mellifluous movements which show elegance and grace, like in ice skating or lawn tennis. One does not like to see athletic exercises performed by a woman. This use of strength is, however, necessary when jumping with snowshoes. And it is not enjoyable or aesthetic to see how a representative of the fair sex falls when jumping from a hill, flips over and with mussed-up hair glides down towards the valley in a snow cloud.[32]

However, not all of the baroness's jumps ended successfully. At an event at which she and five men started, at the Arlberg, a ski resort about 200 km west of Kitzbühel, Paula Lamberg fell in all of her three jumps. Still, her style was praised, and her length mentioned in the official report. She had reached 19.5, 20.5 and 21 metres.

Some of these jumps were longer than some of the men's.[33] A special highlight for Lamberg took place in February 1913. According to Wirtenberger, Princess Viktoria, a sister of the German Kaiser, and His Highness Prince Adolf spent some time in Kitzbühel. Here they also watched a jumping event in which the baroness participated.

After 1913 there are no more sources that mention any ski jumping activities of the baroness. She took up other sports. She became known as a skier and tennis player and, in the 1920s, as a bobsleigh and car racer. In the latter two sports she competed together with her future husband, Earl Franz Schlik (1882–1963). Together with Schlik and friends she also founded the Kitzbühel Sport Club, where international tourists gathered.[34] The year of their marriage, 1927, was a very active year for Schlik and his wife. In bobsleighing the baroness usually occupied the braking position. In the beginning of the year the couple won the Tyrolean Championships in the 'Two-Person Bobsleigh'. That year they also participated together in car races. However, the 3.5 kilometres *Salzbergrennen*, organised by the Bavarian Automobile Club for the third time in the German Berchtesgarden on 4 September, ended tragically. Schlik and the 40-year-old baroness, being considered the favourite team, started last. In order to keep her balance in a curve, the baroness leaned too far out of the car. As a result she fell; a few minutes later she died of her head injuries.[35]

This was the tragic end of a Kitzbühel legend. Whereas nobody talks about the Comtesse's achievements in bobsleigh and car racing any more, she is still remembered today for her performance in ski jumping. Still in 1981, Hans Lackner, a well-known local ski instructor, was quoted as having said that in the 1920s the Comtesse was his role model in ski jumping.[36] The Norwegian press was very much impressed by Paula Lamberg's jumping performances and gave her the nickname the 'Floating Baroness', a name that persists until today.

Paula von Lamberg's funeral service was a big event in Kitzbühel. In appreciation of her contribution to the local winter sports, members of the Winter Sporting Club[37] carried her coffin to her grave. The popular baroness was not only a great local athlete of the time, but also had been very active in promoting tourism in Kitzbühel.[38]

An article in *Der Winter* summarised Lamberg's performances in ski jumping shortly after her death:

> In the years 1908–11 she was a very engaged jumper in Kitzbühel, the only lady, at least in Middle Europe, of whom this can be said. Not only did she jump very well, but also during competitions her jumps reached respectable 20–28 metres, lengths that at that time were extraordinary. Later she became an enthusiastic tourist and was always engaged in the development and well-being of Kitzbühel as a place for winter activities. The 'floating baroness', as the Norwegian press once called her, will thus be held in good remembrance there and by jumpers who appreciated her courage and camaraderie.[39]

Johanne Kolstad

As already mentioned, in Norway one can find several examples of ski-jumping women. Probably the most famous women who performed this sport during the 1930s were Hilda Braskerud (1916–1996) and Johanne Kolstad (1913–1997) from Dokka in Southern Norway. They started ski jumping when they were children and became stars in Norway and abroad. At the age of 17 years Johanne already jumped

46.6 metres. Although she jumped as far as the boys, she and the other Norwegian women jumpers – just like the baroness – had to start 'outside' the competitions, meaning they had to jump during the breaks. Still, they were very successful. Hilde and Johanne became so-called 'trail jumpers' to entertain the spectators during breaks. These two women became celebrities of a sort. A reason for this is – besides their athletic performance – that they always dressed identically. They became the first female media stars of Norwegian ski jumping. Kolstad especially reached international fame. The main source of the following notes on her can be found in the book *Hopp Jenter-Hopp!* by the Norwegian ski historian Karin Berg.

Johanne's most active jumping years lasted the decade: between 1930 and 1940. Through her outstanding jumping performances in Norway she became internationally known. She became famous for travelling together with other Norwegians. She went on several tours abroad: England and four trips to North America.[40] During her visits to the US Kolstad demonstrated her best ski jumping: In February 1936 she reached 53 metres in New Boston. With a jump of 72 metres in 1938 in Berlin, New Hampshire, Kolstad broke her own world record.[41] From that moment she became known as 'Queen of the Skis'. Her record was not beaten until over 30 years later, in 1972 by Norwegian Anita Wold from Trondheim with a jump of over 80 metres.

In the 1930s ski jumping was performed not only outdoors; indoor ski events in major cities around the world took place. Just to mention a few examples: In 1937, besides jumpers from the US and Canada, at least three Norwegian ski jumpers, 'The Flying Norsemen', entertained the spectators at New York's Madison Square Garden: Tomme Murstad, Johanne Kolstad and Ella Gulbrandsen. Johanne did a few parallel jumps with Tomme Murstad, and she competed against other women; one was the American Dorothy Graves, who recalled in an interview given in 1974 that this was the first time that she competed with another woman.[42] Also London had an indoor event: 'Bringing the Alps to Town' could be found as a headline in *The Daily Mirror* of 26 November 1938, announcing an indoor ski-jumping event for a month later at London's Earls Court. It also mentioned that 'famed skiers from all over the world' would come to this 'Winter Cavalcade', among them Johanne Kolstad, holder of the world record jump for women.

Kolstad's last public appearance was at a jumping event in 1940 in her home country. She reached the 70 metres line at Oslo's Midtstubbakken and finished her active career.[43]

After 1940 there are no more sources that tell of Kolstad jumping. The war might have interfered, or meanwhile 27-year-old had decided for a more settled life. Eventually she married Ole Aastal and had a daughter in 1947.

How do Paula Lamberg and Johanne Kolstad fit into the picture of the (sporting) women of the time?

Ski jumpers as the 'New Woman'

Industrialisation, urbanisation, scientific progress and various bourgeois women's movements of the nenteenth and twentieth centuries have led to a change in gender relations over the years on an economic political, social and cultural level. Additionally, the First World War contributed to it, at least for some time. Through the absence of husbands, fathers and brothers, women had to take over typical men's tasks. The number of women working outside their households rose and women gained access to university education.[44] After the war, it was necessary to redefine the role of men and women in European societies. Although women had proven they could do the same work as men, they did not reach gender equality after the war. In many cases they had to return to bringing up their children and return their working place to the men again. Still, a few goals were reached: the possibility of an university education and, in many countries, the right to vote. 'The Victorian mold had been broken', as Allen writes.[45] The public picture of women and their role in society had also slowly started to change, at least among urban middle-class women in the 1920s, the so-called 'Golden Twenties'. This is mirrored in magazines, films and advertisements that spread a new body and beauty ideal for women. No longer was the long-haired 'chubby' woman the beauty ideal, but a thin, boy-like one. The 'new woman' or 'garçonne' showed youthfulness, androgyne behaviour, such as wearing trousers, smoking, having short haircuts and participating in sports. Allen summarises these changes: 'The New Woman reinvented herself by constructing an outward person to fit the new social relationships she was forming with male and female friends.'[46]

Certainly, not all women fulfilled the above-mentioned beauty ideal, but diets, cosmetics, clothes and, last but not least, exercise and sports helped to meet it.[47] The participation in sports and physical activities had already become more and more popular at the turn of the century. During the decades following women slowly gained access to a variety of sports. However, competitions for women still continued to be sparse. As shown above, moral reasons or medical arguments were used to keep them away from exhausting sport participation. Despite these arguments some women broke the gender barrier in sports, and could be found in male sports such as soccer, ice hockey and ski jumping.

Baroness Lamberg can certainly be viewed as an early example of the 'New Woman', a woman who broke the gender barriers of her time already before the First World War. She not only participated in many sports; she also was the founder of a local sports club.

Looking at the existing photos of the jumping baroness one can usually see her in a long black dress. Until the 1920s the dress was a symbol of female morality and decency. Trousers for women were seen in connection with emancipatory movements and not appreciated by society, even when they were more comfortable and practicable for their sporting activities.[48] In skiing there were many discussions on whether they could be useful. Women who wore the male outfit of the time were often ridiculed. The fear existed that trousers would de-sex women, and it was perceived as unaesthetic and not elegant. However, from 1906 on, the first women skiers dressed in trousers could found on the slopes.[49] The impression that the Baroness adjusted at least through her clothes to the conventions of the time cannot be fully supported. There is one picture in existence that shows her jumping in trousers. The year is not known, but considering the fact that her father was among the spectators, it must have been before 1913. His presence can lead to the conclusion that he approved his daughter's activities and lifestyle. The Norwegian Kolstad, however, lived at a time when she no longer had to worry about her outfit for jumping. For her and her female jumping mates it was normal to perform their sport in trousers.

When looking at Paula von Lamberg it has to be taken into consideration that she was an aristocrat belonging to the leading social class of Kitzbühel. When as a 20-year-old adult she entered the world of ski jumping with boys, no one dared to object her doing so. It was a time when Kitzbühel was just beginning to become known as a winter sport resort. Paula's family played an important role in supporting the growth of tourism; the baroness, with her unusual hobby and as a public figure through her social standing, might have even drawn some attention to this city as well. Hierarchy and social class certainly account for the fact she seems to have been accepted by male ski jumpers and also by the public. At least the sources revealed no negative arguments.

Not much is known about Kolstad's background, but it can be assumed that she was not from an upper-class family. Her public acceptance can be drawn back to other reasons. Taking a glance at the history of ski jumping, no other country had as many women ski jumpers in the first part of the twentieth century as Norway did.[50] An assumption might be that for the Norwegians it was less a problem to have women jumping than in many other countries. The fact that Johanne Kolstad was jumping as far as many men probably also helped her to be accepted in this male sport. Through her travelling and her many records she represented her country worldwide and became something like a national heroine or icon in Norway, a person the Norwegians were proud of. Norway was a country that was occupied for centuries by the Danes and later by the Swedes. In 1905 it reached independence. Norway is the origin of skiing and ski jumping. Skiing played an important feature in developing an national identity in the later nineteenth and early twentieth century.[51] Usually women have to fight their way into the national sports of their country and are not easily accepted. In Kolstad's case it might have been different due to the fact that Norway was searching for its identity and skiing played an significant part of Norway's nation-building process, as for instance Goksøyr and Allen have shown.[52] To draw a connection to the 'new woman', Kolstad not only through her sport, but also through her various trips abroad, showed her independence, which was generally not usual for women of the time.

Baroness Lamberg with all her various upper-class sports, and Johanne Kolstad with her independent travels around the world to perform ski jumping and represent her country, embodied both character traits of the 'new woman'. Additionally, with their ski jumping both athletes entered a male domain and broke gender barriers and thus were important forerunners and role models for later generations of women (and men) ski jumpers. Both women were accepted by the public; their performances were watched by the royalty of their countries. Both had their jumping careers just before the outbreak of a world war. It is not known whether this was a reason for them to end their jumping careers or not.

Still, it should be pointed out that it is hard to compare these two women. They lived in different decades, they came from different countries and different social classes. They are perfect examples to show that women could find self-fulfilment and acceptance in sports in the first part of the twentieth century.

Concluding Remarks

Paula Lamberg and Johanne Kolstadt were chosen to show that women's ski jumping is not an entirely new sport that only rose in the 1990s. It also mirrors the fact that these women – although ski jumping was not considered being an appropriate pastime for women in the 1910s or 1930s – had the courage to perform their sporting hobby despite moral and medical restrictions of the time. Both of them travelled and became successful in their sport, reached fame and even became role models not only for women but men as well. However, their success and personal power did not suffice to open this sport to girls and women in general. Until today ski jumping remains an outsider sport for women due to the fact that it is still under hegemonic masculine dominance. Later ski jumpers, such as the Finnish Tiina Lethola, who broke the 100-metre barrier in 1981 with 110 metres, Austrian Eva Ganster, who was the first to be allowed to ski-fly, Austrian Daniela Iraschko, who broke Ganster's record with a distance of 200 metres,[53] the Norwegian Anette Sagen, the German Ulrike Grässler and world champion Lindsay Van, still have to fight gender discrimination in their sport. Although women have their own jumping competitions today, they still often jump as pre-jumpers at men's events or in the interlude. This is especially the case when it comes to ski-flying, where lengths of over 200 metres can be reached. Still the medical argument was used until recently to keep women out of the sport. The notion that jumping would cause uterine displacement remained a point of debate well into the 1990s; the most prominent supporter was FIS president Gian Franco Kasper, who now states that he is a supporter of women's ski jumping.[54] Also the clothing has been discussed again, when Walter Vogler, FIS representative of Nordic sports, suggested in 2009 tighter outfits for the women, to raise media interest.[55]

It will still be a rocky road until women are fully acknowledged as ski jumpers. Although there are no sources, it is almost certain that Paula Lamberg and Johanne Kolstad must have encountered at least some difficulties and most probably hostility during their jumping careers; nevertheless, they certainly laid a foundation stone for future women ski jumpers to build on.

Notes on Contributor

Annette R. Hofmann is professor for Sports Studies at the Ludwigsburg University of Education. She is the president of the International Society of the History of Physical Education and Sport (ISHPES). She has published numerous articles on sport historical, sport sociological and sport pedagogical topics with a special focus on ethnicity, gender and health.

Notes

1. For more detailed information see Hofmann et al., 'Dear Dr. Rogge', and Vertinsky et al., 'Skierinas in the Olympics'.
2. Falkner, 'Von den Anfängen', 536.
3. Allen, *The Culture and Sport of Skiing*, 141.
4. Schneider, *Katechismus des Wintersports*, 31.
5. It was organised by Andreas Bakke. The jumping table is still today called *bakken*.
6. Falkner, 'Streiflichter der Entwicklung', 32; Jahn and Thiemer, *Enzyklpädie des Skispringens*, 11.
7. Ashburner, *The History of Ski Jumping*, 29.
8. Berg, 'Jump, Girls Jump', 12.
9. Von der Lippe, 'Ski Jumping', 1046.
10. Berg, *Hopp, Jenter-Hopp*, 13–18.
11. Falkner, 'Von den Anfängen des Frauenskilaufens', 536–7.
12. *Der Winter* 1909, 537.
13. Ashburner, *The History of Ski Jumping*, 58.
14. Quote from the *Ashland Daily Press*, 10 March 1904.
15. Scott, *Powder Pioneers*, 33.
16. Ball, *I Skied the Thirties*, 80.
17. Thabault, George, 'Dot Graves – "A" Jumper', 9.
18. Berg, *Hopp, Jenter-Hopp*, 69.
19. Berg, 'Jump, Girls Jump', 64.

20. Von der Lippe, 'Ski Jumping', 1046.
21. Lenskyj, 'Common Sense and Physiology'.
22. Hall, *The Girl and the Game*.
23. Vertinsky, *The Eternally Wounded Woman*.
24. Klein-Doppler, 'Die Damen im Skisport', 16.
25. Hoek, *Skiheil Kamerad*, 13.
26. Cranz, *Skilauf für die Frau*, 20.
27. The author wishes to express special thanks to Arno Klien, the Stadtarchiv Kitzbühel, especially Dr. Wido Sieberer and Hans Wirtenberger, for supporting her with sources on Baroness Lamberg.
28. Stadt Kitzbühel, 'Schriftleitung Eduard Widmoser', 399.
29. Kitzbüheler Ski Club, *Hahnenkamm*, 18–27.
30. Schmitt, *Kitzbüheler Winterlob*, 41.
31. The baroness's record was broken in 1926 by the Norwegian Olga Balsted Eggen, who jumped 4.5 metres further: Jahn and Theiner, *Enzyklopädie des Skispringens*, 394.
32. *Illustrierte Sportzeitung*, 9 Oct. 1910, 305.
33. Wirtenberger, 'Sportlady internationaler Klasse'; also Wirtenberger, 'Letzer Schlossherr auf Lebenberg'.
34. The marriage only lasted four months. Paula von Lamberg married in 1927 in Prague Franz Graf Schlik zu Bassano und Weißkirchen. In 1920 he had moved with his first wife to Kitzbühel. Schlik became an important figure in the city's sporting society. Not only was he an active car and bobsleigh racer and tennis player, he also found the Kitzbühel Sport Club together with the comtesse and others. He was involved in building tennis courts, a first ski lift for tobogganing and the cable car at the famous Hahnenkamm. By 1917 Paula and her mother were the owners of Schloss Lebenberg. After her tragic accident Schlik inherited her 50%. Three years later he also was handed over the possessions of his mother-in-law. Thus he became the sole possessor of Schloss Lebenberg. By 1961 he had sold all the property and buildings connected with it. See Wirtemberger, 'Letzter Schlossherr auf Lebenberg', and Stadt Kitzbühel, 'Schriftleitung Eduard Widmoser', 378.
35. *Kitzbüheler Anzeiger*, 21 Dec. 1963.
36. *Kitzbüheler Anzeiger*, No. 23, p. 18, 1981; see notes on orbituary of Hans Lackner.
37. This club has different names in the sources. One finds it under Kitzbühel Sport Club as well as Winter Sporting Club Kitzbühel.
38. Winterberger, 'Letzter Schlossherr auf Lebenberg', no page.
39. *Der Winter* 1927/8, 256.
40. The Norwegians are known to have introduced skiing to North America. The American-Norwegians were eager to supported such events with visiting Norwegians; see Berg, *Hopp, Jenter-Hopp*.
41. Berg, *Hopp, Jenter-Hopp*, 64; 94.
42. Thabault, 'Dot Graves – "A" Jumper', 9.
43. Berg, *Hopp, Jenter-Hopp*, 68; 94.
44. Pfister, 'Die Balance der Differenz', 210–11.
45. Allen, *The Culture and Sport of Skiing*, 176.
46. Ibid.
47. Pfister, 'Sport Befreiung des weiblichen Körpers', 226; Pfister, 'Die Balance der Differenz', 220; Duerr, *Der erotische Leib*, 168–9.
48. Günter, *Geschlechterkonstruktion in Sport*, 106.
49. Allen, *The Culture and Sport of Skiing*, 144–84. Allen devotes a whole chapter on the dress code of women in the early decade of skiing.
50. Still in recent years, one of the strongest opponents of women's ski jumping was the Norwegian FIS representative Torbjorn Yggesett; see Vertinsky et al., 'Skierinas in the Olympics', 38–9.
51. Goksøyr, 'Winter Sports and the Creation of a Norwegian National Identity' 30ff.
52. Goksøyr, 'Winter Sports and the Creation of a Norwegian National Identity', and Allen, *The Culture and Sport of Skiing*.
53. Hofmann and Preuß, 'Amazonen der Lüfte', 105–14.
54. Vertinsky et al., 'Skierinas in the Olympic', 37.
55. Hofmann et al., 'Dear Dr. Rogge', 42.

References

Allen, E. John B. *The Culture and Sport of Skiing*. Amherst, MA: University of Massachusetts Press, 2007.

Ashburner, Tim. *The History of Ski Jumping*. Bath: Bath Press Ltd., 2003.

Ball, William L. *Skied the Thirties*. Ottawa, ON: Deneau Publishers & Co. Ltd., 1981.

Berg, Karin. 'Jump, Girls Jump. Ski Jumping is for All!', in *History of Skiing Conference*, ed. Ski Museum Holmenkollen. Oslo: Holmenkollen Ski Museum, 1998, 64–9.

Berg, Karin. *Hopp, Jenter-Hopp! Historien om Johanne Kolstad og Hilda Braskerud – et annerledes skieventyr*. Oslo: Chr. Schibsted Forlag, 1998.

Cranz, Cristel. *Skilauf für die Frau*. Aalen: Willy Henne, 1936.

Duerr, Hans Peter. *Der erotische Leib. Der Mythos vom Zivilisationsprozeß*. Frankfurt: Suhrkamp, 1999.

Falkner, Gerd. 'Von den Anfängen des Frauenskilaufens'. *Körpererziehung* 39 no. 6 (1989): 536–7.

Falkner, Gerd. 'Streiflichter der Entwicklung des Skispringens'. *Körpererziehung* 41 no. 1 (1991): 36–8.

Goksøyr, Matti. 'Winter Sports and the Creation of a Norwegian National Identity at the Turn of the 19th Century', in *Winter Games. Warm Traditions. Selected Papers from the 2nd International ISHPES seminar Lillehammer 1994*, eds Matti Goksøyr, Gerd Von der Lippe and Kristen Mo. Lillhammer: The Norwegian Society of Sports History/The International Society for the History of Physical Education and Sport, 1994, 26–34.

Günter, Sandra. *Geschlechterkonstruktion im Sport. Eine historische Untersuchung der nationalen und regionalen Turn- und Sportbewegung des 19. und 20. Jahrhunderts*. Hoya: NISH, 2004.

Hall, Ann. *The Girl and the Game: A History of Women's Sport in Canada*. Peterborough, ON: Broadview Press, 2002.

Hoek, Henry. *Skiheil Kamerad. Skikurs für eine Freundin*. Hamburg: Enoch Verlag, 1940.

Hofmann, Annette and Alexandra Preuß. 'Amazonen der Lüfte. Geschichte und Entwicklungen im Frauenskispringen', in *Internationale Skihistoriographie und Deutscher Skilauf*, ed. G. Falkner. München: ILDA Druck, 2005.

Hofmann, Annette, Patricia Vertinsky and Shannon Jette. '"Dear Dr. Rogge": Die Skispringerinnen und die "Human Rights"'. *Sportwissenschaft* 40, no. 1 (2010): 39–45.

Jahn, Jan and Egon Theiner. *Enzyklopädie des Skispringens*. Kassel: Agon, 2004.

Kitzbüheler Ski Club, ed. *Hahnenkamm. Chronik eines Mythos*. Innsbruck: Tiroler Repro, 2003.

Klein-Doppler, Gustav. 'Die Damen im Skisport', in *Amtliches Jahrbuch des Wintersports*, ed. Emil Peege. Wien: Buch- und Kunstverlag, 1926, 16.

Lenskyj, H. 'Common Sense and Physiology: North American Medical Views on Women and Sport, 1890–1930'. *The Canadian Journal of History of Sport* 21 no. 1 (1990): 49–64.

Peege, Emil and Josef Noggler, eds. *Jahrbuch des Wintersports für 1910/11*. Wien: Gerlach & Weidlang, 1911.

Pfister, Gertrud. 'Sport-Befreiung des weiblichen Körpers oder Internalisierung von Zwängen?', in *Zivilisierung des weiblichen Ichs*, eds Gabriele Klein and Katharina Liebscha. Frankfurt: Suhrkamp, 1997, 206–48.

Pfister, Gertrud. 'Die Balance der Differenz – Inszenierungen von Körper und Geschlecht im Sport (1900 bis 2000)', in *Menschenbilder im Sport*, ed. Michael Krüger. Schorndorf: Hofmann Verlag, 2003, 197–234.

Schneider, M. *Katechismus des Wintersports*. Leipzig: Verlagsbuchhandlung von J.H. Weber, 1894.

Schmitt, Fritz. *Kitzbüheler Winterlob. Skispuren durch ein Schneeparadies*. München: Bergverlag Rudolf Rother, 1942.

Scott, C. *Powder Pioneers: Ski Stories from the Canadian Rockies and Columbia Mountains*, Calgary: Rocky Mountain Books, 2005.

Stadt Kitzbühel. 'Schriftleitung Eduard Widmoser', in *Stadtbuch Kitzbühel Band III*. Kitzbühel: Eigenverlag der Stadtgemeinde, 1970.

Thabault, George. 'Dot Graves – "A" jumper'. *Skier* 34, no 4 (1974).

Vertinsky, Patricia. *The Eternally Wounded Woman: Women, Doctors and Medicine*. Urbana, IL and Chicago: University of Illinois Press, 1994.

Vertinsky, Patricia, Shannon Jette and Annette Hofmann. 'Skierinas in the Olympics: Gender Politics at the Local, National and International Level over the Challenge of Women's Ski Jumping'. *Olympika XVIII* (2009): 25–56.

Von der Lippe, Gerd. 'Ski Jumping'. In *International Encyclopedia of Women and Sport*, vol. 2, edited by Karen Christensen, Allen Guttmann and Gertrud Pfister, New York: MacMillan References, 2001, 1046.

Wirtenberger, Hans. 'Sportlady internationaler Klasse'. *Kitzbüheler Heimatblätter* 17, no. 7 (2007).

Wirtenberger, Hans. 'Letzter Schlossherr auf Lebenberg'. *Kitzbüheler Heimatblätter* 17, no. 7 (2007).

The Development of the Female Scouting Movement: Evidence of Female Emancipation in Italy

Roberta Vescovi

'Carlo Bo' University of Urbino, Italy

At the beginning of the twentieth century the female Scouting movement in Italy had only a few members, because of some traditional preconceptions about character training, open-air activities, sport and affiliation to youth groups as elements having no bearing on girls' education. During the Second World War and the years after it, Italian women entered a period of 'female self-promotion'. The birth and renewal of Scouting groups became part of female efforts to achieve equality and self-fulfilment. Thus, although the Italian female Scouting movement was brought back to more traditional female models by the Church and moderate conformists, the new progressive stances could not be neglected. Actually, female Scouting education was tied to traditional women's competences, but at the same time girl scouts acquired a new awareness of their rights and role in society, leading them at the end of the 1960s towards a 'feminist-liberal' trend. The aim of this study is to analyse how female involvement in the Scouting movement contributed to women's self-fulfilment and to their cultural and political equality in twentieth-century Italy.

The Advent of Scouting for Girls in Italy

Scouting started in Italy in 1910, due in part to the meeting of English gentlemen, influenced by Lord Baden-Powell's work and ideas, with Italian educators, and it turned out to be a powerful means of educating young people. The official birth-date of Italian scouting is often listed as 1912, when doctor Carlo Colombo wrote the statute of his youth movement, dividing it into male and female sections, with the common aim for it to be an instrument used to educate Italian boys and girls. In 1913 the first experiment of Girl Guiding took place within the *Corpo Nazionale Giovani Esploratori Italiani* (CNGEI – Italian National Young Explorers' Corp) with a female branch. The activities of girl Scouts were undertaken separately from those of boy Scouts, but maintained the same features. In November 1914, thanks to Colombo's work, a female Scout section, called *Unione Nazionale Giovani Esploratrici Italiane* (UNGEI – Italian National Young Female Explorers' Union) was established. Its general officer was Mrs Mary Rossi, who had collaborated with Lady Baden-Powell in England, and its first general president was Princess Anna Maria Borghese de Ferrari. A great supporter of UNGEI was Sidney

Sonnino, who suggested the young Female Explorers' motto 'Be prepared!' which was taken from Marcus Aurelius's words. At the beginning Catholic circles and press expressed a strong opposition to scouting and especially female scouting, which was defined as 'indecorousness' and an 'unbelievable impudence'. In spite of this opposition the CNGEI and the UNGEI reached its greatest expansion during the Fist World War, with 400 sections and sub-sections, many of them situated in Italian colonies and communities abroad. In July 1920, the first congress of female Scout associations was held at St Hugh's College, Oxford, and the Italian UNGEI 's delegation participated in it. In 1922 the CNGEI's review *Sii Preparato!* ('Be Prepared!') introduced a 'female page', dedicated to the UNGEI's activities. This organisation had modest success, reaching only ten units in a few big cities; its pedagogical aims were modest too, because among its female leaders there was neither a deep knowledge of Baden-Powell's Scout movement nor an autonomous reassessment of Scout methods for girls.[1]

After the First World War the UNGEI, as well as the CNGEI, suffered a difficult period which led to the reduction of its feeble strength, so that in 1920 its headquarters were moved from Rome to Rovereto. It was here, in the patriotic environment of the Trentino region, that the UNGEI came under the leadership of a famous personality, Mrs Antonietta Giacomelli. She was a writer, polyglot, sportswoman and one of the most important exponents of the Catholic movement against the fundamentalism and temporal power of the Church. She had always been described as a strong, tenacious, trustworthy and sincere woman who served her religious creed and her homeland with all her might. She brought winds of change to the Italian girl scouting organisations, following the International Scout Conference in Paris in July 1922, which stated that male and female Scout movements had to be clearly separate and totally independent from each other. Mrs Giacomelli also changed the name of the girl scouting movement to *Unione Nazionale Giovinette Volontarie Italiane* (UNGVI – Italian National Young Female Volunteers' Union). She changed the programmes of activities too, and officially and publicly wanted to clearly separate her association from both Colombo's CNGEI and UNGEI. However, not every section changed the name 'Female Explorers' to 'Female Volunteers' and some sections didn't join Giacomelli's association. In the autumn of 1925 some Female Explorers' sections continued their activities within the CNGEI while Mrs Giacomelli and her volunteers carefully kept their distance from them. The girls were divided into groups, 'Primroses', 'Volunteers' and 'Fides', according to their age and training. They served God, their homeland, the family, their brothers and sisters and were trained for everyday life. In 1924 Mrs Giacomelli founded a Girl Scout Review, *Sii Preparata!* ('Be Prepared!'), which was issued every two months from 1924 to 1926. She also wrote a manual for leaders' training, a book of prayers and organised two national camps near Rovereto. The UNGVI formed international relationships starting from 1924 when Mrs Giacomelli and some girl guides took part in the Third International Conference for Girl Scouts in Foxlease, England, where she presented a paper about education for patriotism. Mrs Giacomelli came from a family of great patriots and for this reason she gave to girl scouting civic, social, patriotic and religious values with an ecumenical and democratic spirituality. She claimed her female scouting movement to be anti-denominational with no political colour and having a democratic and Christian imprint. The main aims of the movement were to be found in the shaping of worthy and strong democratic values and in solidarity which had to overcome every barrier, fusing the love for God and the homeland with the love for mankind. Girl Guiding was not considered as simply open-air sports activities but as an education for moral discipline and health, real democracy, brotherhood, self-sufficiency, generosity, a simple and austere life, practicality, goodness and helping others, with a Franciscan spirit. What Mrs Giacomelli proposed in her effort to reform the movement caused some new Girl Guide units to flourish in the 'Triveneto' region (in Verona, Trent, Riva del Garda, Rovereto) and in Sardinia (in Cagliari and Sassari).[2]

The aims of the Scout movement were exactly the same as those proclaimed by the *Opera Nazionale Balilla* (ONB – National Balilla Movement), from 1926 onwards. It was precisely this coincidence of operational methodology between the scout movement and the ONB, but in the face of a different ideological and political framework, which condemned the Scouts in the eyes of Mussolini. In 1927 Italian Girl and Boy Scout organisations were dissolved by the *Partito Nazionale Fascista* (PNF – National Fascist Party) on the orders of the party's general secretary Augusto Turati.[3] Between 1927 and 1930 Mrs Giacomelli succeeded in keeping her girls together in a series of excursions.[4]

The Struggle of Italian Girl Scouting for Emancipation

The aim of the Scout and Guide organisations was to prepare good young boys and girls, forming their characters, developing a group spirit, a sense of responsibility and of honour, teaching them practical skills of use to themselves and others, promoting their physical development, getting them used to open-air life, and developing personal hygiene and sobriety.[5]

The Girl Guide movement was very successful, even more so than the Boy Scouts in many different countries, as Lord Baden-Powell acknowledged in his writings.[6] Unfortunately this was not true for Italy because as far as Italian Girl Guiding was concerned, it had only a limited importance, with a few hundred members enrolled initially in the UNGEI and later in the UNGVI.[7]

The reasons for this lack of interest in female youth organisations were manifold, but among them the most outstanding was the traditional conception, still alive in Italy, that female education had nothing to do with character building, open-air life, sports activities etc. So enrolment in youth organisations was less widespread and mainly addressed issues to do with domestic economy, child care and gymnastics.[8]

Moreover the opposition of Catholic circles to Girl Guides was strong. It was basically an opposition to all sports and open-air activities for girls. Many exponents of the Italian Scout movement, such as Mario di Carpegna of the *Associazione Scout Cattolici Italiani* (ASCI – Italian Catholic Scout Association) were sympathetic to that problem and they didn't have any kind of hostile prejudice as far as Girl Guiding was concerned, but they were actually aware that considering the predictable opposition of the Catholic clergy, it would have been better not even to consider guiding, as in the past even the Boy Scout movement had faced the same opposition from the Church in Italy. It should also be remembered that, during the Fascist period, the dissolution of the few Girl Guide groups restricted the natural development of the Italian Girl Guides, which might otherwise have taken place in the 1930s.[9]

The Revival of Girls Scouting after the Second World War

The history of the long, difficult and in some way painful journey of Italian Scouting through Fascism makes a short reference to Fascist organisations for Italian youth appropriate, as Fascist pedagogues sometimes cited scouting among the youth movements, claiming to be inspired by their philosophies. The confirmation of how dangerous the Scouts were to the monopolistic plans of the Fascist regime with respect to education became apparent to Mussolini in the report on the Scout movement by a commission of experts whom he had asked to carry out an inquiry into the situation regarding sport and gymnastics in Italy in 1925:

> The organisation of the Young Explorers takes its place between the home and the school. The latter as it is at present is separated from the rest of the children's lives. Given this kind of school, the Young Explorers offers something of an extension and something complementary. They teach a way of life and are in fact a real school of character building.[10]

This was an extremely positive evaluation, but in fact it was turned against the Scouts, because the aims described as being those of the Scouts were exactly the same as those that were proclaimed as its own by the ONB from 1926 on. The theory of Fascism explicitly stated the political nature of the educational process. Fascist education was based on the idea of an ethical and totalitarian state, by means of the identification of Fascism with the state, and on the claim that the Fascist Party was the primary educator. From the beginning of the 1930s, enrolment in the ONB, which was originally voluntary, came to be automatic and obligatory. Once the empire was proclaimed, the ONB was absorbed into the *Gioventù Italiana del Littorio* (GIL – Italian Youth of the *Littorio*) in 1937. Its motto was 'To believe, to obey, to fight'; the education philosophy of this movement had a strong military component. The ONB-GIL had over seven million members, but the educational results were nil

> because the educational aims were subordinate to those of propaganda, because of the authoritarianism which did not shrink from using external and humiliating constriction, and also due to the lack of preparation, tact and intelligence with respect to the majority of managerial staff. The Regime did nothing but adapt scouting to its own particular needs ... transforming a liberal association, which was aimed at promoting independence, creativity, a humanitarian and collaborative approach, into a coercive situation which was to strengthen the group instinct, aggression and the taste for pompous display. ... The leaders of the youth organisations were mainly instructors with a rigid overbearing mentality, only able to discuss political honours. ... In contrast with the prevailing ideas of educational method, they educated the young by changing the joy of free time into a tedious servitude.[11]

Although the Scout movement was formally dissolved in 1927 and was not absorbed into Fascist youth organisations, it did not die out in Italy. Amid various difficulties and risks, several groups continued Scouting activities under various guises. The distinctive feature of the 'clandestine' Scout movement was its spontaneity. The boys and girls and their leaders wanted to continue in spite of legal prohibition, because the ideal expressed in the Scout Law and Promise seemed to them to be irreplaceable and they felt that they had been subjected to an unjust condemnation. The spontaneous reaction of young people to the dissolution of the Scouts proved that during the brief period of its existence, the Italian Scout movement had succeeded in transmitting values such as strength of character, moral responsibility, attachment to the ideals of self-improvement and a willingness to help one's neighbour. The lack of central coordination and the evident danger inherent in making contact resulted in clandestine activity of the surviving Scout groups being carried out in isolation, apart from a few rare exemptions. The ultimate outcome for the groups was also different. Some groups disbanded before the Second World War; others kept going until the start of it, and then either changed or suspended their activities.[12]

In December 1943 there was a second establishment of the Girl Guides, thanks to the care and dedication of two women: Mrs Giuliana di Carpegna and Mrs Josette Lupinacci, who fought to keep Italian girls far removed from the Fascist GIL. When they decided to create the Italian Girl Guides, they didn't have in mind either the UNGEI or Mrs Giacomelli's pioneering experiences but their personal interpretations of Baden-Powell's scout movement. Giuliana di Carpegna was supported in her enterprise by the Dominican monk Agostino Ruggi, who was an ex-Scout of the 5th Rome Group, and he became the main ecclesiastic inspector of that new Catholic girl guide movement, called the *Associazione Guide Italiane* (AGI – Association of Italian Guides). On 9 September 1943, while Nazi troops were attacking Rome, Giuliana and Josette held an organising meeting in the city centre. So during the German occupation of Rome their work had to become clandestine, but it didn't stop and on 28 December 1943, in Priscilla's Catacombs (there was a curfew and meetings with more than three persons were forbidden) Fr Ruggi received the promise from Giuliana di Carpegna and seven other young women and the 'Squirrels' squadron was born, followed by the 'Halcyons', the 'Fireflies' and the 'Swallows', who were formed by female leaders and by young women between 20 and 21 years of age. With the arrival of the Allied forces, Girl Guides could meet openly and the first units were established in Rome. In August 1944 the first central commission was established with Princess Maria Massimo Lancellotti as president and Giuliana di Carpegna as international officer. In that period there were seven Guides' units and two 'Sentries' units. The commission chose the name AGI for the new association. This name was chosen with the aim of organising the association as a free movement outside of organised Catholicism. The founders of AGI wanted to form a unitary association that welcomed Jewish, Protestant, agnostic and Catholic girls in distinct units so that every group could live their spiritual life according to their religious creed and that all together could prepare for the common ideal of becoming citizens at the service of their national community.[13]

A statute was issued and it received the Holy See approval on 8 December 1944. The association was created with the approval of the Church and without those disputes that had characterised the birth of the Scout movement in the Catholic world. According to Monsignor Montini the Girl Guide movement was to educate Italian girls in the Catholic tradition, creating girls and young women with frank and open character; with noble and gentle feelings, with a good-natured and equal minds and with a true religious spirit.[14]

In February 1945 the former girl Explorers of the UNGEI reorganised.[15] There were few contacts between the UNGEI and the AGI until Lady Baden-Powell's visit, when the two associations were asked to form a federation and on 27 July 1945 the agreement creating the new federation, called the *Federazione Italiana Guide ed Esploratrici* (FIGE – Italian Federation of Girl Guides and Explorers) was signed by representatives of the AGI and UNGEI. In 1948 the FIGE was recognised as a full member by the World Organisation of Guides. For a long time Italian Girl Guiding remained an insignificant appendix, from a numerical point of view, of the Boy Scout movement. As it was unknown and misunderstood by the public, it came up against considerable obstacles and prejudices concerning girls' education and the role of women in Italian society of those times. For instance, the problem of its leaders was a real issue in a country of strong traditions that did not normally allow its women to engage in commitments outside their immediate family environment. The UNGEI became part of the CNGEI in 1945 and it always remained part of that organisation without either its own publications or its own specifically adapted rules. Even the Catholic Guiding movement had some difficulties in growing, even though it had a promising beginning. However, step by step the work carried out in the training camps, in the international meetings for leaders and in the press saw the creation, in lots of cities, of some well-organised groups which eventually helped Catholic Guiding to grow in other environments too.[16]

Growing Emancipation

With the collapse of Fascism, their participation in the underground movement and their gaining of the right to vote, Italian women entered a season of 'female self-promotion' during the post-war years.

The birth of AGI and the renewal of UNGEI became part of this general surge in the growing emancipation of women. But almost immediately that surge was slowed down and brought back into line with traditional female models (this was more evident in AGI than in UNGEI). The Church, and moderate public opinion in general, accepted female associations that were to follow traditional and habitual patterns. The associations promoted therefore a traditional view of women based on the concept of 'femininity' intended as submission, dependence, acceptance and implied assent.[17] (Actually there was a reaction against the above-stated view, but only at the end of the 1960s.).

An extraordinary mixture of old and new was born. Of course the aim of Girl Guides' and Explorers' education remained linked to the traditional tasks of women such as domestic activities, but at the same time a new profile of the Girl Guide appeared; the profile of a woman aware of her own rights and of her own role in society and in her community. Another traditional aspect of Guiding was to provide role models, but at the same time there was also the desire to educate girls to be self-sufficient, to take and to become used to responsibilities and to be protagonists in their social environment and in their working place. Moreover the role models, above all in the AGI, were Christian laywomen who represented a dynamic Christianity full of taste for adventure and fun. The books *Stella in alto mare* ('Stars Offshore') by Guy de Larigaudie (everyday mysticism of a lover of God and life) and *Il gioco della gioia* ('The Game of Joy') by Henry d'Hellencourt (the joy discovered in the small everyday things) became the books of reference for the Italian Guides. Later *La spiritualità della strada* ('The Spirituality of the Street') by J. Folliet became very popular. Translated from French into Italian in 1959, it was a book that was not specifically for or about Guiding, but was surely born in the spiritual difficulties of the French *routes* – very different from traditional pietism.[18]

There was also great international influence on Italian Girl Guides. The references to experiences of Girl Guides in other countries (France, Belgium) were fundamental. Italian Guide leaders came from the noble and upper classes and they had a taste for inter-cultural contact and the sharing of experiences; and they could speak foreign languages. In particular the French language was a kind of second language for the Guides: they read, sang and prayed in French. Moreover, a strong international dimension remained a feature of Italian female scouting.[19] The AGI and UNGEI were both born in an elite circle and in the opinion of many, such as the Dominican monk Ruggi, that posed a limit. Italian guiding was accused of being neither involved nor interested in the real world, in everyday issues. In the girls' recruitment there was no class-oriented impediment; on the contrary, there was an effort to bring Girl Guiding to those girls of more modest financial circumstances. Nevertheless it cannot be denied that a certain number of elements (the knowledge of foreign languages, the availability of spare time, the financial charges for some activities, the way to deal with certain problems) were discriminating against working-class girls and for those from poorer backgrounds. For this reason too, the Girl Guide movement was stronger in big cities than in smaller towns. Its development had been more dynamic in the north-central part of Italy than in the south-central part, where public opinion was not only indifferent but even suspicious of it. In part these problems were also present in male scouting associations, but they were more visible in the female movement.[20]

UNGEI and AGI Educational Methods

The renewed Italian Girl Guide movement had to face the problem of educational method: that is, the aims and pedagogical content of Scouting for girls. As far as the choice of aims was concerned, the founder Baden Powell could offer some solutions. In fact for Baden Powell, the aim of Girl Guides was and should be to contribute to the shaping of harmonious female personalities, prepared to fulfil their traditional roles to become wives and mothers and to carry out their social duties as citizens. That was also considered the right aim by the renewed Italian Girl Guide movement.[21]

The real problem concerned the educational aims and the means of achieving them, as Lord Baden-Powell had been a bit vague in his definition of aims and means. His views were mainly inspired by those of the Boy Scouts and were therefore considered, in a Latin country such as Italy, to be too 'masculine' and Girl Guiding was accused of 'masculinising' girls. The UNGEI and AGI were perfectly aware of that and Lord Baden Powell's manual, *Girl Guiding*, was not in fact translated into Italian. They used different manuals. The FIGE used *Sii Preparata!* by Mrs Maynard and the AGI used the Dominican monk Ruggi's manual, *Le guide di oggi, le donne di domani* ('Today Guides, Tomorrow Women'). UNGEI kept quite close to the Boy Scout movement as far as the method was concerned, following its evolution between 1946 and 1970 (when the two UNGEI regulations were issued). On the contrary AGI's method developed from ASCI's experiences without referring to the previous experiences of Italian or British Girl Guides. As a consequence the Guides initially had to carry out 'male' activities such as going out alone, carrying a heavy rucksack, setting up camp, doing heavy work and taking more care of practicality than of elegance. All those activities were important breakthroughs in view of traditional women's education.[22]

At the beginning of the 1950s, during the period of anarchy, another tendency appeared, This was dominated by the concern to avoid the 'masculinisation' of girls and therefore to differentiate between the methods appropriate for Girl Guides' methods and those of the Boy Scout movement in order to find a female solution (for instance a rucksack made for girls). This led to careful choice and selecting only those considered useful for specific purposes with reference to the female personality. Some activities were eliminated and others, more suitable for the female nature, were retained.[23] For girls between eight and 11 years of age the English terms 'Brownies', suggested by Baden-Powell, was considered unfit; the Dominican monk Ruggi suggested the theme of the ladybird, which is a nice and useful insect considered a traditional sign of good luck and happiness. The method of the second branch (from age 12 to 15) followed the traditional lines of the intermediate Boy Scout, with some differences as far as the 'spirit of adventure' was concerned. The aim of adventure in Guiding was above all to test 'femininity', that is to place it in a hostile environment such as that of the camp. The third educational layer, that is the branch of 'Sentries' (aged 16 and up) was greatly influenced from France and Belgium. The book mainly used by the 'Sentries' was *La spiritualità della strada* by Folliet, soon supplemented by *Strade aperte* ('Open Streets') by Pignedoli. The 'street' (i.e. life) had to be experienced with its difficulties to be overcome, to reach personal advancement; the 'street' became a way out from the personal environment, and personal confidence in order to acquire self-sufficiency and experience self-discovery. Moreover, the 'Sentry' was taught how to make her life a service to her association and to her community. Other characteristics of Guiding were reflected in demonstrating a spirit of simplicity, poverty and a communitarian unity as in the Franciscan tradition. This was similar to that of the male 'Rover'. Therefore Italian Scouting and Guiding, which started their educational method from very distinctive atmospheres, converged in their final phase. The Sentries' concept of service to community reflected the values of their male counterparts.[24]

The Unification of Girl Guides and Boy Scouts in Italy

In the second half of the 1960s Italian Scout associations began to experience ferment and unrest, which became stronger after the youth protests of 1968. This unrest can be traced back to three main factors:

(1) The discovery of a political dimension in the Scout movement;
(2) The search for a different relationship between sexes, both within the Scout movement and also in society;
(3) Finally (for the ASCI and AGI) the desire for a new relationship with the Church.

There was a clear interrelationship among those main themes that led to a global conception of the Scout movement in relation to society and in sharp contrast to its traditional view. The nature of the Scout and Guide movements were defined as non-political by their statutes, but political values had always been present:

The scout law, which states the duty to brotherhood apart from social position, religion and race;
The civic value of human solidarity through good deeds and service;
The education for responsibility, self-determination and freedom;
The commitment to leave the world a bit better than it was found.

In the 1960s there was an awareness that a Scout association should be related to every day life, and that they should not be places of escape.[25]

As a matter of fact those concepts are far removed from Baden-Powell's apolitical position. He, and many others of his time, were not able to recognise the true dimension of political structures and powers. This was evident when he met Mussolini in 1933 and misunderstood the real aim of the Fascist Balilla movement. There he stated that:

> In Italy, the Balilla are the equivalent of the Boy Scouts, who are absorbed into the Balilla about four or five years ago. I expected to find a movement of cadets, but on the contrary I found an organization largely based on our ideas, both as regards structures and with respect to the training, above all for the wolf cubs and the scout; whereas for the older boys, the rovers, the training assumed a more decisively military character. ... Balilla have more or less the same activities as our boys, they have their rules and laws and their oath ... just like our Scouts.[26]

Among the unexpected similarities with Baden-Powell's concepts there were: personal development; a uniform; the system of patrols; the activities (physical health, manual dexterity, life in the open-air, games, camps); the decentralisation of the organisational structure. However, he conceded that some important differences existed: the fact that the ultimate aim for the ONB remained the development of the nationalist spirit and military efficiency; and the fact that the ONB was a state organisation with paid instructors. Scouting was intended to be a free movement with voluntary leaders and promoted individual freedom as opposed to the mass instruction and education of the Balilla.[27]

Baden-Powell's political ideal (which he preferred to call 'civic') was to shape men and women of a strong character, encouraging them to do their best for their communities and to better their own personal conditions. The improvement of society was to be realised as a consequence of the increased number of active adult Scouts and Guides in it. He was not interested in educating young people to be aware of the many unjust aspects of society and to change them.[28]

The desire for a political education was meant to be an education for the *polis*, for the community. Where they lived; the city or the neighbourhood, were the fields of action, especially for Rovers and Sentries. Parallel Scout publications, especially those connected to the Rovers and Sentries branches, addressed important political issues such as the Vietnam War, world famine, under-development and Czechoslovakia. There was a new awareness of the political value of education. The Scout movement could not teach the members to transform the world into a better place if it didn't educate them about the many unjust aspects of society. From such considerations some leaders, groups or units went further, crossing the borders between political education and political action. The 1968 spirit acted with much irritability against the established order. They acted against the established order of traditions, authorities, structures, jurisdictional laws, while supporting different political parties and unions.

The movement towards co-education provided a possible answer to a new relationship between genders in the Scout movement as well as in society. The CNGEI and UNGEI experienced the gradual unification of the male and female Explorers with less controversy than was the case in the Catholic Scout movement, and in 1976 they reformed their statute, adopting the name of CNGEI.

The ASCI and AGI had more difficulty in their unification as the Pope wanted a clear separation between Catholic Guides and Scouts. In 1969, in the post-Vatican council atmosphere, the desire to give women the same dignity as men and to help them to overcome their traditional roles, led, inside the Catholic youth associations, to the necessity of co-education. In 1974 the AGI and ASCI were merged and the *Associazione Guide e Scout Cattolici Italiani* (AGESCI – Association of Catholic Italian Guides and Scouts) was created. In 1976 the AGESCI gave itself three years to approve a unitary educational method for its three parallel branches (Wolf Cubs/ Ladybirds; Explorers/Guides; Rovers/Sentries). The Explorers-Guides branch met the deadline in 1979, while a unitary method for the Rovers-Sentries branch was approved in 1980 and finally the Wolf Cubs and Ladybirds had to wait until 1983. One of the most important issues of the unification of ASCI and AGI was to avoid one association imposing its values upon the other. For this reason there were some precise measures in order to ensure women remained active in leadership within the organisation. Without doubt, the merger was a good deal from the point of view of scale. But there was and still is a problem for both the AGESCI and the CNGEI regarding female leadership. A much smaller number of women were active in the leadership of units and of association structures. Moreover female leaders often had and have specific features. They are either not married or women whose husbands are also active in the movement. This issue cannot be connected to male chauvinism within the structures, but it is due in part to female nature (which has to deal with necessities such as maternity) and in part to the position of women both in society and in the Church.

Actually co-education came about as a consequence of social change. After the unification of male and female scout associations there was a certain confusion about whether to educate boys and girls in isolation whilst helping them to be able to interact with the other sex or as 'young people' whereby they would enjoy the same educational experiences in a common pedagogical project, which implies their learning together on a regular and continuous basis. This confusion led to the elimination of gender considerations and it was decided that boys and girls should be treated as one 'asexual' entity. Today we can talk about 'pedagogy of the difference' and even in schools male and female values are rediscovered and appreciated. Even in the Scout movement it is important to educate boys and girls to accept and appreciate such differences. Nowadays in particular, inside the AGESCI there is a male quest. It has been found that in some ways the mixed units of the 11 to 16 age group 'discriminate' against male teenagers. So in order to help a complete development of sexual identity, above all for boys, it is very important to have some activities for boys only or for girls only.

Finally, the Italian Catholic scout movement tried to develop a new relationship with the Church. Above all AGI clearly expressed its denial of all theocratic and fundamentalist inclinations and chose to side with the poor, the humble and the needy. The Sentries asked for broader piety, which was seen as an important value to believe and follow. Girls belonging to other religious denominations or no denomination at all were admitted to AGI. The most important goal for the association was to teach its Sentries to understand, to serve and to take an active part in their society.[29]

Conclusion

The first experiments with Girl Guiding had only modest success in Italy for many reasons. First of all there was the traditional prejudice that female education had nothing to do with character building, open-air life, sport activities or enrolment in youth associations. Secondly, among its first female promoters and leaders there was neither a deep knowledge of Lord Baden-Powell's Scout movement nor an autonomous reassessment of scouting methods as they might apply to girls. Thirdly, in the recruitment of girls there was no class restriction but certain aspects of Girl Guiding were discriminating against working-class girls and those from poor financial backgrounds. Nevertheless, those pioneering female associations helped Italian girls to embrace civic, social, patriotic and religious views, to shape strong democratic values and solidarity which helped them to overcome the traditional prejudices and barriers imposed by public opinion and by the Church, which was strongly opposed to female youth organisations.

Although the Scout movement was formally dissolved by the Fascists in 1927, it did not die out. The boys and girls and their leaders continued in spite of legal prohibition because they believed in the ideal expressed in the Scout Law and Promise. Undoubtedly one of the best articles on the Scout movement was written in 1936 by a young teacher, Teresa Gamboni, in the *Rivista Pedagogica* ('Pedagogic Review') entitled: *Scoutismo e campeggi scolastici nella didattica moderna* ('Scouting and School Camps in Modern Teaching'), where she wrote that the marvellous aspect of the Scout movement was that

> it was not an association either imposed or supported by the state, and yet if has been successful ... based on real and intrinsic value, it has gone far and achieved much! It is an educational system and a movement for universal peace! We hope that this beneficial movement will be able to resume its activity so as to spread throughout the world, with great success, the evangelical precept, which makes all education beautiful, great and true: Love thy neighbour as thyself.[30]

During the post-war years the birth of AGI and the resumption of UNGEI could be considered part of the general movement towards women's growing emancipation, which led to a mixture of 'old' and 'new' in Guiding associations, as the public opinion and of course the Church imposed traditional models of 'femininity' upon Italian Guides, linked to women's traditional tasks. At the same time however, Italian Guides acquired a new attitude; that of women aware of their rights and active roles in society.

In the second half of the 1960s new elements were added to both Guiding and Scouting, which were in sharp contrast to their traditional philosophies. Both movements were meant to be non-political but in the 1960s there was a new awareness of the political value of education and Guiding, even more than Scouting, was affected by issues associated with equal rights and opportunities. Moreover, equality between sexes led to an increase in co-education within the two movements and to the unification of Italian Guides and Scouts in the 1970s. Italian Guides had reached their goal of emancipation inside both the Scout movement and society.

More than 20 years ago, during the years of strong political commitment and totalitarian ideologies, Scouting could not agree with those who wanted to change the structures of society in a rapid way, as it was meant to help individual minds to mature and improve. Today, with the crises of ideologies there is the desire to change human relationships more than social structures and for this reason the quest for education is growing but is not always provided for. In this contest scouting might be a solution that should be reconsidered. Men and women will continue to face and confront values such as solidarity, justice, respect for others, loyalty, responsibility, honesty and peace. So that Scouting and Guiding will maintain a good educational process, shaping boys' and girls' personalities, in a free but responsible way and in a universal brotherhood.

These movements cannot be considered a solution to socio-political problems but they can offer a lifestyle that does not want to teach things to do, but it can suggest the right way to do them.

Notes on Contributor

Roberta Vescovi is a teacher of history of education and sport history at the 'Carlo Bo' University of Urbino, Italy. Her recent publications focus on Italian sports history in connection with politics, education and gender in the nineteenth and twentieth centuries.

Notes

1. Sica, *Storia dello Scoutismo in Italia*, 188–92.
2. Bedeschi, *I pionieri della DC*, 287–302; P. Mazzolari, 'Antonietta Giacomelli', *Adesso*, 1 Jan. 1950; Michieli, *Una paladina del bene*, 92–3; Giacomelli, *Manuale per le organizzatrici, dirigenti e istruttrici*; Lambertucci, *Alle origini del movimento scout in Italia*, 38, 221–5.
3. Vescovi, 'Boy Scout Associations and the ONB'; Vescovi, ˜Children into Soldiers: Sport and Fascist Italy', 166–82.
4. Michieli, *Una paladina del bene*, 93.
5. Vescovi, 'Boy Scout Associations and the ONB'.
6. Baden-Powell, *La mia vita come un'avventura*, 252.
7. Sica, *Storia dello Scoutismo in Italia*, 18.
8. Vescovi, 'Boy Scout Associations and the ONB'.
9. Sica, *Storia dello Scoutismo in Italia*, 191–206.
10. Commissione Reale per lo studio di un progetto relativo all'ordinamento dell'educazione fisica e della preparazione militare del Paese, 1925, 73.
11. Tomasi, *Idealismo e fascismo nella scuola italiana*, 150–2.
12. Vescovi, 'Boy Scout Associations and the ONB'.
13. AGI, *Vent'anni di vita AGI*; Casella, *L'Azione Cattolica alla caduta del fascismo*, 337, 504.
14. Morello and Pieri, *Documenti Pontifici sullo Scoutismo*, 97–9, 132–3.
15. CNGEI, *Cronaca rievocativa a ricordo ed onore*, 122–5.
16. AGI, *Vent'anni di vita AGI*, 15–21; Sica, *Storia dello scoutismo in Italia*, 313–16.
17. Trova, 'Associazione Guide Italiane', 384; Trova, *Alle origini dello scoutismo Cattolico in Italia*.
18. Sica, *Storia dello Scoutismo in Italia*, 316–18.
19. Giuntella, 'Virtù e immagine della donna nei settori femminili', 286.
20. Giuntella, 'Virtù e immagine della donna nei settori femminili', 286–9; Folicaldi and Granello, 'La questione della donna nell'AGI'; Basodonna, *Un annuncio del regno di Dio*; Severi, *Lo scoutismo cattolico italiano*, 154, 184.
21. CNGEI, *Cronaca rievocativa a ricordo ed onore*, 122–5; AGI, *Vent'anni di vita AGI*, 182–7.
22. Folicaldi and Granello, 'La questione della donna nell'AGI'; Basadonna, *Un annuncio del regno di Dio*, 154. Sica, *Storia dello Scoutismo in Italia*, 318–24.
23. Ibid.
24. Severi, *Lo scoutismo cattolico italiano*, 184–186; Giuntella, 'Virtù e immagine della donna nei settori femminili', 292.
25. Sica, *Storia dello Scoutismo in Italia*, 339–52; Morello and Pieri, *Documenti Pontifici sullo scoutismo*, 98, 207, 241.
26. *The Scouter*, April 1933, 190.
27. R. Baden-Powell, 'Lord Robert', *Daily Telegraph*, 28 March 1933; Baden-Powell, *Scouting Around the World*, 25.

28. Sica, *Storia dello Scoutismo in Italia*, 340–52.
29. Ibid., 365–73.
30. Gamboni, T. 'Scoutismo e campeggi scolastici nella didattica moderna', 123.

References

AGI. *Ventanni di vita AGI, 1943–1963*. Roma: Nuova Fiordaliso, 1964.

Baden-Powell, R. *La mia vita come un'avventura*. Milano: Ed. Paoline, 1985.

Baden-Powell, Lord Robert. *Scouting Around the World*, London, 1935.

Basodonna, G. *Un annuncio del regno di Dio: il guidismo*. Milano: Ancora, 1970.

Bedeschi, L. *I pionieri della DC, 1896–1906*. Milano: Il Saggiatore, 1966.

Casella, M. *L'Azione Cattolica alla caduta del fascismo. Attività e progetti per il dopoguerra (1942–1945)*. Roma: Nuova Fiordaliso, 1984.

CNGEI. *Cronaca rievocativa a ricordo ed onore del prof. Carlo Colombo*. Vicenza: A. Viezzoli, 1962.

Commissione Reale per lo studio di un progetto relativo all'ordinamento dell'educazione fisica e della preparazione militare del Paese, Roma, 1925.

Folicaldi, A. and Granello, E. 'La questione della donna nell'AGI'. *EP* 147 (1970): 452–70.

Gamboni, T. 'Scoutismo e campeggi scolastici nella didattica moderna'. In *Rivista Pedagogica* (May/June 1936).

Giacomelli, A. *Manuale per le organizzatrici, dirigenti e istruttrici del UNGVI (già esploratrici)*. Rovereto and Milano: Vallardi, 1924.

Giuntella, M.C. 'Virtù e immagine della donna nei settori femminili nell'Italia del secondo dopoguerra (1945–1958)', in *Chiesa e progetto educativo*. Brescia: La Scuola, 1988.

Giuntella, M.C. 'Virtù e immagine della donna nei settori femminili', in AA.VV., *Chiesa e progetto educativo*, Brescia: La scuola, 1988.

Gori G. *L'atleta e la Nazione. Saggi di storia dello sport*. Rimini: Panozzo, 1998.

Gori, G. *Italian Fascism and the Female Body. Sport, Submissive Women and Strong Mothers*. London and New York: Routledge, 2004.

Lambertucci, R. *Alle origini del movimento scout in Italia*. Ancona: Leonardo, 1955.

Michieli, A.A. *Una paladina del bene, Antonietta Giacomelli*. Rovereto: Accademia degli Agiati, 1954.

Morello, G. and F. Pieri. *Documenti Pontifici sullo Scoutismo*. Milano: Ancora, 1991.

Severi, P.P. *Lo scoutismo cattolico italiano*. Modena: Toschi, 1969.

Sica, M. *Storia dello Scoutismo in Italia*. Roma: Nuova Fiordaliso, 1996.

Tomasi, T. *Idealismo e fascismo nella scuola italiana*. Firenze: La nuova Italia, 1969.

Trova, A. 'Associazione Guide Italiane: gli albori dello scoutismo cattolico femminile (1943–1948)'. *Il risorgimento* 2/3 (1994).

Trova, A. *Alle origini dello scoutismo Cattolico in Italia*. Milano: Angeli, 1986.

Vescovi, R. 'Children into Soldiers: Sport and Fascist Italy', in *Militarism, Sport, Europe. War without Weapons*, ed. J.A. Mangan. London: Frank Cass, 2003.

Vescovi, R. 'Boy Scout Associations and the ONB: The Struggle between Two Systems of Youth Education in Fascist Italy', in *Sport and Education in History, Proceedings of the 8th ISHPES Congress*, ed. G. Gori and T. Terret. Sankt Augustin: Academia Verlag, 2005.

From Women's Exclusion to Gender Institution: A Brief History of the Sexual Categorisation Process within Sport

Sylvain Ferez

University of Montpellier, France

It was not until the 1920s that the slow and long process of women's accession to the Olympics began: a progressive yet still uncompleted conquest. But the integration of women was not taken for granted. It was initially just a concession in reaction to the strategy of a separate female games. Besides, the progressive integration of women took place together with the institutional necessity of segregation between male and female events. Thus sport remains a place where gender division is institutionalised from a legal and an organisational point of view. The aim of the paper is to investigate the means employed by the sporting establishment to preserve this gender division in spite of the contradictions it has to face. This means covering the whole spectrum of the practice to control the body, symbolic as well as legal.

The process of the acceptance of women in the Olympics has been long and slow. It began only in the 1920s, and is by no means over. The integration of women has never been taken for granted. It was initially conceded in reaction to a threat of a separate female games being staged. Moreover, the progressive integration of women has taken place alongside the institutional necessity of segregating male and female events. Thus sport remains an area where gender bi-categorisation (the logical basis of rules defining the official status of citizens) is institutionalised from both a legal and organisational point of view.

Such an investigation is a matter of analysing not only the way in which this institution manages the numerous challenges in respect of its bi-category organisation but also to identify the strategies that underpin it. From a cultural point of view, the paper will examine various strategies of masculinisation or feminisation (including the emphasising of gender features) to create gender bi-categorisation; in particular homophobic abuse among sportsmen and suspicions of lesbianism among sportswomen. However, from a legal and statutory point of view, the analysis will focus on the debates involved by the introduction of 'femininity testing' for sportswomen since the late 1960s. It will show how these debates testify to a determination to establish gender bi-categorisation biologically, despite the difficulties and dead-ends in the way.

The Institution of Good Looks: An Aesthetic Exclusion ...

There is a historical basis in the difficulty, largely but not wholly experienced by men, of accepting the female body participating in sporting activities. When Baron Pierre de Coubertin modernised the ancient Olympic Games, the possibility of women's participation was initially excluded. In 1912 during the Stockholm Olympics he declared:

> A Female Olympics would be inconvenient, uninteresting, un-aesthetic and not correct. The true Olympic hero is, in my opinion, the individual male adult. The Olympic Games have to be restricted to men, the role of women should first be to crown the winners.

> [*Une olympiade femelle serait impratique, inintéressante, inesthétique et incorrecte. Le véritable héros olympique est à mes yeux, l'adulte mâle individuel. Les Jeux Olympiques doivent être réservés aux hommes, le rôle des femmes devrait être avant tout de couronner les vainqueurs.*][1]

Despite a context characterised by women's claims for equal rights, modern sports were based on a reference to an ideal of masculinity.[2] It was not until the 1920s that we began to observe the beginning of a long and slow process of women's integration into the Olympic movement: a process that is still not complete. While there was an increase in the number of women gaining access to sport during the second part of the twentieth century, it remained one of those specific areas where manliness and virility were expressed exclusively.

In spite of the emergence of a new ideal of feminine beauty linked to 'sportswomen' in the work of writers such as Paul Morand or Henry de Montherland in the 1930s, the old norms of setting women's beauty in the context of modesty and fragility tended to keep them away from sports grounds through much of the twentieth century.[3] Nevertheless, these norms go back a long way, perhaps to the 16th Century, confining beauty to femininity and with man being destined to be fearsome rather than handsome:

> A 'finite' being, motionless and closed, woman is perfection of the scene; 'self-sufficient', she is also totally 'given'. While 'man is what he becomes', he is challenge, enterprise, even insult. So many differences underlie the vision of gender in modern times.

> [*Être 'fini', immobile et clos, la femme est perfection de décor: 'suffisante à elle-même', elle est aussi tout entière 'donnée'. Alors que 'l'homme est ce qu'il devient', dépassement, entreprise, voire affrontement. Autant de différences fondant la vision des genres dans la modernité.*][4]

Vigarello's cultural story of beauty points to an important shift in the 1930s, following the 'civilising process' studied by Norbert Elias. But how is this evolution to be understood? Is it sufficient to refer beauty and ugliness to the mere division of cultural norms? How can we understand the issues governing their transformation? If Norbert Elias and Eric Dunning have themselves studied the role played by the sports establishment in the 'civilisation trial', which leaves its mark on the long story of Western society, it is from the point of view of acceptance and management rules of roughness and brutality.[5] But what about control of the norms of beauty?

In the description of the various 'appalling cases' presented in the Leviticus bestiary, Mary Douglas points out how monstrosity relates to the impossibility for these things to be part of the orderly universe of a symbolic order. It is because monstrosity is a fundamental *disorder* that it eventually refers to impurity and dirtiness (Douglas uses the words 'dirty', 'uncleanness' and 'pollution' indiscriminately). She goes further, however, and shows, beyond the question of symbolic disorder and monstrosity, how institutions think and make people think through nomenclatures and the classifications that they produce.[6]

Her thought can in a way be connected with the one initiated by some little time earlier by Foucault after he had read a text by the Argentine writer Jorge Luis Borgès in which he quoted from 'some Chinese encyclopaedia' a list of incongruous animals brought together. According to the philosopher, monstrosity associated with the reading of this passage would depend on the closeness of elements, the proximity of which is unthinkable, and on the anxiety generated by their 'heterotopy':

> For a long time this text made me laugh, not without a certain uneasiness that was difficult to overcome. Maybe because in its wake the suspicion was born that there is no worse disorder than the incongruous and the bringing together of what is unacceptable; disorder would be what brings into light the fragments of a great number of possible orders in the lawless and unlimited dimension of the abnormal.

> [Ce texte m'a fait rire longtemps, non sans un malaise certain et difficile à vaincre. Peut-être parce que dans son sillage naissait le soupçon qu'il y a de pire désordre que celui de l'incongru et du rapprochement de ce qui ne convient pas; ce serait le désordre qui fait scintiller les fragments d'un grand nombre d'ordres possibles dans la dimension, sans loi ni géométrie, de l'hétéroclite.][7]

At the same period Georges Canguilhem was more particularly interested in the weight of the medical institution in defining not only what is normal and what is pathological, but also in defining monstrosity. That is how, in a chapter entitled 'Monstrosity and what is Monstrous', he analyses more specifically the notional and classificatory efforts made by teratologists since the Middle Ages.[8]

Following this reflection, a study of the way in which the sporting institution participates in the construction of the social norms of ugliness and beauty, together with other social institutions (such as the registry office and the medical profession), in aiming to preserve the symbolic gender order becomes important. Thus the main topic of this article is to analyse how sport, as an institution, agrees with the integration of women, provided that gender division is institutionalised and legitimised. In that context, as long as sportswomen's bodies appear as a threat or a challenge to this division (or as long as they disturb the gender norms) sporting institutions reject them as something associated with abnormality and monstrosity.

The Feminine Conquest of Sports

In 1919, although the participation of women was explicitly forbidden by Olympic rules, Alice Milliat asked the International Olympic Committee to organise women's competitions for the Olympic Games in Antwerp (1920). Its refusal finally convinced her to create an independent and self-governing international movement.[9]

In France, she had already created the *Fédération des Sociétés Féminines Sportives de France* (FSFSF) together with Faivre du Bouvot in 1917. This took place in a context of growing women's participation in sporting activities and aimed to facilitate their involvement in athletics, pushball, hockey, basket-ball, swimming and rowing.[10] For Alice Milliat the sportwomen's situation was very clear:

> As they are forbidden access to official sports federations, they will have no solution other than to create their own societies and own sports federations.

[*L'accès des femmes aux fédérations sportives officielles étant interdit, elles n'auront d'autre solution que de créer leurs propres sociétés et leurs propres fédérations sportives.*][11]

This process continued despite considerable opposition from doctors to the opening of sporting competition to women. In France, many doctors declared their concern about the impact of this kind of activity on women's biological reproductive function. In fact, at that time, both proscription and prescription of physical activity for women were legitimised by a central preoccupation with the preservation and development of [female] reproductive organs.[12] After the First World War, the question of motherhood was a common concern, apart from a small number of feminist activists:

> Even Alice Milliat defends the idea that to give France the physical supremacy necessary to its well-being and for posterity, and to raise it to the status the country already has in artistic and intellectual fields, we need strong women who can produce plenty of sound and vigorous children. It is a patriotic and practical duty. Special attention has to be given to health of the mother. Regenerating and perpetuating the race by the development of the woman's body involves taking care of the abilities of this sex. Physical appearance is also important in the question of health and reproduction because of the role appearance plays in relations between men and women.
>
> [*Même Alice Milliat défend cette idée que pour donner à notre France la suprématie physique nécessaire à sa tranquillité et à sa postérité, pour la hisser à ce point de vue au rang qu'elle occupe déjà dans l'ordre artistique et intellectuel, il nous faut des femmes robustes et capables de lui donner des enfants sains, vigoureux et nombreux. C'est un devoir patriotique et utilitaire. Une attention particulière à la santé de la mère doit être apportée. Régénérer et perpétuer la race par le devenir du corps féminin revient à s'attacher aux performances de ce sexe. L'apparence physique prend aussi toute son importance pour la santé et la reproduction en raison du rôle de l'apparence dans la relation entre homme et femme.*][13]

There was therefore the feeling that it was highly necessary to lessen the 'fragility' of women. In that context, from 1915 onwards, some French doctors gave their support to Alice Milliat's initiatives. For them, the main aim of activity remained eugenic, as it had been before the First World War, underlining the desire to reinforce the role of women as future mothers. Alice Milliat largely conformed to that perception, accepting the logic of medical advice that the rules of sport should be adapted for women. This logic was linked to the defence of a specifically defined graduate physical education programme for women that needed to be inferior to such programmes for men and adapted to the supposed fragility of women's bodies.[14]

On 31 October 1921, Alice Milliat created the *Fédération Sportive Féminine Internationale* (FSFI) in Paris.[15] The FSFI rapidly decided to limit women's cross-country to five kilometres and to abandon pole vault and triple jump competitions. The separatist strategy promoted by Alice Milliat led to specific events being held during the 1920s: the Women's Olympic Games taking place in Paris in 1922 and in Gothenburg in 1926. Consequently, women were allowed to compete in five athletics events in the Amsterdam Olympic Games (1928). Nevertheless, female-only Olympic festivals still took place: in Prague in 1930 and in London in 1934. It should of course be pointed that the 800 metres disappeared from the women's track programme following the Amsterdam Olympics after IOC members and team managers (as well as journalists) were shocked by women's participation, declaring they were 'not sweet', breathless and streaming with sweat. In addition to ongoing medical concerns about their reproductive faculties, their pained expressions and grimaces appeared to be an offence to both feminine beauty and role. It was not until 1960, in Rome, that women would be seen running the 800 metres again in an Olympic Games.[16]

In 1984, more than half a century after Amsterdam, the same types of comments were made about the first female Olympic marathon: only the distance had changed. What had become acceptable for the 800 metres was not certain to be accepted for the marathon. Something inscribed within the 'nature of things' constituted a mental barrier to women's participation in such an event. Twenty years earlier, Kathy Switzer had used a subterfuge to participate in the Boston marathon in 1964 by hiding her sex and starting the race dressed as a man. Upon discovering the farce, the International Association of Athletics Federations (IAAF) punished her heavily. International athletic authorities nevertheless gradually accepted women, permitting longer and longer international races: 1,500 metres in 1967, 3,000 metres in 1974, 3,000 metres steeplechase in 1987 and 5,000 metres and 10,000 metres in 1981. The most recent competitions opened to women in the Olympics were the hammer throw and the pole vault in the 2000 games in Sydney.

However, the history of athletics, though it is particularly significant, is not the only example of women's difficult conquest of sports. Whereas fencing has been practised in the Olympic Games by both men and women since 1924, only the foil was open. Women had access to the epée in 1996 and to the sabre in 2004.[17] Louveau and Davisse observe that the weight of the weapons was given as the main justification for this. In fact, the foil weighs 500 grams, the epée 750 grams and the sabre less than 500 grams. Pictures and representations thus seem to weigh heavier than realities.[18] Nowadays, women are still not authorised to compete in the decathlon, as it is considered the summit of the Olympic ideal. On the other hand, men were excluded from synchronised swimming for a long time, and are still not involved in rhythmic gymnastics competitions. More globally, gymnastic apparatus is clearly gendered.

To understand how the sporting establishment organises and constructs gender relations and interactions, it is necessary to go beyond the simple question of whether access is permitted to different activities. Even when both sexes participate in the same activity, they rarely compete together. Very few federations do not differentiate between the sex of adult competitors within their rules[19] and nearly all of them refuse to mix men and women. In a few cases co-presence is accepted with a strict arrangement of dissymetric roles, as for example, in figure skating.[20]

The thought that obligatory sex segregation in sports (forced separation of girls and boys into separate teams) could be a disservice to female athletes is very recent.[21] At the same time, some studies reveal (paradoxically) that gender equity policy can be far from effective in producing equality. On the contrary, in Swedish sports, it seems to have become a new way of emphasising gender difference and to reinforcing constructions of 'manliness' and 'womanliness'.[22]

The Feminisation of Sportsmen and Lesbianism Suspicions of Sportswomen

In fact, women's access to sporting competition (particularly since the 1960s) is significantly associated with masculinity. In that context, the feminisation of sportsmen only occurs either as irony or as an insult. Homosexuality is in the shadows, one of the most common depictions of the sportsman as anti-hero. For a long time, homosexuality in sport was almost totally unthinkable.[23]

On 18 April 1887, in a lecture about 'English education', Baron Pierre de Coubertin suggested the introduction of sport as an excellent means to solve the twin problems of 'overworking' and 'vice' in boarding schools. Strongly opposed to the educational trends of that period, including the promotion of sex education, he considered sport to be a way of diverting young people from sexual 'perversion' and 'pornography' (homosexuality and onanism being the most often described perversions at the end of the nineteenth century).[24]

In traditional sport, homosexuality will remain invisible for a long time. Due to the intensification of manliness, the world of sport will constantly manage to establish heterosexuality as the norm. It is a heterosexist universe in the sense that heterosexual norms are taken for granted. 'Compulsory heterosexuality' is evident everyday through social interactions and role identification. Sportsmen are sometimes portrayed in the reassuring role of head of the family or being associated with authority.[25]

In that context, when homosexuality does appear, it is always in the shade, portrayed negatively, as a counter-model. The 'queer', 'poof' or 'fag' are always the 'opponents', the 'enemies': those who are failing or who are not successful. The insult is diffuse and redundant, and is often uttered as an insignificant habit without any sexual ulterior motive. It often doesn't mean that people are actually homosexual, but *suggests* that they are cowardly and weak. No matter that the *actual* sexual identities and practices of those who are so depicted, or those around them: they are, in fact, presumably heterosexual.[26]

In such a hostile environment, it is very difficult to find sportsmen who are openly gay. The situation is different in women's sports, where the heterosexual norm is not taken for granted at all. Masculinisation strategies are sometimes used to run sportswomen down, with the suspicion or suggestion of lesbianism in the background. This lesbian 'label' corresponds to the 'falsely accused deviant' described by Becker, or, in Goffman's case to a 'stigma' that has to copied,[27] as it is associated with their participation in sport.[28]

Such treatments of certain sportsmen and sportswomen are in fact inverted. On one side we have the feminisation of men who fail, and on the other, the masculinisation of women who succeed.[29] Femininity testing for sportswomen (while there are no masculinity tests for sportsmen) has to be understood from the perspective of women within sports institutions and the gender strategies that go with that. Whereas sporting activity sometimes generates doubts about femininity, the old imagery of hermaphroditism seems to guarantee masculinity. In other words, all by herself, the sportswoman seems to challenge perceived gender allocation.

Are Sportswomen 'Real' Women? The Exclusion of the Hermaphrodite

In July 2009, the South African athlete Caster Semenya participated in the African Junior Athletics Championships in Mauritius. She won the 800 metres, beat the South African record of Zola Budd, and qualified for her first senior competition: the Berlin World Championships:

> Since the day Semenya broke Zola Budd's record, people in South Africa had been talking about her. Semenya does not look like most female athletes. People questioned whether she was really a woman. Some even e-mailed the International Association of Athletics Federations, the worldwide governing body for track and field, with their doubts. Before *Semenya* was awarded her gold medal in Berlin, on August 20th, a

reporter asked about a story that had been circulating at the Championships, that Semenya's sex was unclear and that she had been required to undergo gender-verification testing before the race. The IAAF confirmed the rumor, arguably in violation of its confidentiality policies.[30]

The arguments supporting the questioning of the sex status of Semenya were simple: winning with a physical appearance resembling that of a male and having a 'surprising voice'. Ariel Levy mentions that a rumour relayed in Australia by the *Daily Telegraph* reported that she had neither ovaries nor a uterus, and triple the testosterone level of a typical female. Her victory in the 800 metres in the Berlin World Championship in August 2009 reinforced the suspicion of hermaphroditism. The Sports Confederation and the International Olympic Committee (IOC) then asked for the results of the 'gender verification test' that had been ordered before the competition.

This was by no means the first controversy about the sexual identity of a sportswoman, and was, as usual, followed by the broader question of 'What makes a woman a woman?' [31] In December 2006, the Indian athlete Santhi Soundarajan had to give back the silver medal she gained in the 800 metres at the Asian Games in Doha after the results of her(/his?) 'gender verification test' were made available to the authorities.

The use of femininity tests, discontinued by the IOC in 2000 because of juridical and ethical problems, was coming back. Despite intense efforts and reflections of the sporting institutions, the question of gender control seems to be back, because these institutions haven't managed to solve a problem that is probably bound to rise again. As early as the 1930s and 1940s, the domination of urchin profiles within the emerging women's competitions created some trouble and uneasiness:[32]

(1) In the 4th Women's World Championship in London (1934), Sdena Koubkova won the 800 metres but the truth burst into the media: 'she could be a man'. This was soon confirmed by so-called 'delicate surgery'.
(2) Two years later, in the Berlin Olympic Games (1936), the Polish delegation accused the American winner of the 100 metres, Helen Stephens, to be a 'dressed-up man'. In the 1980s, the autopsy following her/his murder would give rise to a rumour of hermaphroditism.
(3) One has to say that during the same 1936 Olympic Games, Dora Ratjen, 4th in the high jump, was in fact Hermaan Ratjen. The young man had been forced by the Nazi Party to compete with women, hiding his real sex, to increase the number of German medals. S/he would nevertheless carry on her/his feminine career, and even beat the world record during the European Championship in 1938 (jumping 1.67m).
(4) The last example is the one of the French runners Léa Caurla and Claire Bressolles, who ran the female 4 × 100 metres (relay) in the European Championship in 1946. Some years later, they had surgery and became Léo Caurla and Pierre Bressolles.

Most of the discussions about these athletes were based on rumours that were relayed by journalists. Doctors were very discreet.[33] During the whole period of the 1930s and 1940s, doctors just referred to 'doubtful cases' associated with uncertain and vague facts. In 1948, the British Women's Amateur Athletic Association was nevertheless led to ask for a medical certificate testifying that those who wanted to compete were authentic women.

Many new suspicious and 'doubtful cases' occurred during the 1950s. However, in 1964, it was finally the subterfuge employed by Kathy Switzer's to run in the men's marathon that caused both the IAAF and IOC to extend the principle of femininity testing. The official issue is clear: be sure that athletes are 'real women' for a fair competition (with 'equal weapons'). When Semenya's case came on the agenda, in 2009, Alice Dreger thus declared in the *New York Times*:

'Let's start with the reasonable assumption that we want to maintain gender segregation in most sports. It provides girls and women – half the planet's population – a real hope of winning. Without that hope, many may not bother.'[34]

Bi-categorisation and Introduction of 'Femininity Testing' by the Sports Institutions

The final decision concerning Caster Semenya was taken in July 2010 after approximately a year of procrastination and several 'false starts' by the IAAF, due to the fact that members of the federation had been unable to reach a decision.[35] On 14 July 2010, Jo Proctor, a board member of the activist intersex group, 'OII Australia', reacted vigorously to the decision of the IAAF, which had just indicated the complete acceptance of a report from its own medical experts and which finally authorised Caster Semenya to compete. The international federation concluded with the statement that any medical details were to 'remain confidential and the IAAF will make no further comment on the matter'. For Jo Proctor, it was both too little and too late: 'Looking back over the past 11 months, no institution and no organisation emerges with any honour.' Moreover, the activist group said they suspected that there may have been secret surgical or medical intervention on the South African athlete:

> Caster Semenya, as a female, was accused of possessing biologically male attributes – a clear issue of intersex – which, according to her accusers, gave her an unfair advantage. Although she has been cleared fit to race 'as a female' it is still by no means clear what, if any, surgical or other medical intervention has taken place to remove those so-called 'advantages'. ... Most OII members have personal experience with the medical profession's erratic moral and ethical compass when it comes to intersex issues. It is quite common for dubious statistical 'evidence' to be used to pressure parents into allowing surgical intervention on their intersex babies. All too often that surgery either goes bad, or no real benefit can be attributed to it in later life.[36]

The bi-categorical institution of gender is first of all a state institution, and more exactly an institution of civil status as recorded by the registry office. Reproducing Herculine Barbin's autobiographical private diary, Foucault tried to analyse the effect of medical discourse on this state institution, and consequently its impact on the construction of sexual and gender identity.[37] Herculine was born in 1838. In 1860, after several medical visits because of health problems, the doctor asked her to change sex with regard to civil status. She became Abel Barbin on 21 June 1860 and from then on dressed as a man. S/he finally committed suicide in 1868 because of the disorientation, confusion and isolation generated by the change of gendered and sexual status.

In addition to the material from Barbin's private journal, Foucault presented the medical files and considerations on other cases that qualified as hermaphroditism and that had 'disturbed law and medicine' in their desire to distinguish between men and women since the sixteenth century. For a long time, the anatomic examination was the main means to check sex, with the invention of special technologies and instruments. For example, in the nineteenth century, Joseph Récamier invented the vaginal speculum in order to explore all the openings and examine their extension and direction, and identify any false congenital malformations that might be hiding the real sex. Murielle Salle studied the evolution of medical technologies used to allocate an unequivocal sex (in order to conform to the bi-categorisation of the registry office).[38]

In sport, the many doubts concerning the requirement for a medical certificate, instituted in 1964, led the IAAF to organise a gynaecological examination in 1966. In 1967, the Federation finally decided to try out a chromosomal test, as athletes had unanimously condemned the gynaecological examination, considering it to be too invasive and violent.[39] The Barr corpuscle test (which looked for the presence of the second X chromosome within saliva) replaced the gynaecological examination in 1968, but genetic specialists considered it non-reliable and recommended that it be stopped.

However, the inability of the Barr corpuscle test to scientifically identify gender bi-categorisation produced progressively problematic cases.[40] It did not consider chromosomal abnormalities such as transsexualism and intersexuality, and in fact three kinds of participants in women's competitions challenge the will to identify two gender categories:

(1) The first group represent the various types of intersexuality:
- Genetic disorders without physical advantage (testicular feminisation syndrome, mosaic forms XXY type, gonadal dysgenesis etc.);
- Genetic 'abnormalities' giving a physical advantage (as in congenital suprarenal hyperplasia which generates a muscular mass growth sometimes going with hirsutism);
- Men with genetic troubles who have passed the Barr test (Klinefelter's syndrome);
- Hermaphrodites (characterised by a co-presence of ovarian and testicular tissues);
- Pseudo-hermaphrodites (characterised by the presence of genital organs of the other sex).

Muriel Salle speaks about 1% to 2% of children being born intersexed. Elizabeth Badinter reminds us that one woman in 2,700 lives with only one X chromosome (Turner's syndrome) and one out of 500 has three X chromosomes. The XYY case would apply to one man in 500, and the XXY case (Klinefelter's syndrome) to one in 700.[41]

(2) The second group of participants are transsexuals.
(3) The third group concerns men trying to compete as women.

The Medical Legitimisation of the Instituted Bi-categorisation

The category involving men attempting to compete as women is the only one explicitly targeted – to avoid cheating – but since the Kathy Switzer scandal (Boston marathon, 1964), no case of a 'dressed-up' man has ever been detected. In fact, the use of a test reinforces the bi-categorical principle. The impossibility of distinguishing the two groups of intersexed and transsexual people from tricksters or cheats functions as a symbolic exclusion. These two groups represent both unthought-of and unthinkable aspects of a binary gender system that tries to hide the social construction that it produces.

In France, at the beginning of the 1990s, the National Ethics Committee (*Comité National d'Ethique*) and the National Board of Doctors (*Conseil de l'Ordre des*

Médecins) recommended a cessation of the test in sport for two reasons. One was scientific (the test is not reliable from a scientific point of view) and the other ethical (the test being restricted to medical research and medical action). However, the French sports federations were reluctant to follow this recommendation, maintaining that sex division was part of the statutory requirements in the rules governing their competitions.

Finally in 1992, the federations reluctantly agreed to change the test and modified its name at the same time. 'Femininity testing' became 'gender verification test', even though it still only applied to women's competitions. Seventeen years later, when the IAAF revealed that Caster Semenya was tested as a hermaphrodite, some voices pointed out the problematical aspect of the gender designation of the test. The argument was that in this particular case 'sex testing' should be preferred to 'gender testing', with particular regard to the right of the athlete to define herself/himself and make it known to other people of her/his own volition.[42] Nevertheless, a similar sequence of events occurred at international level at the same period:

'Faced with the case of a competitor whose genes and genitals were clearly at odds, the IAAF in 1990 convened an international group of experts – geneticists, a psychologist, an endocrinologist – to answer the question of how to determine, once and for all, if a woman is a woman.'[43]

The IAAF finally heeded the group's recommendation and got out of the sex-verification-testing business. In 1991, it abandoned this method as unreliable and nine years later in 2000, so did the IOC. Between 1992 and 2000 other federations used the new PCR/SRY – as did the IOC – to check the presence or absence of the Y chromosome (and not the presence of the second X chromosome, as in the Barr test).[44]

More deeply, however, sports doctors were not at ease when faced with sex determination. The multi-dimensional nature of sex identity was accepted with some difficulty by the field of sports medicine.[45] The binary vision of the establishment persists, without giving a single thought to the recognition of a (biological) sex continuum with different levels, crossing an anatomic sex, a gonadic sex and a genetic sex: a continuum that is nowadays made more complex by new considerations of both the psychological and social aspects of sex.

Of course the IOC decided to temporarily stop the use of the 'gender verification test' in 2000, but this was conditional upon finding some other means of testing/controlling gender. However, five international sports federations (basketball, volleyball, skiing, judo and weightlifting) decided to continue with the PCR/SRY test. After 2000, sports authorities and their medical experts remained much divided on the topic. While some federal doctors defended the test in the name of equity, justice and the fight against cheating, others criticised it as discriminatory. In that context, the IOC asked its Medical Commission to gather together some experts to establish rules on the participation of athletes who had had a sex change.

The recommendations suggested by the group in 2003 would be applied in 2004. They proposed regulations and procedures to guarantee that transsexual athletes did not benefit from physical advantages with respect to the other athletes. However, the various debates within sports institutions since the 1990s, and the institutional changes consequently adopted, did not solve the problems. Gender control came back onto the agenda in the 2006 Doha Asiatic Games (the Santhi

Soundarajan case) and in the 2009 Berlin Athletics World Championship (the Caster Semenya case).

After the Caster Semenya 'affair', some articles again insisted that 'gender control' is both not reliable and complicated because of the philosophical consequences and bio-ethical questions to which it is linked. In that context, the IAAF was strongly criticised for its handling of the Semenya case. But it also appears that the implications of this case for the ethics of sport could not be separated from the debates concerning gender and enhancement nor from the broader philosophical debate about the nature of categories and the classification of people. Three main questions then arise: What about the reality of intersexuality? Could a scientific or medical test offer uncontroversial answers regarding Caster's gender? And ... isn't the concept of gender a social construction?[46]

Prescription and Proscription

Gender bi-categorisation as a state institution is constantly reasserted and this is never so clear as when problems occur. These problems throw up institutional analyses revealing the very basis of these organisations. A parallel can be drawn between hermaphroditism debates about sportswomen and the legal process leading to the annulment of the marriage of Camille and Monica in Ruel-Malmaison in 2005 mentioned by Eric Fassin.[47]

There was no problem as regards the registry office; the two contracting parties being officially a man (Monica) and a woman (Camille). However, the physical appearances and the declared identities were much more controversial. Camille being transsexual and Monica transgender, the civil ceremony apparently involved two 'women'. The legal decision to dissolve the marriage was justified by the *trouble à l'ordre public* (disturbance or breach of the peace) it represented. One can here observe a state reaction to 'trouble' introduced within the norms of gender, of sexuality and of marriage.

This kind of appearance-prescription logic is well known in the sphere of sport. As soon as women had access to sport in any numbers, as early as the 1930s and the 1940s, they caused suspicion about their 'real' sex. Doctors immediately become 'moral entrepreneurs', speaking in the name of science to stipulate (otherwise prescribe) what 'real' women should be, and how they should behave.[48] They thus use medical legitimacy to set out the various kinds of sporting activities that are (or not) fully compatible with their own gender norms. This prescriptive action is quickly reinforced by proscriptive measures, on the basis of a bi-categorical approach that is blind to the scientific developments on which they nevertheless simultaneously base their own authority.

The virilism process (a slow biological convergence of women's and men's morphologies) that is generated by the access of women to the same sports competitions as men, also generates attempts to limit this proximity by using aesthetic judgements or legal proceedings against women's virilism. Inherently biased towards gender bi-categorisation, the establishment does not easily accept this gradual convergence of male and female morphologies. On one hand, legal sport jurisdictions and courts officially exclude those who do not fall within a social norm that is presented as a biologically rooted rule. On the other hand, an everyday basic justice operates on the doubts and the suspicions of hermaphroditism and lesbianism.

This is the way in which the sports establishment, to a certain extent, is involved in socially defining beauty and ugliness. Though it does not have either monopoly or legitimacy in this matter, it can nevertheless be perceived as a normative authority which, in linking with the registry office and the medical establishment, produces aesthetic and legal judgements aimed at establishing the institution of gender as something 'natural' and as a universal category.

Notes on Contributor

Sylvain Ferez is a lecturer at the University of Montpellier, France. A member of the Health, Education and Situations of Disability research group (SANTESIH), he works on discriminations and on the various barriers to social participation to sports and leisure.

Notes

1. Coubertin, 'Discours des quarante années d'Olympisme', 69.
2. Cf. 'urchin' fashion in France, where Victor Margueritte, in his novel *La Garçonne* (1922), invented and made the word *garçonne* popular. A million copies were sold between 1922 and 1929. It was essentially related to a physical choice, in which the haircut was the main characteristic. Moreover, this new female haircut spread widely all through the 1920s.
3. Gaucher, *L'Écriture de la sportive*.
4. Vigarello, *Histoire de la beauté*, 36.
5. Elias and Dunning, *Sport et civilisation*.
6. *Douglas, Danger and Purity*; Douglas, *How Institutions Think*.
7. Foucault, *Les Mots et les choses*, 9.
8. Canguilhem, 'La monstruosité et le monstrueux'; Canguilhem, *Le Normal et le pathologique*.
9. Devron, *Alice Milliat*.
10. Bohuon, 'Entre santé et pathologie', 262–3.
11. Arnaud, 'Le genre ou le sexe?', 163.
12. Bohuon, 'Entre santé et pathologie', 273.
13. Prudhomme-Poncet, *Histoire du football féminin au XXe siècle*, 111–12.
14. Bohuon, 'Entre santé et pathologie', 278, 287.
15. Laget et al., *Le Grand livre du sport féminin*, 28.
16. Arnaud and Terret, *Histoire du sport féminin*; Louveau and Davisse, *Sports, école, société*.
17. Ottogalli-Mazzacavallo et al., *Pour une histoire des championnats du monde d'escrime*.
18. Louveau and Davisse, *Sports, école, société*.
19. Only the three federations of shooting, horse-riding and sailing.
20. Cf. Goffman, *L'Arrangement des sexes*.
21. McDonagh and Pappano, *Playing with the Boys*; Kaufman, 'Playing with the Boys'.
22. Larsson, 'A History on the "Sportsman" and the "Sportswoman"'.
23. Pronger, *The Arena of Masculinity*.
24. Boulongne, *La Vie et l'œuvre pédagogique de Pierre de Coubertin*.
25. Baillette and Liotard, *Sport et virilisme*.
26. Ferez, *Le Corps homosexuel en-jeu*.
27. Goffman, *Stigma*.
28. Blinde and Taub, 'Women Athetes as Falsely Accused Deviants'.
29. Griffin, *Strong Women, Deep Closets*.
30. Ariel Levy, 'Either/Or', *New Yorker* 85, no. 39 (30 November 2009), 48–9.
31. Black, 'The Not So Curious Case of Caster Semenya', 41; Orenstein, 'What Makes a Woman a Woman?', *New York Times Magazine*, 13 Sept. 2009, 11.
32. Ritchie et al., 'Intersexe and Olympic Games'.
33. Parienté, *La fabuleuse histoire de l'athlétisme*, 731.
34. 'Seeking Simple Rules In Complex Gender Realities', *New York Times*, 25 Oct. 2009, 8.
35. 'Verification Results on South African Runner Awaited', *New York Times*, 19 Nov. 2009, 16; 'South African Runner's Sex-Verification Result Won't Be Public', *New York Times*,

20 Nov. 2009, 10; 'Semenya Won't Receive Results of Sex Verification Tests Until June', *New York Times*, 1 April 2010, 14; 'South African Is Cleared to Compete as a Woman', *New York Times*, 7 July 2010, 13.

36. OII Australia, 'Caster Semenya: Post-mortem of a debacle', 19 July 2010, available at http://oiiaustralia.com/oped-caster-semenya-postmortem-debacle.
37. Foucault, *Herculine Barbin dite Alexina B.*
38. Murielle Salle worked on 19 books of the Dr Lacassagne collection and nine articles published in *Annales d'hygiène publique et de médecine légale* between 1866 and 1906. Cf. Salle, 'Assigner un sexe sans équivoque'.
39. Louveau and Bohuon, 'Le test de féminité', 88–89.
40. Bohuon, 'Les enjeux d'une "bicatégorisation" par sexe dans le champ sportif'.
41. Salle, 'Assigner un sexe sans équivoque'; Badinter, *XY*, 61–2.
42. Black, 'The Not So Curious Case of Caster Semenya', 41.
43. D. Epstein, 'Well, Is She Or Isn't She?', *Sports Illustrated* 111, no. 9 (2009), 25.
44. Ljungquist and Simpson, 'Medical Examination for Health of All Athletes'; Vignetti et al., '"Sex Passport" Obligation for Female Athletes'.
45. Bohuon, 'Le test de féminité ou la définition médicalement légitime des corps féminins sportifs'; Bohuon, 'Le "test de féminité" dans le monde du sport'; Fox, 'Gender Verification'.
46. John Lanchester, 'Short Cuts', *London Review of Books* 31, no. 19 (2009), 28; Camporesi and Maugeri, 'Caster Semenya'; Anon, 'Is She or Isn't She?', available at: http://www.highbeam.com/doc/1P3-1887473641.html, 8.
47. Fassin, *L'Inversion de la question homosexuelle*, 12.
48. Becker, *Outsiders*.

References

Arnaud, P. 'Le genre ou le sexe? Sport féminin et changement social. 19ème–20ème siècle', in *Histoire du sport féminin*, vol. 2, eds P. Arnaud and T. Terret. Paris: L'Harmattan, 1996, 147–83.
Arnaud, P. and T. Terret, eds. *Histoire du sport féminin*, 2 vols. Paris: l'Harmattan, 1996.
Badinter, E. *XY. De l'identité masculine*. Paris: Odile Jacob, 1992.
Baillette, F. and P. Liotard. *Sport et virilisme*. Montpellier: Quasimodo & fils, 1999.
Becker, H. *Outsiders. Études de sociologie de la déviance*. Paris: Métailié, 1985.
Black, S. 'The Not So Curious Case of Caster Semenya'. *Canadian Dimension* 43, no. 6 (2009): 41.
Blinde, E.M. and D.E. Taub. 'Women Athetes as Falsely Accused Deviants: Managing the Lesbian Stigma'. *Sociological Quarterly* 33, no. 4 (1992): 521–33.
Bohuon, A. 'Les enjeux d'une "bicatégorisation" par sexe dans le champ sportif : l'exemple du test de féminité'. *Nouvelles Questions Féministes* 27, no. 1 (2008): 80–91.
Bohuon, A. 'Entre santé et pathologie: discours médical et pratique physique et sportive féminine (1880–1922)'. PhD diss., Paris: Université Paris Sud XI, 2008.
Bohuon, A. 'Le "test de féminité" dans le monde du sport: une absence de réglementation et un bouleversement de l'ordre sportif'. *Revue Juridique et Economique du Sport* 96 (2010): 42–5.
Bohuon, A. and C. Louveau. 'Le test de féminité ou la définition médicalement légitime des corps féminins sportifs', in *Sport et homosexualités*, ed. P. Liotard. Montpellier: Quasimodo & Fils, 2008, 95–109.
Boulongne, Y.P. *La Vie et l'œuvre pédagogique de Pierre de Coubertin 1863–1937*. Otawa: Ed. Leméac, 1975.
Camporesi, S. and P. Maugeri. 'Caster Semenya: Sport, Categories and the Creative Role of Ethics'. *Journal of Medical Ethics* 36, no. 6 (2010): 16.
Canguilhem, G. 'La monstruosité et le monstrueux', in *La Connaissance de la vie*, ed. G. Canguilhem. Paris: Librairie philosophique J. Vrin, 1965.
Canguilhem, G. *Le Normal et le pathologique*. Paris: PUF, 1966.
Coubertin, P. de. 'Discours des quarante années d'Olympisme', in *Le Vrai Pierre de Coubertin*, ed. J. Dury. Paris: Comité Français Pierre de Coubertin, 1994, 69.
Devron, A. *Alice Milliat: La pasionaria du sport feminine*. Paris: Vuibert, 2005.
Douglas, M. *Danger and Purity*. London: Routledge and Kegan Paul Ltd., 1967.
Douglas, M. *How Institutions Think*. Syracuse, NY: Syracuse University Press, 1986.

Elias, N. and E. Dunning. *Sport et civilisation: La violence maîtrisée*. Paris: Fayard, 1994.

Fassin, E. *L'Inversion de la question homosexuelle*. Paris: Editions Amsterdam, 2005.

Ferez S. *Le Corps homosexuel en-jeu. Sociologie du sport gay et lesbien*. Nancy: Presses Universitaires de Nancy, 2007.

Foucault, M. *Les Mots et les choses. Une archéologie des sciences humaines*. Paris: Gallimard, 1966.

Foucault, M. *Herculine Barbin dite Alexina B*. Paris: Gallimard, 1978.

Fox, J.S. 'Gender Verification; What Purpose? What Price?'. *British Journal of Sports Medicine* 27 (1993): 148–9.

Gaucher, J. *L'Écriture de la sportive. Identité du personnage littéraire chez Paul Morand et Henry de Montherland*. Paris: L'Harmattan, 2005.

Goffman, E. *Stigma. Notes on the management of spoiled identity*. New York: Anchor books, 1964.

Goffman, E. *L'Arrangement des sexes*. Paris: La Dispute, 2002.

Griffin, P. *Strong Women, Deep Closets. Lesbians and Homophobia in Sport*. Champaign, IL: Human Kinetics, 1998.

'Is She or Isn't She?. Tests Raise Ethical Questions'. *Contemporary Sexuality* 43, no. 10 (2009): 8.

Kaufman, P. 'Playing with the Boys: Why Separate Is Not Equal in Sports' (book review). *Sociology Of Sport Journal* 27, no. 1 (2010): 105–7.

Laget, S., F.Laget and J.-P. Mazot. *Le Grand livre du sport féminin*. Belleville, Saône: FMT éditions, 1982.

Larsson, H. 'A History on the "Sportsman" and the "Sportswoman"'. *Historical Social Research* 31, no. 1 (2006): 209–29.

Ljungqvist, A. and J.-L. Simpson. 'Medical Examination for Health of All Athletes Replacing the Need for Gender Verification in International Sports. The International Amateur Athletic Federation Plan'. *JAMA* 267, no. 6 (1992): 850–2.

Louveau, C. and A. Davisse. *Sports, école, société. La différence des sexes*. Paris: L'Harmattan, 1998.

Louveau, C. and A. Bohuon. 'Le test de féminité, analyseur du procès de virilisation fait aux sportives', in *Sport et genre. La Conquête d'une citadelle masculine*, vol. 1, ed. T. Terret. Paris: L'Harmattan, 2005, 87–117.

McDonagh, E. and L. Pappano. *Playing with the Boys: Why Separate Is Not Equal in Sports*. New York: Oxford University Press, 2007.

Margueritte, Victor. *La Garçonne*. Paris: Flammarion, 1922.

Ottogalli-Mazzacavallo, C., G. Six and T. Terret. *Pour une histoire des championnats du monde d'escrime*. Paris: Minuit, in press.

Parienté, R. *La fabuleuse histoire de l'athlétisme*. Paris: Editions de La Martinière, 1995.

Pronger, B. *The Arena of Masculinity. Sports, Homosexuality and the Meaning of Sex*. New York: St Martin's Press, 1990.

Prudhomme-Poncet, L. *Histoire du football féminin au XXe siècle*. Paris: L'Harmattan, 2003.

Ritchie, R., J. Reynard and T. Lewis. 'Intersexe and Olympic Games'. *Journal of the Royal Society of the Medicine* 101 (2008): 395–9.

Salle, Muriel. 'Assigner un sexe sans équivoque. Les médecins et l'hermaphrodisme dans la seconde moitié du XIXe siècle'. Lecture at 'Le Corps sexué et ses constructions' symposium, 18–19 Sept. 2008, MSH Paris-Nord. Available at: http://brouillonpro.blogspirit.com/media/00/01/83808448.ppt#257,13,Diapositive13.

Vigarello G. *Histoire de la beauté*. Paris: Seuil, 2004.

Vignetti, P., A. Rizzuti, L. Bruni, P. Tozzi, P. Marcozzi and L. Tarani, '"Sex Passport" Obligation for Female Athletes'. *International Journal of Sports Medicine* 17, no. 3 (1996): 239–40.

Women in Weapon Land: The Rise of International Women's Fencing

Thierry Terret and Cećile Ottogalli-Mazzacavallo

CRIS, University of Lyon

The world of weapons has always been male-dominated both on the battlefield and in sport. Competitive fencing, born as mimicry of duels, developed throughout the twentieth century as a symbol of masculinity; an embodiment of the notion of manhood and an expression of men's virility. Surprisingly however, female fencing was accepted into the Olympic programme in Paris in 1924, before many other sports, as a result of an ambiguity in the regulations of the International Olympic Committee (IOC) and the International Fencing Federation (FIE). The full integration of female fencing took much longer according to the diverse weapons used in the competitions. Although the individual foil event appeared in 1924, the team foil event was not recognised until 1960 and the other weapons even later. The female epée became an Olympic event only in 1996, the female sabre in 2004, after long discussions both within the FIE and between the FIE and the IOC.

The different stages of the recognition of female fencers by the sporting institutions are the focus of this paper. The analysis of the process, based on the archives of the FIE as well as on the specialised press, reveals the influence of three successive time contexts: the 1920s, the 1960s and the 1990s. The long resistance of the male fencing community to any challenge of the gender order has also been relevant. It is finally argued that, despite the explicit defence of women's sport by the leading sport institutions, women were still until recently the victims of the lengthy negotiations between the IOC and the FIE.

From duels to battles, the world of weapons has always been male dominated, and the world of sport is no exception.[1] Competitive fencing was born out of the practice of duelling and developed throughout the twentieth century, not only as a symbol of masculinity through its embodiment of a particular notion of manhood and male honour,[2] but also as an expression of masculine virility. It is hardly surprising, therefore, that all three fencing weapons rapidly became part of the Olympic Games for men; as early as 1896 for individual events and then in 1906 for team events. As for world championships, the programme of events was finalised a mere dozen years after the competition had been set up: epée, sabre and foil were included in the programme in 1921, 1922 and 1926 respectively for individual events and between 1929 and 1931 into team events.

Epée and sabre fencing were attached to the instrumental mastery of the art of killing or injuring in societies at war and in military institutions, as well as in civilian society through duelling. In contrast foil fencing was historically used in duels and it arrived a little later than the other two forms. From the sixteenth and seventeenth centuries onwards, the three weapons continued to develop like dancing within *academies*, using various technical models depending upon the national cultures in which they grew.[3] As a result, they became symbolically attached to France in the case of the foil, Italy the epée and Hungary the sabre. Such a pattern was based on both objective technical elements and stereotypes. Foils were the weapons used to learn how to fence. They were light, flexible and easy to handle, as well as favouring precision and counter-attacks, and had to observe special conventions that differentiated between the fencer who could attack and the one who did not have 'priority'. Epées had a heavier and longer blade, making the performance more closely linked to power and speediness. Finally, the sabre allowed both the edge and the tip of the blade to be used. They were traditionally associated with the cavalry, where assaults were quick and needed excellent techniques.

This brief statement aids understanding of both the nature and the differences between the three weapons for women. Female fencing was socially more acceptable if it fitted the stereotypes associated with femininity. Conversely, it provoked greater institutional resistance when it challenged the gender order. By their technical characteristics and connotations, foils were more in keeping with standards of acceptability for women than epées, which were in turn considered more appropriate for women than sabres.

Olympic Female Foil Fencing: Puzzling Result of Dissension during the Roaring 1920s

Despite its masculine legacy and war connotations, the sport of fencing at the beginning of the twentieth century was practised by a small number of women in those countries where the activity enjoyed a well-anchored tradition and where, simultaneously, female sports were developing as areas of resistance to male dominion, particularly in England, Denmark, France and the Netherlands. Denmark, for instance, organised national championships from 1915 until 1918, albeit for foil fencing only. Major figures of post-war female fencing made their appearance here, including future 1924 Olympic champion Osiier-Ellen Ottillia. However, competitions remained infrequent at national level and almost non-existent at international level. Neither the recently created FIE nor the IOC was willing to put the issue on the agenda at this time.[4] Neither institution, widely under French influence, was ready to make any concessions on the subject.[5]

The development of female fencing was also obviously linked to economic considerations. In France, for instance, the pro-female propaganda which appeared in the columns of the magazine *l'Escrime et le Tir* after the Great War referred, at first, to the difficulties of fencing clubs and fencing masters who were faced with declining clientele. The number of special courses for ladies and women fencing masters rose consequently, with women representing a new reservoir of potential members and a potential market that many masters could no longer ignore. Competitions between women were not long in following. A number of them were organised within the framework of the women's multi-sports club *Académia* and opened the way to the first international foil fencing competition for ladies held in June 1921. The event was organised with the patronage of the *Fédération Nationale d'Escrime* (FNE – National Fencing Federation) during the *Grandes semaines des Armes* (grand weapons weeks), with European (men's) championships being held in parallel. French, English, Danish and German women competed and witnessed the victory of Uta Barding, the 'strong and scientific Danish fencer', to the sound of the Toselli Serenade. Osiier-Ellen Ottillia was also rewarded for the aesthetic quality of her techniques. In the small world of Parisian fencing, however, the fact that women had been granted the right to compete did not mean that they also had the right to give up their femininity.

Tournaments were staged in Paris, Ostend, London and so on and a number of the sport's leaders even believed that European championships would shortly follow. Not everyone, however, was convinced of the idea. In France, even the strongest defenders of women's fencing, including the young fencing master Albert Lacaze, perceived it all as a way to develop the beauty of the female body and the aesthetics of walking techniques, as well as harmony in general body attitudes; rather than a serious intention to invite women to enjoy the pleasure of competing and fighting. According to the dominant discourse on women's physical exercise in the early 1920s,[6] female fencers were asked to move 'nicely rather than strongly and not to sacrifice everything in order to fulfil the desire of touching the opponent'.[7] On the other hand, England and Denmark favoured a more militant stance which was less narrowly linked to the hackneyed stereotypes of femininity. English and Danish women remained avant-garde by encouraging female fencers to reach technical excellence and compete. The fact that the first official proposal to include a fencing event for ladies in the 1924 Olympics was put forward by Denmark, through the voice of Julie Simonsen in 1921, came therefore as no surprise.[8]

As a result of ongoing discussions among IOC members on the necessity of avoiding increasing the number of events within the Olympic Games, the FIE chose not to forward the demand, officially so as not to receive a potentially negative answer from the Olympic authorities. The defenders of the feminine cause refused to admit defeat and put forward a further application during the FIE congress of the following year. The insistence of both English and Danish delegates forced the FIE general secretary, Frenchman René Lacroix, to acknowledge that the argument given a year earlier as justification for refusing Julie Simonsen's request was not valid, since IOC members had omitted to mention explicitly that it resulted from their refusal to increase the number of events in the 1922 Olympic programme. On this occasion, the French IOC delegate, the Marquis of Chasseloup-Laubat, who was also vice president of the FIE, was able to gain agreement that the question of women fencers would be discussed during a meeting of the FIE at a later date.[9] In reality, the IOC took little risk with this decision since the stance taken by the leaders of international sport federations was generally rather traditionalist. Furthermore, in doing so, the IOC also appeared to leave the responsibility of refusing to include female fencing in the hands of the FIE.

However, the situation gave rise to fierce debate within the fencing community. The FIE Congress in 1922 reflected a clear division. For some leaders, the institutional recognition of female foil fencing had arrived too early, since only a few exceptional participants were able to fence at a high level. In their opinion, organising competitions in such conditions would be counter-productive for the sport. For others, on the contrary, the quantity and quality of many female fencers gave them the right to compete at an international level. The latter argument finally won, thanks to the convincing example of Britain and Denmark. With 39 votes against 22, the FIE adopted the principle of a competition for ladies at the VIIIth Olympiad, in the form of an individual foil event.

The IOC was taken aback by the decision and found itself forced to become part of a movement it had not desired. In 1923, Franz Reichel, who was in charge of organising the Paris Olympics,[10] informed René Lacroix that the ratification of this decision could only become effective after the Prague congress in 1925, i.e. only for the Olympic Games of 1928. Yet who was to decide? Should it be the International Fencing Federation or the International Olympic Committee? Difficult discussions were then held. René Lacroix was not initially inclined to fight and in the annual report of 1922 merely confirmed the decision taken by the IOC. The English delegate Seligman reacted immediately. No! The FIE had voted and the general secretary had, therefore, no choice but to make sure the IOC included a ladies event. René Lacroix returned to battle with Olympic delegates and, this time round, was successful. Between 2 and 4 July 1924, the *Vélodrome d'Hiver* of Paris opened its door to 25 competitors from nine nations, who came to compete in the first Olympic foil fencing event for females. Danes (first, third and fifth place) and Englishwomen (second and fourth place) largely dominated the competition. The French organisers were more than satisfied with the results. Indeed, behind every Olympic medallist there was a French fencing master! Furthermore, in Paris, fencers had managed to escape criticism. Although the technical level of the competitors was considered low, their outfit was, on the other hand, beyond reproach, thanks to both the work of the clothing committee of the French Olympic Committee and the decision to make skirts compulsory.[11]

The Olympic Games of 1924 were an important step towards the recognition of female fencers.[12] With the setting-up of a new foil fencing event and the increase in the number of women participating (177 against 66 in Antwerp), these games confirmed the decline of de Coubertin's influence within the Olympic administration, as well as the growing interest of international federations in female sport.[13]

Controversial European Championships

There was still some way to go, however, and the situation remained difficult for women, until 1932 at least. The integration of women's fencing had been the result of 'dissension' between the IOC and FIE and, for this reason, women's participation was questioned each and every time that sports leaders discussed the possibility of reducing the number of events in the Olympic programme. In 1925, the FIE resisted the pressure being exerted on it and chose to modify the rules and competition format rather than completely remove the women's event and this was upheld for the 1928 Olympic Games in Amsterdam. There, the performance of German Olympic champion Hélène Mayer was enthusiastically welcomed by experienced spectators. The French female competitors, on the other hand, were the focus of criticism: 'French fencing masters give young girls and ladies lessons which are just as serious as those given to their brothers, cousins or husbands! And introduce them to the public only when they no longer look like awkward children with weapons.'[14] Perception of female fencers was further affected by the scandal surrounding the women's 800 metres in the same Olympics, during which one of the runners fell at the end of the race. In spite of this, however, the FIE decided, in a meeting organised during the Amsterdam Olympic Games, to accept an idea launched by the organiser of the games, German Van Rossen, i.e. to organise ladies' European championships the following year based on the model of the male championships.[15] This competition, which was actually more of a world championship at a time when fencing was totally dominated by Europeans, was staged for the first time on 15 April 1929, by one of the leading fencing nations, Italy, in the city of Naples.

This first initiative produced a great deal of criticism. The ladies' event was mercilessly and unanimously condemned by both the Italian and French press, as well as by the new FIE president, Swiss Eugène Empyeta, during the farewell dinner[16] Except for the German Hélène Mayer, who was referred to as 'the best of all'[17] and Dutch woman Johanna de Boer, who was acknowledged as 'knowing the art of foil fencing', the performance level of all the other fencers was considered to be very low. These comments affected the legitimacy of female fencing during the international congress of April 1929, when surprisingly, the delegate of the German Fencing Federation, Van Rossen, regretted that the experience in Naples had been counterproductive for international fencing on account of the poor quality of the women's performances: 'I shall henceforth be of the opinion that the International Federation should not hold European championships for ladies', he concluded.[18] The English delegates stood firm and took offence. For them, the low level of female fencers could be explained by the fact that both judges and organisers failed to take them seriously: 'I can guarantee that if you came to London to see our English *fleurettistes*, you would be amazed and would think twice before fencing against them.'[19] Other delegates were quick to agree, but remained nonetheless aware of the lack of homogeneity among competitors. A number of them, however, expressed a further concern regarding potential concurrence between sexes. Thus, when the English delegate said in Amsterdam that women were 'as strong as men',[20] French delegate René Lacroix immediately commented that

> Female fencing is of importance, and because it is of importance we must not let people think that it is the same as male fencing. People must not be led to think that ladies can be more or less strong in epée or foil fencing just because ladies have begun competing like men in certain countries. It is totally different.[21]

From then on, René Lacroix considered that the ladies' event could only be held if the country hosting it was not the same as the one in charge of the male championships. Female fencing and male fencing were 'two absolutely different things'; they must then be clearly differentiated, whatever the value of fencing for women.[22]

FIE president Swiss Eugène Empeyta confirmed this position. For him it would not go against the interests of female fencing to maintain a separate championship that was as important as the men's. The appropriateness of the format adopted for the championship was even discussed. Why not go back to the previous event format, as organised by the *Société d'Encouragement à l'Escrime* (society dedicated to the promotion of fencing) in Paris, where all high-level fencers remaining in the competition automatically received a medal and a certificate? However, as the English delegate pointed out quite sensibly, such a format would mean totally denying the very principle of the competition, which was to become a champion. 'We already have female Olympic champions, we also have one female European champion. If today you go one step back, you will greatly harm our sport.'[23]

The congress finally voted to continue the ladies event, but decided that the country chosen as the location for the next European championships could decline the offer to stage the ladies' championships in favour of another country: 'And if no other country appears, the female championships will not take place.'[24] Women became dependent upon the goodwill of host countries.

Further criticism focused on the 'inappropriate dress' of a great number of female fencers. Some of the competitors wore skirts that were too short, while others did not wear them at all, preferring trousers. Yet, since February 1928, a number of women had been complaining about the clothing committee, claiming that the skirts they had to wear were uncomfortable, unsightly and dangerous. All to no avail, however. Armand Massard, whose nickname was 'guardian of underwear', was supported by congress members and stood firm, 'for the good image of female fencing and of the fencers themselves, such issues as these should not occur any more'.[25] The Hungarian delegate tried to defend the women's cause, but congress members refused to discuss the matter, in support of their president, who promptly closed the discussion:

> Female issues should not cause us to lose time. We have rules; it is necessary to apply them. ... Since we decided to uphold European championships for ladies, we have expressed the wish and shall require that women's dress code be strictly observed in the future, in order that it may not be criticised.[26]

Sportswear was a symbol in the debate on sportswomen, and fencing reflected its importance.[27]

Rejection of Female Epée Fencing and Integration of Team Foil Events: The Hesitations of the 1930s

In 1929, female fencing reappeared on the agenda of the FIE at the request of Swiss delegate Dr Mende, who had previously initiated epée events for women in his country. He suggested holding similar competitions at the international level, with the support of the FIE. People were astonished by the proposal since the president had already forewarned Dr Mende of the risk of his proposal being refused, while taking care to add that 'refusal would not mean dishonour for our [Swiss] federation'.[28] For Dr Mende, however, epées were no more the weapon used in former duels. They were neither heavy nor rigid and, in addition, their widespread use among women was presented as a potentially interesting way to develop the activity of fencing clubs. Far from any ethical or political arguments related to gender equity, justifications were laden with the supposed fragility and weakness of women, together with the need for men to protect them. Epées, for instance, were said to be more accessible for women in that learning how to use them took less time and was less demanding than for foils. Furthermore, potential dangers associated with their use could easily be reduced with the use of certain kinds of sword tips. Finally, 'there is no reason for women not to use an epée'.[29]

Dr Mende's proposal however, did not simply raise the question of whether women could or could not fence with an epée,[30] but rather what the FIE could do to stimulate their participation, particularly through official recognition within an international competition such as the European championships. Although nothing in the regulations forbade epée use for women, the FIE left the responsibility of trying out such events to the different national federations – 'When we have seen them, we will discuss whether or not we want to support these events more or less officially'.[31] The president did not wish to challenge the many hostile representations with regards to female epée fencing. Discussion of the proposal was therefore postponed to a future congress. Moreover, the context had become altogether more difficult since the place of female sport in general was under debate at the time, and in view of the IOC Congress to be held in Berlin in 1930, with women's participation in future Olympic Games being far from certain.

Although the time of applying for Olympic recognition of female epée fencing was particularly ill-chosen, opportunities existed for foil fencing. Once again, as the result of a proposal by the Danish Fencing Federation, a new ladies' foil team event was approved by the FIE in 1932. Indeed this foil fencing was sufficiently developed in a number of countries to justify the setting up of one team of four female fencers per nation. Although the event was not yet part of the Olympic programme, it was held for the first time in Copenhagen, on 5 May, 1932, during the 25th anniversary of the Danish Fencing Federation, which body had been given a cup by fencing fans, just for the occasion. This award was immediately offered to the FIE for the ladies' European team championships, as a means of encouraging its organisation on a yearly basis, in the same way as other European championships. For once, comments were rather positive, thanks mainly to the high level of skill reached by the participants.[32] Denmark was in charge of this first foil team event and witnessed the victory of its own team. The struggle to victory was hard, however, with fierce competition from female fencers from the east, in particular Austria and Hungary. Women from Hungary took the lead soon afterwards and held on to it until the Second World War, with Germany managing to defeat them in 1936.

In spite of this recognition, female foil fencing still suffered from the supposedly weak nature of women. Many proposals were put forward to adapt, simplify and reduce endurance events, in total concordance with the dominant discourse on sport at the time.[33] Thus, in the same way as limits were imposed on women tennis players by the International Federation of Lawn Tennis, FIE President Empeyta suggested, during its Congress in 1930, that the length of assaults between women be shortened to three times five minutes, under the pretext that they hardly ever reached the five valid hits within the authorised time of ten minutes and, as a result, suffered from excessive tiredness. English opposition to the proposal finally resulted in maintaining the *status quo*.[34] Two years later, it was proposed that women should use a specifically shorter sword (the so-called 'blade no. 3') in order to limit its weight. Congress rejected the idea, but left open the possibility for both women and national federations to decide what was best in each individual case.[35] Although FIE members were concerned about the image of women fencers, the quality of their performance became progressively as important as any aesthetic, moral or hygienic considerations. When, in 1935, Hungarian delegate Doros referred back to the congress the suggestion put forward by his fellow citizen Lichtneckert (and refused) in 1929, namely to wear large trousers closed just below the knee, new advantages were mentioned. Times had changed; 'Social conventions and prejudices will no longer prevent them being worn in fencing'.[36] From that moment on, bloomers became official dress for female fencers, although application of the rule took a long time. It was for concrete reasons – namely the poor economic state of the world of fencing, and not for ethical ones, that the FIE requested, in 1957, that a ladies' foil team event be integrated into the Olympic programme.[37] The organisers of the Rome games accepted the proposal, without attaching any particular conditions, asking only that no more than 21 participants of both sexes per nation be authorised to take part in the fencing tournament. The IOC ratified the decision during its congress in Tokyo in 1958.[38]

The Struggle of Female Epée Fencing

In the middle of the twentieth century, international female fencing was limited to foil fencing. Thirty years later such disparity became more difficult to accept. Thanks to new sensitivity in northern Europe, Canada and the United States, equality of opportunity between the sexes became a leitmotif during the 1980s. Sport, albeit a male preserve, had no choice but to follow suit and did so with more or less enthusiasm depending on the sport. By way of example, the International Athletic Federation, often considered as a reference by other sports bodies, adopted a new position on the subject, and the events which, until now, 'shook organs', 'exhausted the bodies' or were 'inelegant for women', were successively opened up to women, including the 400-metre hurdles in 1976, the marathon in 1980, 10,000 metres in 1985, triple jump in 1990, hammer in 1994, pole vaulting and 5,000 metres in 1995 and, finally, the 3,000 metres steeplechase in 2000.[39] Fencing was engaged in this spiral, although developments at first concerned only epée fencing. The FIE had to take into account the example of the International Union of Modern Pentathlon (UIPM) which already had an epée event in its own competitions,[40] i.e. world cups since 1978 and world championships since 1981.[41] Moreover, the fencing federations of both France and the USA had already inaugurated ladies' epée events, which explained why, in 1983, the executive committee of the FIE asked its regulation committee to reflect upon the issue. This provoked an immediate and indignant reaction from 76-year-old Ilona Elek – the only FIE honorary president – in whose opinion the UIPM were allowing women to take mindless risks with regard to the danger of epées.[42] This was an astonishing and passionate defence from one who was considered at that time to have been the best *fleurettiste* ever!

As the issue was obviously proving to be a sensitive one, a commission was set up to engage with it and encourage debate. It was made up of five women, who were already elected members of the FIE: Ilona Elek (Hungary), Irene Camber (Italy), Kate D'Oriola (France), Mary Glen Haig (Great Britain) and Violeta Katerinska (Bulgaria). The commission was presided over by a man, Italian Edoardo Mangiarotti, and compiled information on the various experiments conducted in Australia, the United States and Great Britain. However, it took a traditional stance when it deemed that more in-depth studies were required into the issues of protection and safety.[43] Obvious and hackneyed stereotypes surrounding the subject of feminine fragility once again reared their heads.[44]

Faced with a lack of recently published reports, except for those about a national competition organised by Great Britain, the FIE Temporary Commission for Female Epée Fencing then decided to send out a questionnaire to the different delegations attending the 1987 FIE Congress. Results indicated that female epée fencing was flourishing with 23 nations already involved and that international competitions had already taken place in France, Austria, Mexico and the United States.[45] The challenge of the French city of Vincennes, where epée fencing by females had been developing relentlessly since the beginning of the 1980s, succeeded in bringing together 70 European and American competitors.[46] As early as 1988, the Netherlands and France explicitly hinted that they were ready to hold a world championship in ladies epée fencing. 'We have reached a turning point', confessed the FIE president. A report in which the scepticism expressed two years earlier was seen to have disappeared provoked a collective reaction during the federation's congress, which voted unanimously (minus three abstentions) for the event to be included in the programme of the world championships.[47] To some extent, this vote was unexpected, since previous debate had never really focused on safety and protection matters, two issues which could clearly not be raised without taking into account outdated and discriminatory discourse. On the contrary, attendees wondered more prosaically about the consequences of this new event for the duration and size of the competitions, at a time when the IOC was expressly requesting that international federations reduce their numbers of Olympic participants. In spite of all the fears, a decision was quickly reached, and women were allowed to compete in epée events during a 'world criterion event' that was held in France in 1988, with the aim of trying out the regulations, with the first official world championships being postponed until 1989. It should be noted, however, that the FIE did not break totally with tradition. During the same congress, when the Romanian Federation delegate requested an increase in the number of executive committee members, in order that two women become members, the proposal did not get beyond the stage of the statutes committee, which decreed that gender should not take precedence over competence when selecting members of the executive council.[48]

Female epée fencing was experimented with in several countries during its early years. The most successful were initially those where a tradition of female foil fencing already existed, i.e. France, West Germany, Cuba, Italy and Hungary, although new nations also made their entrance at the highest level, including the Netherlands and Switzerland, where a small number of female epéeists had been practising the sport since the inter-war period. The range of medallists during the first world championships brought clearly to light the infancy of the weapon and the absence of any established hierarchy. Hence, a number of rather atypical (physiological) profiles which produced comments triggered by 'machismo' rather than objective observation. For instance, the 1.94m height and 84-kilos frame of German Ute Schäper, silver medallist in the 1989 World Championships, were mentioned in the magazine *Escrime* as 'a physical appearance which, it had to be said, is not an excellent advertisement for the sport'.[49] Nevertheless, female epée fencing progressed rapidly and was granted Olympic status in the 1996 games in Atlanta, where French fencers imposed their leadership with Laura Flessel-Colovic and Valerie Barlois respectively winning the gold and silver medals in the individual event and contributing to French victory in the team event.

From Epée to Sabre Fencing: Female Rights to Fence and the Olympics in the Turn of the Century

The successes of female epée fencers paved the way for sabre fencing to quickly follow suit. Hopes were particularly high, given that the gender issue had gained greater visibility in society through obvious discrimination and inequality.[50] Gender equality in sport was one of the main challenges faced by national federations, who often added the issue to their agenda in the 1990s and 2000s and the world of fencing experienced a revolution following decades of patriarchy and machismo. The IOC amended the Olympic Charter in 1994 to assert the requirement for the equality of opportunity for women and from 1996, it regularly organised world conferences on women and sport and requested that national Olympic Committees modify their policies accordingly. The Olympic Charter was soon amended in the same way. Objectives in terms of women's participation in the Olympic Games were fixed and considered as standards that every delegation was expected to meet. Women represented only 15% of the total number of participants at Munich in 1972; that figure rose to 29% in Barcelona 20 years later and then to 35% at Atlanta in 1996. There was however, considerable variation from country to country.[51]

After years of resistance, fencing had anticipated the trend in female epée fencing by becoming much less conservative than many other federations. In a sense, the sanctioning of female sabre fencing would complete the change. Its recognition certainly had to face a number of common obstacles that were reflected in discourses on a weapon that was considered 'too demanding and where the blows are too violent for frail shoulders'.[52] Yet, in spite of all this, several countries succeeded in setting up competitions. It was often those countries that had championed the cause of female foil fencing that also promoted female sabre fencing. France, for instance, first staged a ladies' sabre event in Saint Jean de la Ruelleo on 16 November 1997[53] and both Iceland and Norway developed women's use of the weapon early on.[54] The ever-increasing sensibility of the world of sport and the successful integration of female foil and epée fencing, together with the growing number of events held, convinced the FIE to go one step further. During the congress held on 2 October 1998, they voted in favour of the principle that a female sabre event should be included in the programme of the next world championships in Seoul the following year. Three days after the vote, on 5 October 1998, a pilot competition in female sabre fencing was organised as a prelude to the upcoming fencing world championships in La Chaux de Fonds, Switzerland.

The first world championships were held in Seoul in 1999, where 59 women specialised in sabre fencing and 14 women's teams gathered together. There were 86 sabre fencers and 20 teams respectively in the case of men participants. The results reflected the domination of three nations, Azerbaijan, Italy and France, with each country having a tradition in male sabre fencing and a reservoir of women foil fencers. In the team event, Italy was victorious over France and Azerbaijan, while in the individual event, Azeri Elena Jemaeva, who trained in Moscow and was married to Russian *fleurettiste* Mamedov, won the title by beating Italian Ilaria Bianco. Frenchwoman Eve Pouteil-Noble shared the bronze medal with Italian Anna Ferraro. These results reflected an event where, once again, hierarchies had not yet been established and which opened opportunities for fencers. As a result, the sporting careers of a number of individuals progressed at great speed with, for example, bronze medallist Eve Pouteil-Noble winning her medal at the age of 18, although she had only discovered sabre fencing a mere two years earlier.[55]

Although it appeared that the last stronghold of opposition to women's fencing had fallen,[56] the reality was slightly different since the recognition of female sabre fighting thus far had not encompassed national or world championships. The Olympic Games constituted supreme legitimation and were the main objective of the political manifesto put forward by René Roch for re-election to the FIE presidency in 2000.[57] After the second World Championships held in Nimes in 2001, this objective became more apparent, and women sabre fencers 'knocked at the door of the Olympic Games'.[58]

René Roch succeeded in winning round the IOC when he happened to mention the fact that accepting female sabre fencing would establish gender equality in fencing at long last. The IOC, however, was compelled to limit the expansion of its programme and, for this reason, only authorised a total of ten fencing events. The FIE then found itself faced with a difficult choice: should it add events in female sabre fencing which, in turn, would require the withdrawal of an equivalent number of other events? A few days before the ordinary congress of the FIE held in Havana in December 2001, Roch asked Jacques Rogge if the time had not now come to stop including female sabre fencing events. The president of the IOC replied that to do so would be inappropriate or even impolite, since the principle of including female sabre fencing had already been approved. The addition of individual and team sabre events was finally voted for fairly clearly by the FIE, with 50 votes in favour, 23 against and two abstentions. However, this decision created a new dilemma: should the whole programme be reduced to five individual events and five team events or should two events, preferably team events, be deleted? René Roch came up with the totally unexpected proposal of setting up a mixed team event for teams made up of two women and two men![59] The proposal was finally accepted following a series of lengthy discussions.

The idea was of course seen as somewhat shocking and even regarded as sacrilegious in the world of sport. Barring a few exceptions, there had always been a reluctance to set up mixed events; a division between the sexes always having been favoured. The IOC nevertheless requested that the FIE try out these new mixed events before the Olympic Games and, if necessary, plan alternatives. The matter was once again added to the agenda of the FIE leaders during its extraordinary congress in Antalya in April 2002. There, was much discussion there between those who urged that female sabre fencing should be withdrawn before it became a 'genuinely Olympic' event in Athens in 2004, and those who felt that two other events should be removed. Throughout the debates, the issue of gender equality took second place to considerations of medal-winning consequences if the decision went one way – or the other. The only consensus reached was that the organising of a mixed event (agreed upon four months earlier in Havana) was now unacceptable as it would be too expensive to add an extra day of competition to the next world championships in Lisbon. There was, therefore, too little time to experiment with sabre fencing in two world championships before the Olympic Games, as the IOC had requested in order to avoid making the Olympic Games itself a testing platform. As Jacques Rogge declared rather abruptly to René Roch, 'If you propose a mixed event, we will reject the proposal and go back to the format of the Sydney Games'.[60]

Discussion on the topic was postponed to a future date while, at the same time, the FIE voted to decide on the removal of two team events from the Olympic programme by drawing votes out of a hat.[61] This draw resulted in the withdrawal of the female foil and male sabre events and their replacement by two female sabre events. Reactions were immediate, especially from the nations where male sabre fencing was particularly developed, thus obliging the FIE to reconsider its previous decision during the Lisbon congress.[62]

IOC Sports Director Gilbert Felli insisted that the Olympic programme in fencing be restricted to ten events and that two of the 12 events of the world championships be removed every four years. Beginning with the games in Athens, two team events, the first being female sabre fencing, i.e. one of the two events that had given rise to the problem in the first place, would be deleted. The principle of a draw was discarded for the second event – to be removed only temporarily – and a survey was sent to fencers by the FIE Athletes Commission on 1 June. Fifty-eight people responded, with 39 of them (less than 1% of the 4,900 fencers consulted) suggesting that the female team foil event be removed. However, during the session in Lisbon, new proposals poured in, including that put forward by the president of the Italian Federation, who supported the idea of a ladies' relay in the three weapons. Yet nothing could really justify that the selection of such an event. The congress, therefore, decided to refer to the result of the Athletes Commission's survey and came to the rather astonishing decision that female sabre fencing should remain in the Olympic programme; although this concerned only the individual event and resulted in the removal of the female foil team event.[63] The gender equity issue on which initial arguments had been based had not lasted for long. In the Athens games in 2004, men competed in six fencing events and women in only four.

Both the integration of female sabre fencing into the Olympic programme[64] and the temporary suppression of the female team foil event from the Athens Olympics were confirmed by the IOC executive committee in Lausanne on 28 August 2002. Both female sabre and foil team events had been living on borrowed time and found themselves once again in the modest world championships that were held during the Olympic year. The use of mixed events could easily have solved the problem. Yet a demonstration test in sabre fencing by a team made up of two men and two women was still held on 23 August 2002, during the last day of the world championships in Lisbon, albeit without any title being awarded. During the following FIE congress, however, René Roch gave up completely on his initial idea by promoting the position of the IOC: 'I think that this proposal should be abandoned. ... It does not seem that the International Olympic Committee is favourable to mixed teams.'[65] Although fencing had a unique chance to challenge the traditional sporting gender order, the IOC put up two arguments that clearly revealed that its political orientations had never really moved beyond a boundary that was irretrievably wedded to the separation of the sexes. The first argument, which claimed that mixed teams did not exist in other sports, was hardly realistic bearing in mind developments in rackets sports and activities of an artistic nature (such as skating etc.) that portrayed the image of the ideal couple. The second argument simply demonstrated the strength of discrimination within the sports systems of certain cultures:

'These [mixed] teams are hardly conceivable in countries where it is not suitable to let men and women fence together and in these countries, there is obviously, a certain amount of opposition and lobbying within the IOC, which explains why we cannot suggest mixed teams.'[66]

The idea of a mixed event was likewise rejected by the top sabre fencing nations – notably, Russia, Hungary, Poland and France. Only Germany, China, South Korea, the United States, Great Britain, Japan and Italy accepted the invitation from the FIE to participate in the mixed event in Lisbon.[67]

Conclusion: Social Acceptability, Fencing Techniques and Gender

Although women did not take part in the Olympic fencing events as early as men, it should be noted that female fencing was included in the Olympic programme for Paris in 1924. Rather than being the result of a particularly modern gender approach within the fencing community, this early recognition could actually be explained by the pressure exerted upon the IOC by influential members of the FIE. In reality, much more time was needed for the different weapon events of female fencing to become fully-fledged parts of the competition. Although the individual foil event appeared in 1924, the team event was not recognised until 1960, with events for the remaining weapons following much later. Female epée fencing became an Olympic event as late as 1996 and the sabre event in 2004, after much protracted debate between the FIE and IOC. In general, the inclusion of events in world champion-ships heralded their Olympic recognition.

The different stages of the process whereby female fencing was recognised by international sports authorities and integrated into the programmes of the world championships and Olympic Games were synonymous with the laborious and difficult struggle of women, especially in Europe, to conquer the equality gap in a sport marked by its masculine connotations. Likewise, combat sports often expressed their military legacy with symbolic violence; all sources of masculine domination.[68] The legitimate definition of fencing was socially and historically dominated by a male oligarchy which, beyond the recurrent conflicts linked to issues of national prestige, found an easy consensus in the rejection of women from high-level competitions. Fencing reflected what British sociologist Jennifer Hargreaves describes as 'institutionalised discrimination',[69] i.e. the establishment of a social organisation that creates a patriarchal domination over the sport system.

This first interpretation is limited however, since women had access to the Olympic Games and elite competitions in fencing much earlier than in other sports.[70] In light of such an observation, it has been argued that the differences between the three weapons should then be taken into account by cross-referencing the specific chronology of their recognition as women's events with their symbolic and technical characteristics.

Finally, the integration of team events for women experienced delay in comparison with individual events. This helps complete the recent works of sports historians John Loy, Fiona McLachlan and Douglas Booth, who have analysed resistance towards women in the Olympic Games by revisiting the works of Eleanor Metheny and Pierre Bourdieu.[71] They observe that team games, which supposed confrontation and body contact, systematically took longer to be recognised as part of the Olympic programme in the case of women. Yet team events in fencing are not really 'team sports' in the same way as ball games. They are closer to relays. Nevertheless, the observations of Loy, McLachlan and Booth can be considered justified here, even if contact between opponents is not direct but occurs via use of a weapon. Women succeeded in entering the world of weapons through the main door, although they had not been given the keys.

Notes on Contributors

Thierry Terret is professor of sports history and the director of an interdisciplinary research centre in sport science (Centre de Recherche et d'Innovation sur le Sport – CRIS) at the University of Lyon, France. He is the vice-president of the International Society of the History of Physical Education and Sport (ISHPES) and the president of the French Society of Sport History. His main research focuses on gender, politics and transculturalism.

Cécile Ottogalli-Mazzacavallo is lecturer at the Centre for Research and Innovation in Sport (CRIS, University of Lyon, France). She more especially works on sports history and gender, with a focus on fencing and mountaineering.

Notes

1. For an interesting insight into masculinity and duelling in classical literature, see Low, 'Manhood and the Duel'. For an example of masculine pride and international fencing events, see Terret et al., 'The Puliti Affair'.
2. McAleer, *Dueling*.
3. Cohen, *By the Swords*. On the importance of fencing and dancing in the education of the noblemen see for instance Vaucelle, 'L'art de jouer à la Cour'.
4. The FIE was created in 1913.

5. Coubertin's hostility towards women's sport is well reported. See for instance Rosol, 'Pour une participation des Françaises aux Jeux Olympiques'. On French influence over the FIE at the time of its creation and first regulations, see Ottogalli-Mazzacavallo, 'L'escrime olympique (1896–1936)'.

6. For example: Prudhomme, *Histoire du football féminin*; N. Rosol, 'Une participation contrôlée des Françaises aux épreuves d'athlétisme (1917–fin des années 1950), in 'T. Sabre au féminin dès 1999', *Le Monde*, 7 Oct. 1998).

7. Albert Lacaze, 'L'escrime féminine', *L'escrime et le Tir*, Nov. 1922.

8. Minutes of the FIE Congress, 1921.

9. René Lacroix, 'FIE', *L'escrime et le Tir*, July 1922.

10. On the context of these games, see Terret, *Les paris des Jeux de 1924*, in particular the first volume, 'Les paris de l'organisation'.

11. In 1923, an FIE commission, which included Armand Massard and Paul Anspach, fixed rules on fencers' dress, i.e. skirts hiding underwear from the knee up. These regulations were in line with concerns expressed by several sports federations in France during the period. See Jamain, 'Sport, genre et vêtement sportif'.

12. Ottogalli-Mazzacavallo et al., 'Les jeux des dames en 1924'.

13. Carpentier and Lefèvre, 'The Modern Olympic Movement'.

14. Jean Joseph Renaud, 'Les Jeux de la VIIIème Olympiade', *L'escrime et le Tir*, July–Aug. 1928, 16.

15. Minutes of the FIE Congress, Amsterdam, 26 July, 1928. Archives of the French Federation of Fencing, Paris.

16. Armand Massard, 'En assistant à Naples à une floraison de champions d'Europe', *L'escrime et le Tir*, May 1929.

17. Olympic champion Hélène Mayer is more well-known for her involuntary role in the political instrumentalisation of the 1936 Olympic Games. With a Jewish father, and therefore considered a Jew according to German law, Hélène Mayer was the only member of Jewish confession authorised to take part in the Nazi games for Germany. She was the pretext Hitler was looking for to respond to the criticisms of the IOC and international press on the absence of Jewish athletes representing Germany. Vice Olympic champion in 1936 and world champion in 1937, she then immigrated to the United States to escape Nazi purges. See Mogulof, *Foiled*.

18. Minutes of the FIE Congress, Geneva, 26 and 27 April 1929, 39.

19. Ibid.

20. Minutes of the FIE Congress, Geneva, 26 and 27 April 1929, 40.

21. Ibid.

22. Ibid.

23. Minutes of the FIE Congress, Geneva, 26 and 27 April 1929, 41.

24. Minutes of the FIE Congress, Geneva, 26 and 27 April 1929, 42.

25. Minutes of the FIE Congress, Geneva, 26 and 27 April 1929, 43.

26. Ibid.

27. Jamain, 'Le vêtement sportif des femmes'.

28. Minutes of the FIE Congress, Geneva, 26 and 27 April 1929, 72.

29. Minutes of the FIE Congress, Geneva, 26 and 27 April 1929, 73.

30. The debate was already taking place in the magazine *L'escrime et le Tir*, where Joseph Renaud had been an ardent defender of female epée fencing since 1926.

31. Minutes of the FIE Congress, Geneva, 26 and 27 April 1929, 73.

32. Jean Lacroix, 'Championnats féminins d'Europe de Fleuret', *L'escrime et le Tir*, Aug. 1932.

33. Terret, 'Femmes, sport, identité et acculturation'.

34. Minutes of the FIE Congress, Geneva, 19 and 20 May 1930, 67.

35. Minutes of the FIE Congress, Brussels, 12 and 13 May 1933, 19.

36. Minutes of the FIE Congress, Brussels, 29 and 30 April 1935, 21.

37. Pierre Ferri to Avery Brundage, 3 July, 1957. Correspondance de la Fédération Internationale d'Escrime: FI-ESCRI-FIE-CORR, 1921–1963, 77'770 SIM DGI 9571, IOC Archives, Lausanne.

38. Pierre Ferri to Avery Brundage, sd[1958], Correspondance FIE/CIO, IOC Archives, Lausanne.

39. Rosol, 'L'athlétisme français au féminin'.
40. Modern pentathlon is based on five disciplines, namely shooting, horse riding, running, swimming and fencing.
41. See 'Le pentathlon moderne, le biathlon et l'Olympisme', Revue Olympique 192 (Oct. 1983). As a result of its long military origins and history, modern pentathlon was strongly connected to the cult of hegemonic masculinity. See Heck, 'Modern Pentathlon and World War I'; Heck, 'Modern Pentathlon and Symbolic Violence'.
42. Minutes of the 64th FIE Congress, Al Alghero, 20–21 May 1983, 10. Italian Nostini added that the FIE had to impose its views on the subject over the IUPM and not the other way round.
43. Minutes of the 67th FIE Congress, Paris, 23–24 May 1986, 75.
44. Hargreaves, Sporting Females.
45. Minutes of the 68th FIE Ordinary Congress, Versailles, 5–6 June 1987, 21–3.
46. Michel Salesse, 'Vive les femmes', Escrime 2 (May 1986), 19.
47. Ilona Elek's absence from the discussions undoubtedly had an effect here. The Hungarian passed away a few months later, in May 1988.
48. Minutes of the 68th Ordinary Congress of the FIE, Versailles, 5–6 June 1987, 25. Moreover, the executive committee esteemed that the question was 'not urgent'.
49. 'Epée féminine individuelle', Escrime 20 (Sept.–Oct. 1989), 23.
50. Thébaud, Ecrire l'histoire des femmes et du genre.
51. Smith, Nike is a Goddess.
52. 'Sabre au féminin dès 1999', Le Monde, 7 Oct. 1998.
53. 'Première compétition nationale de "sabreuses"!', Escrime 58 (Feb. 1998), 4.
54. 'Le sabre dame, une utopie devenue réalité', Escrime 63 (March 1999), 8.
55. Françoise Chaptal, 'La nouvelle Eve', Escrime 67 (Dec. 1999), 15–17.
56. Stéphane Lauer, 'Les femmes prennent d'assaut la dernière forteresse de l'escrime', Le Monde, 3 Nov. 1999.
57. Minutes of the 81st Ordinary Congress of the FIE, Paris, 9th December 2000, p. 19.
58. Gilles Van Kote, Le sabre féminin a bénéficié d'une reconnaissance accélérée, Le Monde, 28 October 2001.
59. Minutes of the 82nd Ordinary Congress of the FIE, Havana, 8–9 Dec., 2001, 72–83.
60. Minutes of the FIE Extraordinary Congress, Lisbon, 17 Aug. 2002, 12.
61. Minutes of the FIE Extraordinary Congress, Antalya, 7 April 2002, 17–40.
62. Minutes of the FIE Extraordinary Congress, Lisbon, 17 Aug. 2002, 11–21.
63. Minutes of the FIE Extraordinary Congress, Lisbon, 17 Aug. 2002, p. 21.
64. 'Le sabre féminin presque olympique', Le Monde, 20 Aug. 2002.
65. Minutes of the 83rd Congress of the FIE, Leipzig, 22–23 Nov. 2003, 21.
66. René Roch on the subject of his discussions with the IOC: Minutes of the 83rd Congress of the FIE, Leipzig, 22–23 Nov. 2003, 21.
67. Jean-Marie Safra, 'Examen de passage réussi pour l'épreuve par équipe de sabre masculin et féminin', Escrime internationale 41 (2001), 24.
68. Bourdieu, La domination masculine.
69. Hargreaves, Sporting Females, 174.
70. Earlier female sports events in the Olympic Games were archery, diving, figure skating, golf, swimming and tennis.
71. Loy et al., 'Connotations of Female Movement and Meaning'.

References

Bourdieu, P. La domination masculine, Paris: Seuil, 1998.
Carpentier, F. and J.P. Lefèvre. 'The Modern Olympic Movement, Women's Sport and the Social Order during the Inter-war period'. The International Journal of the History of Sport 23, no.7 (Nov. 2006): 1112–27.
Cohen, R. By the Swords: A History of Gladiators, Musketeers, Samurai, Swashbucklers, and Olympic Champions. New York: Ramdom House, 2002.
Hargreaves, J. Sporting Females. London: Routledge, 1994.
Heck, S. 'Modern Pentathlon and Symbolic Violence – a History of Female Exclusion from Stockholm 1912 to Paris 1924'. International Journal of Sport and Violence, May 2010.

Heck, S. 'Modern Pentathlon and World War I – When Athletes and Soldiers Meet to Practise Martial Manliness'. *The International Journal of the History of Sport* 28, nos. 3–4 (2011): 410–28.

Jamain, S. 'Sport, genre et vêtement sportif. Une histoire culturelle du paraître vestimentaire (fin XIXe siècle– début des années 1970)'. PhD diss., University of Lyon, 2008.

Jamain, S. 'Le vêtement sportif des femmes des "années folles" aux années 1960. De la transgression à "neutralisation" du genre'. In *Sport et genre,* vol. 4: 'Objets, arts et medias', eds A. Roger and T. Terret. Paris: L'Harmattan, 2005, 35–48.

Low, J. 'Manhood and the Duel: Enacting Masculinity in Hamlet'. *Centennial Review* 43, no. 3 (Autumn 1999): 501–12.

Loy, J., F. McLachlan and D. Booth. 'Connotations of Female Movement and Meaning. The Development of Women's Participation in the Olympic Games'. *Olympika* XVIII (2009): 1–24.

McAleer, K. *Dueling: the Cult of Honor in Fin-de-siècle Germany.* Princeton, NJ: Princeton University Press, 1994.

Mogulof, M. *Foiled, Hitler's Jewish Olympian: the Helene Mayer Story.* Oakland, CA: RDR Books, 2002.

Ottogalli-Mazzacavallo, C. 'L'escrime olympique (1896–1936) au temps de l'hégémonie franco-italienne', in *Jeux olympiques, Fierté nationale et enjeu mondial,* ed. C. Boli. Biarritz: Atlantica, 2008, 277–87.

Ottogalli-Mazzacavallo, C., J. Prudhomme-Poncet and A. Velez. 'Les jeux des dames en 1924: Echec et mat à la logique d'exclusion du CIO?', in *Les Paris des Jeux de 1924,* vol. 4: 'Les paris culturels', ed. T. Terret. Paris: Atlantica, 2008, 1189–1216.

Prudhomme, L. *Histoire du football féminin au XXe siècle.* Paris: L'Harmattan, 2003.

Rosol, N. 'Pour une participation des Françaises aux Jeux Olympiques (1900–1928). Un combat mené par Alice Milliat', in *Le sport français dans l'entre-deux-guerres,* eds J-P. Saint Martin and T. Terret. Paris: L'Harmattan, 2000, 15–37.

Rosol, N. 'L'athlétisme français au féminin (1912–fin des années 1970). Des athlètes en quête d'identité'. PhD diss., University of Lyon, 2005.

Smith, L. *Nike is a Goddess. The History of Women in Sports.* New York: Atlantic Monthly Press, 1998.

Terret, T. 'Femmes, sport, identité et acculturation. Eléments d'historiographie française'. *Stadion* XXVI, no. 1 (2000): 41–53.

Terret, T., ed. *Sport et genre.* Paris: L'Harmattan, 2005.

Terret, T., ed. *Les paris des Jeux de 1924.* Paris: Atlantica, 2008.

Terret, T., C. Ottogalli and J. Saint-Martin. 'The Puliti Affair. Fencing Tradition, Geo-Political Issues and National Pride in Paris 1924'. *The International Journal of the History of Sport* 24, no. 10 (Oct. 2007): 1281–1301.

Thébaud, F. *Ecrire l'histoire des femmes et du genre.* Lyon: ENS, 2007.

Vaucelle, S. 'L'art de jouer à la Cour. Transformation des jeux d'exercice dans l'éducation de la noblesse française au début de l'ère moderne (XIIIe–XVIIe siècles). Unpublished PhD diss., Ecoles des Hautes Etudes en Sciences Sociales, Paris, 2004.

The Sports Woman as a Cultural Challenge: Swedish Popular Press Coverage of the Olympic Games during the 1950s and 1960s

Helena Tolvhed

Department of History, Stockholm University, Sweden

In this article, popular press coverage of summer and winter Olympic Games in Swedish popular and illustrated magazines during the 1950s and 1960s is analysed as part of a process of everyday affirmation of national and gender identity. First, it is shown how Swedish male athletes are represented in the media as active and forceful male bodies, competing for national honour. The article then moves on to an analysis of representation of female Olympians, and how 'our' Swedish girls are discursively linked to a Western, attractive and modern womanhood. In the Cold War context of the 1950s and 1960s, female athletes from Communist states were held out as contrasting examples. Media representation focusing on the good looks and attractiveness of female athletes is read as cultural negotiations of the challenge of women's sport. It is argued that female Olympians were visually and textually represented as *women* rather than as athletes. This is related to the Swedish historical context, where the female body was a crucial site and symbol for the separation of gendered spheres. The article concludes that the configuration of femininity does not, as in the decades around 1900, refer to biology but rather to social and cultural necessities.

Introduction

Historically, sport has been a politically useful resource. As a range of practices as well as in its mediated forms, it has served to mark and manifest differences based on nation, gender and class. Sport has been used for training and shaping 'manly characters', and to establish a cultural national identity. It has bridged the gap between the public and the private spheres by providing national symbols (athletes) with whom to identify, and by the sense of national unity instilled by the symbolic 'friendly rivalry' between nations in the sports arena. Like fighting for the nation in military battles, representing it in prestigious sport events was for a long time an exclusively male duty and privilege.[1]

The main focus in this article is how the Olympic sportswoman as a culturally challenging figure was understood and negotiated in 1950s and 1960s Sweden. Media representations of Swedish female Olympians are placed in the historic context of the Cold War and analysed against the background of gender relations that were fundamental to society during this era of the Swedish 'people's home' and emerging welfare state. The research is based on the thesis 'Sporting the Nation', where the source material consists of press coverage of summer and winter Olympic Games in six Swedish popular and illustrated magazines during the 1950s and 1960s.[2] The magazines generally targeted mixed groups of readers with regard to gender and age, although some leaned more towards male, female or younger readers. During this time period, these weekly magazines were at the height of their popularity with very high circulation figures, before declining due to the increased popularity of television. On a global political and cultural level, this is an era characterised by the polarisation of the 'Cold War' and the process of decolonisation. The latter meant that more and more nations from outside the Western world began to compete in the summer Olympics. Competing became symbolically important as a manifestation of being accepted and recognised as a nation in the international community of states. Also, the decades following the Second World War were a period when women became increasingly present and visible as competitors in the Olympic Games.[3]

Following Benedict Anderson's concept of the 'imagined community', *nation* is here understood to be a construction that is not natural, universal or eternal but instead a result of specific developments in European history. Moreover, as feminist scholars such as Nira Yuval-Davies and Anne McClintock have pointed out, gender is central to the national representational system. While men are imagined as the active representatives, subjects and defenders of the nation, women typically have been assigned more passive positions as symbols, and as bearers and mothers of a new generation of men. These are the positions that underpin the imagined belonging to a 'family of the nation'. Differences of gender, and to some extent also differences of class, may, as Yuval-Davies has pointed out, be attributed to a functional need for an organic conception of nation in order to secure a smooth and efficient working of 'the community'.[4] Stuart Hall has formulated the paradox of the nation being founded on difference as well as unity: 'Instead of thinking of national cultures as unified, we should think of them as constituting a *discursive device* which represents difference as unity or identity. They are cross-cut by deep internal divisions and differences, and "unified" only through the exercise of different forms of cultural power.'[5]

Hence, the nation is a homogenising force, the success of which, as a producer of meaning, depends on an ability to suppress internal conflicts and dividing lines. The era in Swedish history known as *folkhemmet* (the people's home) from the end of the 1920s and the growth of the welfare state, makes an illustrative example of this principle, since the ideology of separate gendered spheres was crucial to a functionalist approach to society. The gender ideology emphasised 'harmony-in-difference', where distinct gender spheres were assumed to make up a harmonious whole.[6] Hall also emphasises the symbolic quality of the national community; 'a nation is not only a political entity but something that produces meaning – *a system of cultural representation*'.[7]

In modern society, media representation is crucial to the production of meaning. Media shape our knowledge of 'how the world is', as part of a process where meaning is produced within history and culture.[8] What makes the sporting media an interesting object of study from a feminist perspective is the potential they provide for studying how the bodies and character of athletes are represented and constructed. Historian Joan W. Scott has argued that when our attention shifts to the dynamic question of *how* hierarchies are constructed and legitimised, significance is accorded – more productively – to *processes* rather than origin.[9] It can be argued that sport, and also sport media, is part of a process of everyday affirmation, and naturalisation, of national and gender identity. Through the popular culture present in the everyday lives of citizens, readers are simultaneously positioned as national and gendered subjects.[10] National identity is discursively constructed – in highly gendered ways – through the representation of culturally relevant Others. Who and what *we* are is defined by pointing out who and what we are *not*.[11]

Forms of representation have to be understood as historically specific, and the aim here is to point out how the position of *us* is inscribed and naturalised in the text. Popular magazines are used as sources to study historical cultural contexts and examine the intersecting ways that gendered and national identities are discursively constructed.[12] Theoretically, the study rests on Foucault's understanding of the interconnectedness of knowledge and power, and on cultural studies' conception of representation and the textual and visual address of the reader.[13] The analysis explores how historically specific configurations of Swedish masculinity and Swedish femininity emerge as privileged positions in the text (and images) and are offered to the reader as identities or 'subject positions'.[14]

Sport and Masculinity

Gender is a relational concept. Hence, this article starts with a discussion of masculinity and the male body as a norm in sport with some examples from 'Sporting the Nation'. It then moves on to an analysis of the representation of Swedish female Olympians. As feminist and postcolonial scholars have pointed out, conceptions of the human body have historically been central to the social and cultural construction of gender and race. The characteristics of the female body have been used to explain and justify the social exclusion of women as well as the cultural devaluation of femininity, much in the same way that the black body has been imagined as different, deviant or even abnormal.[15] Thus, the social subordination of women and blacks has been legitimised by claims of deviant and inferior body constitution in comparison to the white man.[16]

But sport has not only been an arena for the display of purely physical accomplishments and capabilities. Part of its historical function as a legitimisation of male social privilege has also been the display of the supposedly 'male' ability to put the body under the disciplining power of the mind.[17] As historian Gail Bederman has shown, seemingly contradictory notions of masculinity – on the one hand Victorian ideals of self-control, and on the other hand the more 'primitive' side of masculinity emphasising physical assertiveness, strength and force – came together in the larger discourse of 'civilisation'.[18] Sport, and especially sport performed at the Olympics, where national identity, glory and tradition were projected and constructed, were ideally suited to represent and affirm this combination of discipline and power.

Research on sport, masculinity and the media has highlighted how the victories of sportsmen have been celebrated and mythologised, while the athletes have been made national heroes and perceived as embodiments of the nation.[19] Swedish popular magazines from the 1950s and 1960s illustrate this close interconnectedness of masculinity and nation. Male athletes are textually and visually represented as embodiments of Swedish strength. These are active and forceful bodies, competing for national honour. The ability to push the body to – and even beyond – its physical limitations is attributed to successful male Olympians, and especially Swedish ones. The pictures in the illustrated magazines show these men in vigorous movement and the physical strain, and the text emphasises the superior determination involved in beating the competitors. The successful male Swedish athlete's excruciating training regime is explained in great detail: typically, getting up early in the morning and then spending hours on the track or in the woods. The strenuous physical work, the sacrifice and the suffering behind success are emphasised, and in this way success is earned. Men's bodies are represented as disciplined and ruled by both strong willpower and sense of national duty.[20]

This active male body is marked as distinctly Swedish but the representation – especially in articles from the winter Olympics – also articulates ideas on a specific Nordic and Scandinavian form of masculinity. Results of the research in 'Sporting the Nation' point to a cultural conception of affinity and the idea of a special bond between countries of the North, constructed most explicitly on the basis of the interest and successes shared by Sweden, Norway and Finland in cross-country skiing. 'Swedishness' and 'Nordicness' seem to overlap as discursive markers of identity in the construction of *us*.[21] At the same time, however, there is also stiff competition between these countries for winter Olympic medals. Throughout the period, a mutual respect and community based on what is perceived as the shared skiing skills and specific stamina of Nordic (male) Olympians is represented in the press material.

'Sporting the Nation' shows a move over time towards a higher degree of complexity regarding masculinity. During the 1960s, the unified ideal of the (successful and male) Olympic athlete as a national hero and personification of national character was paralleled by a newly emerging alternative configuration of masculinity. This was an ideal suited to a young pop-culture generation – the partygoer, drinker and womaniser who could still perform impressively in sports and win the competitions.[22] This hedonist 'playboy-masculinity' was marked by aspects of age, generation and modern, post-war consumption ideals, and appeared in 1964 with the Olympic Games in Innsbruck and Tokyo.[23] This form of masculinity seems in many ways very different from the ascetic self-sacrificing characteristics of earlier masculine ideals. However, the forms and ideals are parallel in their existence. Successful Swedish male winter Olympians were still represented as displaying bodily strength and discipline; the fusion of nation and masculinity remained culturally relevant.

That this construction of male willpower is strongly linked to white maleness is made clear when comparing with representations of black male athletes. The participation and successes of African and African-American male athletes in the summer Olympics are extensively covered in the popular Swedish magazines. A recurring theme in these articles is the posing of the question of how *their* successes are to be made sense of and explained. There are articles speculating on superior uptake of oxygen and genetic advantages, but perhaps the most interesting aspect of this is the formulation of this as a question, even a problem, that should elicit an answer.[24] In stark contrast with representations of white and especially Swedish males, it is not the hard and disciplined work behind the victories that is emphasised in features on black athletes. Instead, they are frequently represented as natural phenomena and found to be lacking when it comes to the mental capability to apply tactics and strategies. This is also illustrated in the use of describing metaphors such as 'black tornadoes' or references to animals. As postcolonial research has pointed out, the concept of black people having 'natural' physical ability has historically been used to legitimise unequal power relations and a colonial world order.[25]

Thus the work behind the achievements of black athletes is concealed, while bodily discipline is reserved and ascribed to a white, Western and Swedish masculinity. The black men pose a challenge through their athletic prominence, and this 'threat' is culturally negotiated in a way that places white and Swedish masculinity above that of black males – regardless of the outcomes of Olympic competition. Issues of race thus pervade these constructions of masculinity, and the white, male and Western body is central to the construction of (successful) Swedish national identity. Although Sweden was never a prominent colonial power, its masculinity is constructed as part of a Western and white community and civilisation. The connection between black male athletes and natural ability is made throughout the period, even in coverage of the 1968 Olympic Games in Mexico City where the magazines generally take an explicit stand for the right of American athletes to protest against racial oppression.

The Sportswoman

Women's sports have been a controversial issue, from their modest beginnings in the end of the nineteenth and throughout the twentieth centuries. Physical activity, strength and assertiveness have generally not been regarded as either commendable or suitable for women, since the possession of such qualities has gone against traditional definitions of womanhood. Modern sports were developed and formed during the second half of the nineteenth century, where the bourgeois feminine ideal dictated a slender, passive and physically weak body, and this ideal has continued to make women's sport problematic.[26] Research on media coverage has shown that female athletes have been, and in fact still are, marginalised in quantitative terms in comparison to males. When represented at all, their sport performances have frequently been trivialised and regarded as less important than for their male peers.[27] Historian Susan K. Cahn has showed how the representation of female athletes in American media throughout the twentieth century was marked by the tendency to represent them well inside the norms of stereotypical femininity. The media focused upon their beauty and on supposedly feminine interests such as cooking, sewing and caring about appearance. In a similar way, those advocating women's sport in the American educational system tried to avoid the stigma and the fear of lesbians through emphasising family ideals and sport as graceful play and enhancer of beauty in accordance with heterosexual norms. Idealised images of the female athlete as a beauty queen and mannequin should, following Cahn, be understood as a way to meet the challenge against the established gender order – inside and outside sport. Furthermore, this construction of women athletes secured the sport hero as a personification of male virtues.[28]

Eva Olofsson has argued that historically, organised sport in Sweden has been lagging behind the progress for gender equality in other areas of society. The reason for this, Olofsson argues, is the strong emphasis in sport on biology and gender separation. This sustained a naturalisation of differences between men and women, which made it possible to neglect women's sport and favour male sport. It was only after external political and social pressure and the arrival of the issue of gender equality on the public agenda that at the end of the 1970s, the Swedish sports movement began to make efforts to have more women participants.[29]

Pia Lundkvist Wanneberg has shown that physical education in Swedish schools in the 1950s and 1960s was aimed at cultivating boys and girls into two different, highly gender-marked groups of citizens, where boys, especially boys from the upper classes, were guided towards exercises emphasising strength, determination and competition, and girls were taught to develop grace and agility through 'aesthetic' gymnastic exercises.[30] The female body was perceived as weak and therefore needed to save strength for reproductive functions. The female character was also presumed to lack competitive instincts. Physical education in schools was designed to respect and preserve these presumably natural 'weaknesses' and 'lacks'. This provides an illustration of how discourses of gender not only shape identities and characters but also materialise in the physical shape and form of the body.[31]

This paper will now turn to representations of female athletes in 1950s and 1960s popular magazines and how they articulate gendered constructions of a national identity. This underlines the understanding of masculinity and femininity as distinct and separate. Feminist historians such as Anne McClintock and Susan K. Cahn have pointed out that idealised femininity has been created through a historical process of distancing it from what it is not (or the antithesis of the white and middle-class respectable woman). Black women, lesbians and working class women.[32] Sociologist Beverly Skeggs has emphasised the importance of respectability, where class, gender, sexuality and race intersect to make up a middle-class marked and heterosexual white femininity.[33]

Feminine Swedish Girls and Muscular Communist Women

In a study of Olympic sports journalism in early-twentieth-century Finland, Mervi Tervo points out the importance of sport to the nationalist project. Tervo's conclusion is that Finnish women athletes were either completely marginalised, or constructed as highly gender-marked and passive symbols of the nation – 'pure Finnish maidens who were symbolically, with their mere presence, representing Finland at the Olympics'.[34] Tervo shows how the commendable character of Finnish women was emphasised through contrasting them with American and Canadian women. The latter were represented as artificial, flirtatious and overly sexual with too much make-up, in comparison to the pure and modest Finnish 'maidens'. Represented as distinctly *modern* women, American and Canadian women thus became symbols of a threatening modernity. Put against these *others*, the Finnish female athletes – whose sport activities in themselves threatened to raise suspicions of their proper womanhood – could be marked as feminine, decent and respectable.[35]

In a similar vein, the sources utilised in writing the thesis to which this paper refers show that in the Cold War context of the 1950s and 1960s, female athletes from Communist states were held out as contrasting examples. In this cultural climate, they emerged as prominent *others* and functioned to elucidate respectable and attractive Swedish and Western femininity. The Soviet Union competed at the Olympics for the first time at the 1952 summer Games in Helsinki. Articles in the Swedish press centred upon this unique meeting and competition between the two political systems of Communism and capitalism. Much curiosity surrounded the Eastern bloc athletes, who were lodged in their own camp, separate from the rest of the Olympic village.

In magazine representations of Eastern female athletes, distance and difference is emphasised. A feature from the summer Olympic Games in Melbourne 1956 includes photographs of Swedish high-jumper Gun Larking and Russian shot-putter Diskowitz – see figure 1.[36] The latter's first name is not mentioned, which renders her 'masculinised' since women generally are referred to by either their full name or their first name only, whereas males often are referred to only by surname.[37] The photograph of the Russian depicts her whole body and captures her just as she is putting the shot, with a strained facial expression, while the picture of the Swede shows only chest and face, and she is smiling, posing and looking straight into the camera. She has her hands in her hair in what might be termed a very 'heterofeminine' pose. The fact that the image of Diskowitz is about twice the size of the image of Larking also suggests that she is physically larger than the Swede and this visual contrast is further emphasised and completed – or in Roland Barthes's terms, 'anchored' – by the accompanying text, which refers directly to the photographs.[38] The Swedish woman Larking is described in the text as 'our own soft and feminine', while Diskowitz is deemed to be 'repelling and ungraceful'. Furthermore, the text explicitly encourages the reader to judge between the two through the ironic formulation: 'It's unnecessary to ask which one you prefer, isn't it?' The boundaries of acceptable and respectable femininity are clearly spelled out here.

This is an example of how the threat of sport to the female body and mind is negotiated through 'masculinised' images of Soviet female athletes. *Contrasting* is used in both visual and textual representation and guides and encourages the reader

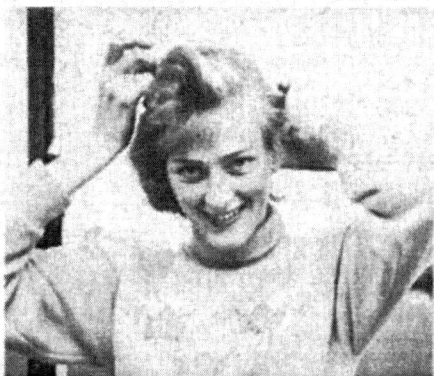

TVÅ OLYMPIAFLICKOR

som båda just har tävlat färdigt i Melbourne. Det är väl onödigt att fråga vilken ni föredrar? För alldeles bortsett ifrån att vår egen mjuka, feminina höjdhoppsflicka *Gun Larking* (som rättar till frisyren härovan) har fått mycket till skänks av naturen, så ligger det något så frånstötande (förlåt vitsen!) och *ospänstigt* över den typ som ryskan *Diskowitz* t. v. representerar. Hennes träningsprogram har tydligen gått ut på att lägga så många kilo som möjligt bakom kulan! Man kommer att tänka på VR:s idrottsföljetong »Olympiad 1996» . . .

Figure 1. 'Two Olympic girls'.
Source: *Vecko-Revyn* (magazine) 49, p. 13 (1956).

towards dissimilarity between the two women: through the difference in sizes of the pictures and the contrasting representations of their bodies. The photograph of Diskowitz, showing her strenuous physical activity in a way not associated with images of Western female athletes at this time, underlines her *otherness*. This representation is also structured by discourses of class: this big, active, muscular body is contrasted with Larking, who embodies the ideal of respectable, middle-class (Swedish) femininity. Representations of the masculinised Communist woman defined the borders of gender as well as nation, and assured the reader that sport would not make *our* women cross the line by becoming muscular, unattractive and uninterested in conveying heterosexual femininity. Susan Cahn has pointed to similar mediated constructions of Soviet women occurring in the 1950s in the United States, where images of mannish sportswomen were conferred upon Soviet 'Amazons'.[39] Thus the occurrence of similar textual and visual representations in Swedish magazines must be understood within the context of the political and cultural climate of the Cold War. They point to a Swedish sense of cultural affiliation to the West, in spite of the official doctrines of Sweden's political neutrality in the Cold War.[40]

Constructing a Swedish and Western Femininity

A similar form of contrasting can be seen in the coverage of another magazine from the Olympics in Helsinki 1952, an article on the female athletes' camp:

> The Swedish sports girls are certainly not masculinised – none of the 500 in this house were. Although, there were a few rather pronounced cases in Otnäs, the Russians and other Eastern states camp, where also their female troupes have stayed. Before the Swedish gymnastic girls competed, a Swedish hairdresser ... came and did everybody's hair. ... All the Swedish girls have done their make-up very well and discretely – or not at all – but they have generally been meticulous with the nail varnish on fingers as well as toes.[41]

Here the contrasting of Swedish, Western femininity with that of women from the Communist East is explicit. *Our* girls are explicitly distanced from *them* – the Eastern female athletes – who are described as 'masculinised' in the quote above. *Our* Swedish girls are associated with Western, modern womanhood through markers such as the attention paid to the body and a 'hetero-feminine' presentation of this body. Femininity is marked by the references to hair, make-up and nail grooming: 'proper women' are expected to take an interest in their physical appearance. This is an attractive Swedish femininity on display. Grooming and body care are also markers of class – a respectable, heterosexual and middle-class marked femininity with discreet make-up (too much or excessive would be a marker of lower class origin). Swedish and Western female Olympians are here constructed as 'proper women' who – although involved in an activity that was coded as masculine – will not pose any threat to the established gender order.

Beauty pageants functioned as a common frame of reference for female participants competing in the Olympics. The media sometimes even portrayed the Olympics as first and foremost a beauty contest for the female participants. The headline of a feature from the magazine *Se* about Swedish gymnast Lena Adler, published weeks before the Olympics in Rome 1960, poses the question 'Will she be the Swedish poster girl of the Olympics?' – see Figure 2. The concept of the Olympic 'poster girl' was well established and recognised at this time, and female Olympians

Figure 2   'Will she [Lena Adler] be the Swedish poster girl of the Olympics?'
Source: *Se* (magazine) 34, p. 18 (1960).

were chosen as possible 'candidates' to the 'title' beforehand. It is not surprising that the woman in question is a gymnast, since gymnastics was traditionally a non-controversial and even commendable sport for women, considered to maintain a 'feminine' character through the emphasis on appealing qualities such as grace, litheness and beauty.[42] Adler is shown in physical activity in the photos, but the inviting smile and the gaze directly into the camera clearly suggests that she is posing for the camera, that these photographs are arranged rather than just snapshots from a practice session. In the text that accompanies the photos, there are further references to the prospect of her becoming the 'beauty queen' of the Olympics, just like the Swedish Gun Larking was claimed to have been at the previous games in Melbourne. Adler is also quoted as saying that she intended to become an airline flight attendant and that gymnastics was just a hobby to her. Athletic achievement is seldom the focus of features on female Olympians, and especially not for Swedish women. In stark contrast with male Olympians, sport competition and national honour were not represented as the main purpose for their presence at the event. Instead, the media coverage emphasises their nice behaviour, popularity among the Olympic audience and fellow Olympians from other nations, and their attractive yet respectable way of presenting themselves in both dress and conduct.

Articles on women athletes in the Swedish popular press tended to focus on their life outside of sport. Their good looks, family, romance or general plans for the future was often the focus of the articles, rather than practice, achievements and results related to their sport. Sport in itself is occasionally represented as being incompatible with, even threatening to, femininity and (the construction of) the character, life, body and dreams of the young woman. The sports activities of female athletes were typically framed as a limited period of play for the young woman, before marriage and the duties of adult womanhood take over.[43] Thus their sport activities were trivialised and represented as 'just a hobby'. Women's participation at the Olympics is described as an exciting experience for them, while the results in the competitions, it is frequently claimed, are not that important. Rather, it is about seeing the world and meeting people from many different countries. This is something very different to articles on male athletes, where the competition (preparations, chances, results) are often the main focus. Sport was also represented as a threat to the supposedly 'natural' and 'truly feminine' body. Female athletes' bodies are often commented upon, through appreciative remarks assuring the reader that this woman has not become too muscular or 'masculinised' through her sport. Also, descriptions of how the practice is adjusted so as not to result in bulky muscles on the legs and arms occur on occasion.[44]

Cracks and Possibilities in Representations of Women's Sport

So far, some illustrative examples of the dominating pattern in the analysis of mediated representations of women's sport during the 1950s and 1960s have been offered. It has been concluded that female athletes are frequently 'sexualised', with coverage focusing on their good looks and attractiveness rather than on athletic performance. But looked at from a critical-analytical perspective, it could be argued that the predominant form of coverage of female Olympians tries so hard to convince readers of their femininity that it actually make it obvious that women in sport poses a kind of cultural challenge. As Sara Mills has emphasised, the historian can interpret such repetitive reassurances of traditional conceptions of femininity as evidence of cultural conflict and challenges. She analyses 'etiquette-books' for young women from the Victorian era in which unwanted behaviours were described and condemned. Mills argues that these sources, through their very existence and content, indicate that the young women of the time were in fact not the docile subjects that this form of literature strived to highlight. Rather, the very *raison d'être* for this genre was the need to foster those subjects who did not comply with its prescriptions. The books occurred as a response to traditional gender relations being challenged at this time in history, and an emerging resistance to the 'established ways'. From a discourse-analytical perspective it is, Mills argues, possible to understand this kind of cultural repetition as something more than merely signs of repression. In the same way, compensatory media representation of the sports-woman as a beauty queen can be understood as a counter to the destabilising force represented by women's sport at the time. These representations point to the instability of gender relations, which, rather than being 'given' or 'natural', needed (popular) cultural reinforcement.

However, Mills also take her argument one step further, in order to emphasise various possibilities when it comes to reception and reading. Readers are able to understand and utilise literature in various ways. Mills argues that the etiquette books carry a destabilising potential since the identification of unwanted forms of female behaviour, traits or physical appearance makes available a range of alternative positions and possibilities besides those normally acceptable.[45] In line with this approach, even negative representations of 'Communist' women athletes can be seen as ambiguous since they display active, strong female bodies. When sport is represented as a threat to respectable femininity, this rests on assumptions that women can in fact be competitive and that the female body can develop muscles, become larger, stronger and faster.

Hence it can be understood why representations of Olympic sportswomen tie them to stereotypical femininity as cultural negotiations of the challenge of crossing gendered borders. Paradoxically, they expose the 'borderlands', the existence of which is denied, as well as the cultural anxiety that this creates. The constant marking of (middle-class, attractive and respectable) femininity exposes how biology, as Judith Butler and R.W. Connell have claimed, in itself makes an uncertain foundation of societal gender order. Hence, a constant cultural reinforcement is necessary in order to maintain gender as a socially relevant classification, so that the boundaries may be 'kept safe'. Hence, the suggestion here is that the gender discourse in the magazines is not founded in biology. Examinations of these magazines has found no discussion on the question of whether women should or should not participate in sport; or any arguments suggesting that sport is physically harmful for women. The configuration of femininity does not – as in the decades around 1900 – refer to biology but rather to *social* necessities and 'facts'. Sport is represented as potentially harmful to women's appearance and their suitability as symbols of the nation, rather than as being detrimental to their health. In this historical context the gendered representation appears to be about the stability and function of society, referring to a social and cultural need for separated gender spaces.

However, culture is always a complex and sometimes contradictory study object. In 'Sporting the Nation', some examples are discussed where the intersections between gender, nation and age seems to result in a break with predominant discourse of femininity. National success (particularly in what was thought of as specific 'national events' such as cross-country skiing) does, in some representations, seem to 'override' the meaning of gender and thus open up for representations of the capable *Swedish* female body. It seems reasonable to understand these representations as outcomes of the intense focus on national sporting success in Olympic coverage. Previous research has shown that coverage of female athletes increases during major events such as the Olympic Games, since the main logic of such events is the competition between countries and number of medals won.[46] On a few occasions when Olympic medals are won by Swedish female athletes, this focus seems to take precedence over otherwise gendered constructions of Olympic athletes. Also, references to a young generation of healthy Swedes seems, as a part of the discourse on public health characteristic of this period in Swedish history, to sometimes make possible a display of the (young) female body as active and physically strong. The magazine most obviously addressing a female audience, *Idun*, also displays the representations of female athletes that are most similar to the general representation of male Olympians. This includes photographs showing activity and movement as well as textual descriptions of bodies as hard-working and disciplined, emphasising their commitment to sport. *Idun* targeted the middle-class, professional woman, and, contrary to what was the case in more family-oriented magazines, the public sphere was familiar territory for the readers of the mildly feminist *Idun*. Here, woman was thought not only – as in dominant discourse and public policy at the time – to belong in the private sphere but also in the public arena. For this reason, elite-level sport was not as controversial in this particular publication as it was in others. This underlines the strong symbolic value of women's sport and the active female body, and how this is connected to the upholding of a separation between a public and a private sphere.

Concluding Discussion: The Sportswoman as a Cultural Challenge

This paper has made the argument that, generally, women's presence and competition at the Olympic Games in the popular Swedish press during the 1950s and 1960s is portrayed in a culturally acceptable and familiar context, bringing them from the masculinised sphere of sport to within a 'safer' sphere of femininity. The Swedish 'girls' represent their country by being attractive, admired by the world and by men from other countries, yet remain still respectable in their behaviour. In this way, however, they are trivialised as athletes and not represented as active, assertive competitors in a public arena in the way that sportsmen generally are. The female body is predominately represented, both visually and textually, as passive, posing and smiling. The appearance of female athletes is commented upon and compared, and the appointment of Olympic 'beauty queens' is a recurrent feature. Women's sports activities are frequently either downplayed or understood as displays of beauty rather than, as for male athletes, sporting performances and purposeful and strained *work* in the *public arena*. This should be understood as part of the specific historical context, where on an ideological level, the concept of female work was controversial and women were assigned to the private social sphere, preferably as home-makers. The importance of female (paid and unpaid) work for the national and household economy was a threatening fact which had to be kept hidden, since *folkhemmet* as well as the welfare state as political and social projects were organised on the basis of a gendered order which placed the married woman at home. The work that the housewife performed at home was not perceived as work but rather as a supposedly 'natural' female sphere of activities.[47]

In this paper it has been argued that the symbolic challenge presented by women's sport was negotiated by means of constructions of women's bodies and characters as being different in comparison to men. In the same way that women's paid and unpaid work and commitment to career was trivialised, so were women's sporting activities and their commitment to competitive sport. In accordance with previous research on gender and nation, women were positioned as passive symbols of the nation, through attractive bodies and respectable conduct, rather than as active representatives. The sportswoman, displaying physical, social and mental strength and assertiveness, not only challenged gendered ideas but also carried fundamental implications for an overall sense of stability, coherence and predictability resting on a gendered division of labour.

The study has shown that while male athletes were represented as *sports*men, with an emphasis on their superior physical abilities and remarkable willpower, female Olympians were predominately represented as *women*. They were often showed in passive and inviting positions, smiling and posing and were thus portrayed as unthreatening and 'regular' women in a way that upheld the boundaries between the sexes. Furthermore, sport as a risk to respectable Swedish and Western femininity was negotiated in way that were highly time and context specific, by displacing the negative images of muscular and unattractive females onto 'Communist' female athletes. This placed the threat of 'masculinised' sportswomen at a safe distance from *our* (Swedish, Western, white) women. By pointing out *their* lack of heterosexual attractiveness, the women of the East were marked as ambiguous – sexually and in terms of gender – while the heterosexuality, femininity and middle-class-marked respectability of *our* female Olympians was underlined through visual and textual contrasts. The representations of Soviet female athletes show how excessive activity and traces of physical work in the form of muscularity on a female body constitutes a threatening transgression of a hetero-normative gender order, and is symbolically neutralised by being cast as repulsive.

Since what is at stake is not actually who *they* are, but rather who *we* are, the characteristics assigned to *others* are historically variable. In the polarised Cold War context, femininity became a central signifier, marking Sweden as a Western modern nation. The study concludes that women are crucial in displaying and embodying the nation's morality and social stability through references to a traditional, heterosexual order within a nationalist discourse. This 'truly feminine' female body is not imagined as being capable of the disciplined and controlled physical work that is ascribed to (Swedish, Western, white) sportsmen. These gendered media representations must be understood against the background of the Swedish era of *folkhemmet* and the emerging welfare state, where the ideology of separate gendered spheres was crucial to a functionalist approach to society. The gender ideology emphasised distinct gender spheres, thought to make up a harmonious whole. The competitive sportswoman – a strained, active body moving through public space and in the public eye – posed a social and cultural challenge not only to gendered ideals but to a deep-set, reassuring conception of society as a stable entity.

However, and in order to conclude on a more positive note for the future, it should be noted how Judith Butler has discussed women's sports as something that challenges dominating ideals of femininity and presses the boundaries of gender in processes of cultural negotiation on the issue of women in sport. Butler understands sport as a cultural arena where gendered norms are played out, thus helping to maintain gender as a socially relevant classification through a process of constant repetition. However, in Butler's thinking, this repetition is never seamless and exact, but does allow for new elements to be introduced and hence for discursive change. History does show us many examples of women's hardships when it comes to the right to participate and be included, and sport is another example of this. Mediated representations have social implications, since characteristics of the female body have historically justified the social exclusion of women and cultural devaluation of femininity. Like Butler, this writer also believe that there has been, and certainly still is, a radical potential in women's sports as an arena where the meaning of gender can be renegotiated and challenged:

> If cultural resources offer conflicted and complicated ideals, ones that call forth a crisis in stable gender norms, then women's sports, which have the power to press the boundaries of gender ideals, not only take place at the cross-roads of conflicting ideals, but constitute one of the most dramatic ways in which those conflicts are staged and negotiated in the public sphere.[48]

Notes on Contributor

Helena Tolvhed is a lecturer and postdoctoral researcher in sports history at the Department of History, Stockholm University. Her work focuses on sport history, gender and nationalism.

Notes

1. Hobsbawm, *Nations and Nationalism since 1780*, 142, 143; Mangan, *Tribal Identities*; Gori, *Sport and Gender Matters*; Tervo, 'Nationalism, Sports and Gender', 365; Hofmann and Trangbæk, *International Perspectives*.
2. The article is based on research published in my thesis (in Swedish): Tolvhed, 'Nationen på spel' (Full title translated into English: 'Sporting the Nation: Gender, "Swedishness" and the Body in the Representation of Olympic Games in Swedish Popular Press. 1948–1972).
3. Young and Wamsley, *Global Olympics*.
4. Yuval-Davis, *Gender & Nation*; Anderson, *Imagined communities*.
5. Hall, 'The Question of Cultural Identity', 297.
6. Hirdman, *Med kluven tunga*.
7. Hall, 'The Question of Cultural Identity', 292.
8. Hall, 'Introduction', 3–5.
9. Scott, *Gender and the Politics of History*, 4.
10. Billig, *Banal Nationalism*.
11. Said, *Orientalism*; Hall, 'The West and the Rest'.
12. Yuval-Davies, *Gender & Nation*. On intersectionality, see Crenshaw, 'Mapping the Margins'; Hill-Collins, 'Its All in the Family'; Nash, 'Re-thinking Intersectionality'.
13. Foucault, *Power/Knowledge*; Hall, 'The Work of Representation'.
14. Fairclough, *Media Discourse*, 5, 17.
15. Gilman, *Difference and Pathology*; Grosz, *Volatile Bodies*, 14.
16. Hall, 'The Spectacle of the Other'; McClintock, *Imperial Leather*; Miller, 'The Anatomy of Scientific Racism'.
17. Dyer, *White*; Tasker, *Spectacular Bodies*.
18. Bederman, *Manliness and Civilization*.
19. Boyle and Haynes, *Power Play*; Whannel, *Media Sport Stars*.
20. Tolvhed, *Nationen på spel*, 95–130.
21. Ibid., 110–22. See also Meinander and Mangan, *The Nordic World*.
22. Whannel, *Media Sport Stars*, ch. 9.
23. Tolvhed, *Nationen på spel*, 131–47.
24. Ibid., 244–51.
25. Patrick B. Miller has pointed out that the overwhelming athletic success of black male athletes made it impossible to imagine their bodies as weak, for how would one then explain how they could beat white men time and time again? Instead, black men's racial inferiority has from the beginning of the twentieth century been imagined to be in a closer relation to nature, which defined black people in opposition to Western culture and civilisation: Miller, 'The Anatomy of Scientific Racism'.
26. Cahn, *Coming on Strong*; Hargreaves, *Sporting Females*.
27. Creedon, *Women, Media and Sport*; Birrell and Cole, *Women, Sport, and Culture*; Birrell and McDonald, *Reading Sport*; Rowe, *Critical Readings*. Natalie Koivula examined a sample of sports news broadcasts on the Swedish public service broadcaster and on one national commercial station during one year (1 Sept. 1995 – 31 Aug. 1996; a total of 1470 minutes). The results showed that less than 10% of sports news air-time was devoted to female athletes. Koivula, *Gender in Sport*.
28. Cahn, *Coming on Strong*, 18–30.
29. Olofsson, *Har kvinnorna en sportslig chans?*
30. Lundqvist Wanneberg, *Kroppens medborgarfostran*.
31. Connell, *Gender and Power*, 81.
32. McClintock, *Imperial Leather*; Cahn, *Coming on Strong*.
33. Skeggs, *Formations of Class and Gender*; Frankenberg, *White Women, Race Matters*.
34. Tervo, 'Nationalism, Sports and Gender', 367.
35. Ibid., 357–373.
36. 'Två olympiaflickor', *Vecko-Revyn* no 49, s. 13 (1956).

37. Rod Brookes mentions the disproportionate use of first names for women as an example of the 'infantilisation' of female athletes. Brookes, *Representing Sport*, 130.
38. Roland Barthes, 'Rhetoric of the Image', in *Image, Music, Text*.
39. Cahn, *Coming on Strong*, 132–3.
40. On Sweden's neutrality doctrine, see af Malmborg, *Neutrality and State-building in Sweden*.
41. *Idun* 30 (1952) (my translation).
42. Trangbæck, 'Gender in Modern Society'.
43. This corresponds with gender historian Yvonne Hirdman's general findings for this historical period: Hirdman, *Med kluven tunga*, 212–13.
44. Tolvhed, *Nationen på spel*, ch. 4.
45. Mills, *Discourse*, 79–81.
46. For an overview, see Bruce et al., *Sportswomen at the Olympics*.
47. Larsson, *En annan historia*. See also McClintock, *Imperial Leather*, 114.
48. Butler, 'Athletic Genders', 108.

References

af Malmborg, Mikael. *Neutrality and State-building in Sweden*. Basingstoke: Palgrave, 2001.

Anderson, Benedict. *Imagined communities: Reflections on the origin and spread of nationalism*. London: Verso, 1983.

Barthes, Roland. *Image, Music, Text*. New York: Hill and Wang, 1977.

Bederman, Gail. *Manliness and Civilization*. Chicago: University of Chicago Press, 1995.

Billig, Michael. *Banal Nationalism*. London: Sage, 1995.

Birrell, Susan and Cheryl L. Cole, eds. *Women, Sport, and Culture*. Champaign, IL: Human Kinetics, 1994.

Birrell, Susan and Mary G. McDonald, eds. *Reading Sport. Critical Essays on Power and Representation*. Boston, MA: Northeastern University Press, 2000.

Boyle, Raymond and Richard Haynes. *Power Play: Sport, the Media and Popular Culture*, Harlow: Longman, 2000.

Brookes, Rod. *Representing Sport*. London: Arnold, 2002.

Bruce, Toni, Jorid Hovden and Pirkko Markula, eds. *Sportswomen at the Olympics: A Global Content Analysis of Newspaper Coverage*. Rotterdam: Sense, 2010.

Butler, Judith. 'Athletic Genders: Hyperbolic Instance and/or the Overcoming of Sexual Binarism'. *Stanford Humanities Review* 6, no.2 (1998).

Cahn, Susan K. *Coming on Strong: Gender and Sexuality in Twentieth-Century Women's Sport*. Cambridge, MA: Harvard University Press, 1995.

Connell, R.W. *Gender and Power. Society, the Person and Sexual Politics*. Cambridge: Polity in association with Blackwell, 1987.

Creedon, Pamela J., ed. *Women, Media and Sport. Challenging Gender Values*. Thousand Oaks, CA: Sage Publications, 1994.

Crenshaw, Kimberlé. 'Mapping the Margins: Intersectionality, Identity Politics, and Violence Against Women of Color', in *The Public Nature of Private Violence. The Discovery of Domestic Abuse*, eds Martha Albertson Fineman and Rixanne Mykitiuk. New York: Routledge, 1994.

Dyer, Richard. *White: Essays on Race and Culture*. London: Routledge, 1997.

Foucault, Michel. *Power/Knowledge: Selected Interviews and Other Writings 1972–1977*. New York: Pantheon, 1980.

Fairclough, Norman. *Media Discourse*. London: Edward Arnold, 1995.

Frankenberg, Ruth. *White Women, Race Matters: The Social Construction of Whiteness*. London: Routledge, 1993.

Gilman, Sander L. *Difference and Pathology: Stereotypes of Sexuality, Race, and Madness*. Ithaca, NY: Cornell University Press 1985.

Gori, Gigliola, ed. *Sport and Gender Matters in Western Countries: Old Borders and New Challenges*. Sankt Augustin: Academia Verlag, 2008.

Grosz, Elizabeth. *Volatile Bodies: Toward a Corporeal Feminism*. Bloomington, IN: Indiana University Press, 1994.

Hargreaves, Jennifer. *Sporting Females. Critical Issues in the History and Sociology of Women's Sport*. London: Routledge, 1994.

Hall, Stuart. 'The West and the Rest. Discourse and Power', in *Formations of Modernity*, eds. Stuart Hall and Bram Gieben. Cambridge: Polity Press in association with the Open University, 1992.

Hall, Stuart. 'The Question of Cultural Identity', in *Modernity and its Futures*, eds Stuart Hall, David Held and Tony McGrew. Oxford: Polity in association with the Open University, 1992.

Hall, Stuart. 'Introduction', in *Representation. Cultural Representations and Signifying Practices*, ed. Stuart Hall. London: Sage, 1997.

Hall, Stuart. 'The Work of Representation', in *Representation. Cultural Representations and Signifying Practices*, ed. Stuart Hall. London: Sage, 1997.

Hall, Stuart. 'The Spectacle of the Other', in *Representation. Cultural Representations and Signifying Practices*, ed. Stuart Hall. London: Sage, 1997.

Hill-Collins, Patricia. 'Its All in the Family. Intersections of Gender, Race and Nation', in *Decentering the Center. Philosohy for a Multicultural, Postcolonial and Feminist World*, eds Uma Narayan and Sandra Harding. Bloomington, IN: Indiana University Press, 2000.

Hirdman, Yvonne. *Med kluven tunga. LO och genusordningen*. Stockholm: Atlas, 1998.

Hobsbawm, Eric. *Nations and Nationalism since 1780. Programme, Myth, Reality*. Cambridge: Cambridge University Press, 1990.

Hofmann, Annette R. and Else Trangbæk, eds. *International Perspectives on Sporting Women in Past and Present: A Festschrift for Gertrud Pfister*. Copenhagen: University of Copenhagen, Institute of Exercise and Sport Sciences, 2005.

Koivula, Natalie. *Gender in Sport*. Stockholm: Stockholms Universitet, 1999.

Larsson, Lisbeth. *En annan historia. Om kvinnors läsning och svensk veckopress*. Stockholm: Symposion, 1989.

Lundqvist Wanneberg, Pia. *Kroppens medborgarfostran. Kropp, klass och genus i skolans fysiska fostran 1919–1962*. Åkersberga: Stockholms universitet, 2004.

Mangan, James A., ed. *Tribal Identities: Nationalism, Europe, Sport*. London: Frank Cass, 1995.

McClintock, Anne. *Imperial Leather. Race, Gender and Sexuality in the Colonial Contest*. London: Routledge, 1995.

Meinander, Henrik and James A. Mangan, eds. *The Nordic World. Sport in Society*. London: Frank Cass 1998.

Mills, Sara. *Discourse*. London: Routledge, 2004.

Miller, Patrick B. 'The Anatomy of Scientific Racism. Racialist Responses to Black Athletic Achievement', in *Sport and the Color Line. Black Athletes and Race Relations in Twentieth-Century America*, eds Patrick B. Miller and David K. Wiggins. New York: Routledge, 2004.

Nash, Jennifer C. 'Re-thinking Intersectionality'. *Feminist Review* 89, no 1 (2008)89, no 1 (2008): 1–15.

Olofsson, Eva. *Har kvinnorna en sportslig chans? Den svenska idrottsrörelsen och kvinnorna under 1900–talet*. Umeå: Universitetspress, 1989.

Rowe, David, ed. *Critical Readings: Sport, Culture and the Media*. Maidenhead: Open University Press, 2004.

Said, Edward W. *Orientalism*. New York: Pantheon Books, 1978.

Scott, Joan W. *Gender and the Politics of History*. New York: Columbia University Press, 1988.

Skeggs, Beverly. *Formations of Class and Gender: Becoming Respectable*. London: Sage, 1997.

Tasker, Yvonne. *Spectacular Bodies. Gender, Genre and the Action Cinema*. London: Routledge, 1993.

Tervo, Mervi. 'Nationalism, Sports and Gender in Finnish Sports Journalism in the Early Twentieth Century'. *Gender, Place and Culture* 8, no. 4 (2001)8, no. 4 (2001): 357–73.

Tolvhed, Helena. *Nationen på spel. Kropp, kön och svenskhet i populärpressens representationer av olympiska spel 1948–1972*. Umeå: Bokförlaget h:ström Text & Kultur, 2008.

Trangbæck, Else. 'Gender in Modern Society: Femininity, Gymnastics and Sport', in *The Nordic World. Sports in Society*, eds Henrik Meinander and J.A. Mangan. London: Frank Cass, 1998.

Whannel, Garry. *Media Sport Stars. Masculinities and Moralities*. London: Routledge, 2002.

Young, Kevin and Kevin B. Wamsley, eds. *Global Olympics: Historical and Sociological Studies of the Modern Games*. Amsterdam: Elsevier, 2005.

Yuval-Davis, Nira. *Gender & Nation*. London: Sage, 1997.

Breaking Down the Sex Barrier: The Emancipation of Female Modern Pentathlon in West Germany (1967–1981)

Sandra Heck

Ruhr-University Bochum, Germany

Fencing, shooting, horse-riding, swimming and running – five good reasons for men to argue that women are wrong when asking to be modern pentathletes but also five good reasons for women to counter that they are definitely right. Even though as early as 1912 a British woman had asked to compete in the sport, another 69 years passed until the first female World Championships were held in London in 1981. This paper deals with women's struggle towards an equal participation in modern pentathlon. Whereas the development of men's modern pentathlon remained for the first 37 years exclusively within the Olympic domain, the female movement primary gained ground through regional and national activities. Germany was among the most active countries. After the president of the German Modern Pentathlon Federation had paved the way for women's participation by fighting for its administrative recognition at the end of the 1960s, the strength of female modern pentathlon slowly increased at home as well as abroad. However, men still stood against an equal sports practice of both sexes for more than a decade. The creation of female modern pentathlon World Championships in 1981 was finally not only a result of women's enthusiasm, tenacity and patience but also of men's concession to a female competency which could not be denied any longer.

Despite a strong male resistance, courageous women increased their participation in sports in Western Europe and North America during the course of the twentieth century. This came along with other general social achievements on the road towards emancipation. From the 1960s onwards a second wave of feminism manifested itself in various movements fighting against discrimination:[1] In the United States, Title IX[2] and on the European continent, in France, the *Mouvement de Libération des Femmes* (MLF – movement of women's liberation).[3] Those developments assisted in the overcoming of paternal control and the assertion that women were more than domestic slaves. As Germany had been divided into two parts since 1949, two geographically separate movements towards women's liberation existed. Passed as law by four female and 61 male delegates in 1949, article three of the Basic Constitutional Law of the Federal Republic of Germany (FRG) formally gave equal rights to both sexes. From 1945 onwards several women's federations were created in West Germany and led to the formation of the so-called *Autonome Frauenbewegung* (autonomous women's movement). Like the FRG, the constitution of the German Democratic Republic (GDR) established a law of equality as early as 1945 and also highlighted support for women both in professions and in society as state issues.[4]

Despite these positive developments towards female emancipation, women's social participation remained restricted in many spheres. In sport, several federations refused to establish competitions for women by using pretexts originating in the nineteenth century; labelling female sports activity as an excessive demand and thus harmful; or as immoral and unfeminine, and thus reducing the chances of marriage.[5] Modern pentathlon, a combined sport composed of fencing, shooting, horse riding, swimming and running, was among those pure male fortresses. Born as an Olympic sport in 1912, modern pentathlon was primary practised in military circles.[6] Moreover, Baron de Coubertin, as IOC president responsible for the implementation of modern pentathlon, was generally against women's inclusion into the Olympics. Thus it is not surprising that in the year of modern pentathlon's Olympic debut in Stockholm in 1912 no rule for the case of a female participation request existed. Despite the lack of a particular rule, Helen Preece's request was confronted with a unanimous hostile refusal.[7] After this bad experience, no woman tried to enter the modern pentathlon again for decades. Female modern pentathletes were finally not allowed to compete in the Olympics until the year 2000 in Sydney. However, the base for women's Olympic participation was laid down some 20 to 30 years earlier.

This paper deals with women's struggle towards equal participation in modern pentathlon between 1967 and 1981. In 1967, one year after Wilhelm Henze had taken the presidency of the German Modern Pentathlon Federation (Deutscher Verband für Modernen Fünfkampf) (DVMF), he put the topic of female participation on the agenda for the very first time. The idea was not warmly welcomed. Nevertheless, Henze did not hesitate to raise the issue at national and international meetings. These organisational struggles were accompanied by women's sports events, concentrating on single European focus venues. One such place was Bensheim, FRG, from where the movement encouraged girls and women across the country to take up modern pentathlon. In contrast, East Germany suspended its modern pentathlon teams after 1968 due to a low expectation of medals and hence did not take part in the emancipation movement.[8] So, in the 1970s, West Germany was among the most active countries fighting for women's emancipation in modern pentathlon. Despite these efforts, the supporters of a ladies' competition still had to struggle against remaining resistances and discriminations so that it was not until 1981 that the first female World Championships took place. Surprisingly enough, even though modern pentathlon is the masculine sport par excellence, the topic has not yet been included either in gender studies or in sports history research.[9] In attempting to fill the gap, this paper also aims to point out that the gender relations created through modern pentathlon are worthy of a historical text.[10]

Wilhelm Henze: the Father of Women's Modern Pentathlon

Peter-Wilhelm Henze (1910–2004) was the first person to officially pursue the issue of a ladies' modern pentathlon in Germany.[11] He spent much enthusiasm on the implementation of a women's modern pentathlon and is hence, with good cause, called the 'father of women's modern pentathlon'.[12]

Having mastered swimming, cross-country running and handball as a child, Henze developed diversified skills early. During his studies he even widened his range of sports and was especially attracted by fencing. Even though he had never been a modern pentathlete, he had dabbled in modern pentathlon's sports individually and appreciated the idea of all-round athleticism. In the summer of 1939 Henze was drafted to serve in a 'short-term exercise' as an infantryman, which led to more than seven years of service. The fact that as a well-trained athlete he survived the war proved of the value of a diversified sporting preparation, especially for a soldier.[13] However, due to injuries sustained in his military service Henze had to give up his own sporting career after 1950 but this would not be the end of his involvement with sport.

When in 1955 the question of allowing a women's event in modern pentathlon arose during the eighth congress of the *Union International de Pentathlon Moderne* (UIPM) in Macolin, Switzerland,[14] it seemed like a change of opinion was close. But these theoretical discussions did not lead to actions and for the next 12 years nothing further happened. Hope for the beginning of a new era was raised in 1961 when the Allied boundaries eased and allowed the creation of the DVMF (*Deutscher Verband für Modernen Fünfkampf*) in Warendorf on 27 May. Even though the German states were allocated responsibilities, the police and the Federal Armed Forces kept control. As neither domain had career opportunities for women,[15] it was likely that they would be treated in the same misogynistic manner as the modern pentathlon board. The first president of the DVMF, Major-General (retired) Heinrich-Georg 'Heinz' Hax,[16] underlined this attitude. Hax's leadership focused on boosting male modern pentathlon competitions and in helping German competitors catch up to the standards of international elite sport. These goals did not change between 1964 and 1966 during Gerhard Stabenow's two-year presidency, so that the possibility of a female modern pentathlon event was not pursued at all in the first five years of the DVMF.[17] Henze, in contrast, had no practical experience in modern pentathlon. Nevertheless, when, after the Second World War, the future of modern pentathlon in Germany seemed to be threatened, he became involved in the reconstruction of the sport by organising seminars and competitions in Göttingen, Warendorf and Berlin.[18] As well as being a member of the NOC (national Olympic committee) board for modern pentathlon and chairman of the inaugural meeting of the DVMF, Henze was also vice president and leader of the German modern pentathlon delegation at international competitions. His position as professor at the Georg-August-University of Göttingen provided him with social influence and his research for his doctoral thesis on the history of fencing, showed a deep interest in sport history, and particularly in military disciplines.[19] The question remains: what made Henze, a sports official and professor, turn out to be one of the greatest supporters of women's modern pentathlon?

Firstly, he was generally opposed to injustice and considered the exclusion of women from sport generally and modern pentathlon in particular to be unjust.[20] As he mentioned in an interview in 1999, Henze was sure that women were 'one of the most beautiful of God's inventions'[21] and thus felt obliged to respect ladies' concerns. His chosen topic in the German *Abitur*, 'Goethe and the women',[22] already indicated his particular interest and people still testify today that his intense relations with the opposite sex were not only theoretical.[23] Even though he was expecting great resistance when supporting women in sport, he didn't care about being his own popularity and thus said what many women were too afraid to say and most men did not want to hear. Looking back on his life, he described his character as follows: 'I never avoided difficulties. When I have noticed something as right I have fought for it with all means that were available and [made sure] that injustice ends.'[24]

When Henze was elected as DVMF president in 1966, he had not only the will but also the means to take up the battle for women's recognition as modern pentathletes. Triggered by several requests, Henze put the question of a ladies modern pentathlon up for discussion at a press conference on the occasion of the German Modern Pentathlon Championships in 1967.[25] The timing was excellent, as in the late 1960s 'there was a sense of a new era about to dawn in German society and in the sport system'.[26] These changes manifested themselves for instance in the declaration of women's sport as one of the seven German Sports Federation (DSB) departments.[27] Also the male German modern pentathletes – supported by the German Football Federation (DFB) – seemed to forge ahead, achieving fourth place in the team rankings at the World Championships in Jönköping, Sweden and being honoured with the cup for the best development work within the *Union International de Pentathlon Moderne et Biathlon* (UIPMB).[28] Despite these positive developments, the German delegates did not take Henze's proposal seriously.

Even though the national federation showed little interest in his idea, Henze tried 'without fear of big animals'[29] to broaden his activities at international level by suggesting the opening up of modern pentathlon to women at the UIPMB congress in Mexico in 1968.[30] As the German president expected counter-arguments, he underlined his proposal by naming five reasons why women should be included in modern pentathlon.[31] In addition to arguments from the general female equality movement, such as the claim for equal rights and self-determination, Henze gave special emphasis by urging the UIPMB to 'convince the IOC to maintain our sport on the Olympic programme',[32] at the end of his speech. Furthermore, his arguments were intended to confront delegates with the reality of contemporary sports which indeed mirrored progress for women in several sports, among which were the five disciplines of which modern pentathlon was composed.

During the course of the twentieth century, the sex barriers within the five single sports slowly began to crumble. Female swimming was included for the first time in the Stockholm Olympics in 1912, fencing in Paris in 1924 and shooting (in a mixed team) in Mexico in 1968. The horse-riding regulations were changed in 1952, allowing civilians and women to compete without separation between the sexes in the same competition.[33] Cross-country running was an Olympic sport for men only from 1912 to 1924 and never included women.[34] Besides the practice of single sports, women also discovered other multidisciplinary events. Originating in Germany in 1928, a pentathlon based on the athletic disciplines of shot-put, long jump, 100-metre sprint, high jump and javelin became popular among female athletes. While this athletic-based pentathlon became an Olympic sport for women in 1964, modern pentathlon remained a male preserve. Nevertheless, the UIPMB president Sven Thofelt made a joke out of Henze's proposal by commenting 'Now the problem: modern pentathlon for ladies' – which led to great laughter in the audience.[35] The major objections centred on the fact that the delegates considered modern pentathlon still to be 'men's business'.[36] Thus, Henze did not immediately achieve the implementation of female competitions, but was ready to continue fighting for recognition in the years to come.

However, as a result of his request in Mexico, a special commission, responsible for creating regulations for women's modern pentathlon, and composed of representatives of Germany, Finland, France and Switzerland, was elected.[37] Its all-male composition was not queried, especially after Jean de Beaumont's proposal at the IOC to co-opt women as members had recently been abruptly rejected.[38] Even though the newly-created working group was spearheaded by Henze himself, who surely aimed at quick decisions, it took three years until a first draft of the regulations was presented at the UIPMB congress in San Antonio in 1971.[39]

The commission had put special emphasis on the integration of girls and women into the existing modern pentathlon system rather than building a new separate women's federation. This goal was pursued in the ensuing years and led for instance to the introduction of epée fencing for female modern pentathletes in 1977, although female fencing specialists exclusively used the floret during that time.[40] Since men and women could theoretically use the same equipment and coaches, this decision made the implementation of a women's event easier but increased the difficulties of élite female fencers: whether to switch their sports practice to modern pentathlon only or train for fencing *and* for modern pentathlon.

In the 1970s Henze did not give up promoting the idea of a women's modern pentathlon. From 1968 onwards he was a member of the organising committee for the 1972 Olympic Games in Munich and responsible for the modern pentathlon competition. Internationally, between 1969 and 1971, Henze took the chance at every UIPMB congress to promote women's modern pentathlon and report about ongoing activities. Due to women's increasing level of education and integration into the labour market, female emancipation grew in sport generally. Ladies football, for instance, was officially recognised from 1970.[41] Despite these improvements, Henze's ideas still met with resistance. The Eastern bloc countries especially showed little interest as they could not win medals in a non-Olympic and unrecognised sporting domain.

In 1972, a 62-year-old Henze could have been satisfied with having initiated the female modern pentathlon movement. However, he was not. Even after he had relinquished his presidency to Walter Grein in the very same year, he continued his work as UIPMB council member and thereby reaffirming his great tenacity and passion for the recognition of women's pentathlon. He remained a UIPMB council member, which had a greater influence with regard to the question of the admission of women than the national boards.

When a meeting of the international federations took place in his home country during the Olympic Games of Munich in 1972, the professor used the chance to make a plea for the inclusion of women into the UIPMB. Despite the scepticism of many countries, his proposal to include women's modern pentathlon and the combined competition regulations into the federation were unanimously accepted and member countries were asked to collect experiences according to the newly fixed rules.[42]

During the years that followed Henze began another attempt to support the female development by sending out questionnaires to 25 UIPMB member federations in order to collect and evaluate experiences of women's modern pentathlon.[43] Of the 13 responses, ten federations stated that there was currently little or no women's modern pentathlon activity.[44] Among those ten, eight nations could not register any women practising modern pentathlon at all[45] and only Switzerland and Sweden reported an active female participation which meanwhile, due to (unspecified) problems, had stopped. Finland had at least two passive female federation members. Three nations, namely Australia, the Soviet Union and the

USA, declared their intention to start developments in women's modern pentathlon that year. Thus, by 1975 an active female modern pentathlon movement had developed only in Germany, Great Britain and France.[46] Very good progress was made with co-educational modern pentathlon training in Germany which proved that girls and women were physically and psychologically as well suited to modern pentathlon as boys and men.

In addition to this survey on the quality and expansion of women's modern pentathlon, the participating countries gave recommendations for future improvements. Their was a stated intention to aim at a higher influence for women within the UIPMB, and to request support for the development of regular training as well as on the establishment of frequent international competitions.[47] The latter was highlighted by Henze at the end of his speech when he imagined ladies participating in World Championships and Olympic modern pentathlon competitions in the future. Those ideas testified that he aimed at more than including women in non-competitive training. At the end of his report, written in July 1976, Henze expressed his future aims: World Championships and Olympic Games for women.[48]

Even though Henze could not be present, his survey results were probably also discussed at the UIPMB congress held in Montreal, Canada in July, where consequently a women's competition was considered for the time of the 1977 men's World Championships.[49] Two months later, at the UIPMB General Assembly in Rome on 29 September 1976, Henze was willing to present his results in person. Despite the lack of any travel support through the DVMF, he financed his journey privately. As representatives of the German federation, Grein and Krickow, were also participating in Rome. They probably left the room as a sign of protest during Henze's presentation.[50] Due to the increasing internal discordances, Germany's seat in the administrative council was lost.[51] Nevertheless Henze's enthusiasm, sustainability arguments and persistent support convinced the delegates present in Rome with the result that his report was seen by the UIPMB as a positive step in the right direction.[52] Meanwhile, during the 1970s, the European Community had taken important general decisions with regard to gender equality. Adequate legislation texts were integrated in several European countries. These texts were not necessarily aligned to sport in particular, but nevertheless contributed positively to the female emancipation movement generally.[53]

Despite this international recognition, the national federation of Germany, headed by Walter Grein, remained sceptical and pointed to existing difficulties with regard to the men's event.[54] While Henze was promoting ladies' modern pentathlon, Leo Becker, the first deputy of Warendorf, stated that 'we have enough to do with the men: we cannot also deal with the chicks'.[55] Henze's successor in the DVMF shared the same opinion and expressed quite clearly in 1974 that at the current moment the DVMF was not able to care for the pentathlon for girls and women.[56] The president supported his statement by pointing at the lack of money and manpower. Keeping male modern pentathlon on the Olympic programme had priority. Thus, between Grein and those members in favour of an exclusion of women and Henze and those supporting women's inclusion there existed an ongoing quarrel.

On the one hand, Grein tried to show diplomacy through praising the regional and local developments, while on the other it seemed that he actively tried to hinder the development of women's modern pentathlon. Henze further argued that the DVMF wanted to keep him away from the UIPMB congresses by discontinuing his financial travel support.[57] Henze also claimed that during several UIPMB congresses his ideas were portrayed as private opinion, rather than those of the DVMF. Henze was reputedly even asked to give up his seat in the UIPMB and hand it over to Grein in case he would like support for his national claims.[58] Knowing that in any case his UIPMB position was not in his personal gift and that his resignation would have necessitated an election, Henze did not engage with that proposal.

With regards to these machinations Henze saw Grein as a victim of extortion rather than as a hostile decision-maker. Grein and the DVMF depended on the municipal financial support of Warendorf, so in Henze's opinion it was Leo Becker who was the puppet-master and who worked against him whenever he could. For example, on the occasion of an international congress in Warendorf, Becker refused Henze's participation by arguing that the room would be too small for him to fit in. Finally, the Swedish delegates Sven Thofelt and Wille Grut nevertheless took Henze into the room and introduced him, to much applause as, 'father of the ladies' pentathlon'.[59]

Despite disagreements, in the aftermath of the 1972 UIPMB congress a special German commission, composed of Wilhelm Henze, Wolfgang Goedicke[60] and Fritz Kirsch, was elected to deal with the particular development in Germany.[61] As the gap between Henze and the DVMF was only growing as a result of such activities, Henze initiated a new national strategy which was mirrored in a letter to the DVMF's National Associations on 18 October 1976.[62] The DVMF, however, remained stubborn with regard to the 'women question'. Meanwhile, with a background of the UIPMB's general recognition, the practice of female modern pentathlon had increased and this clearly hinted at the fact that the DVMF could not maintain its hostile position forever.

Henze's struggles were important in paving the way for women's recognition in modern pentathlon. Convincing male delegates was only possible for a man, as women had no voice; moreover it had to be someone of a strong fighting character such as Henze. However, his activities were mainly at an organisational level and could not substitute the practical enhancement of women's modern pentathlon performance.

Pioneers of Women's Modern Pentathlon

In the 1960s, while both the UIPMB and the DVMF had not yet given yet their blessings to ladies' competitions, a handful of women trained for fun together with men.[63] However, the first official competition for women took place in Berlin in 1971. On the occasion of a triathlon (shooting, swimming, and running) for mini-pentathletes, included among the 19 participants was 12-year-old Martina Goedicke, a daughter of the former modern pentathlete Wolfgang Goedicke.[64] After Martina achieved a sixth place, the DVMF newsletter reported in an appreciative but at the same time sexist way that she indeed 'could show to some of her male contemporaries her beautiful girl heels'.[65]

A year later, when the UIPMB included a ladies' modern pentathlon in their programme, four Regional Associations, namely Bavaria, Berlin, North Rhine-Westphalia and Rhineland-Palatinate, were already dealing with girls' and women's modern pentathlon.[66] Uncharted terrain was explored when the Berlin Association organised a special girls' competition within the pupils' championships in June 1973.[67] In the following years further youth competitions, duathlons, triathlons and quadrathlons, open for boys and girls, took place in Germany.[68] The German Championships in Youth Quadrathlon (fencing, shooting, running, and swimming) has existed since 1974[69] but even though a ladies' pentathlon was officially integrated into the UIPMB program in 1972, no national championships were organised, either in Germany or elsewhere. Nevertheless, in the meantime, women began to prove that their performances could be at least equal if not even better than those of men.[70]

A further step towards women's pentathlon was reached in January 1974 when for the first time female modern pentathletes from the associations of Berlin, Baden-Württemberg, North Rhine-Westphalia and Rhineland-Palatinate came together in Wittlich-Wengerohr for a *Landesleistungslehrgang* (national performance seminar).[71] Rositha Kirsch, who took the silver medal in the triathlon (shooting, swimming, running) in Wittlich, later became one of Germany's pioneer modern pentathletes. As there were not many women competing frequently at that time, Kirsch additionally took the chance to take part in girls' competitions.[72] At that time however, girls' and women's entrance into modern pentathlon was limited to a restricted discipline scope.

In 1975 a complete pentathlon was organised for the first time within the International German Junior Championships in Leverkusen-Opladen, even attracting participants from Great Britain.[73] At that time modern pentathlon for girls and women was already established in eight of the nine existing German regional associations.[74] Despite these positive developments, prejudices against women remained. The youth officer of the Bavarian Modern Pentathlon Association wrote in a letter to Henze in 1975 that he was generally in favour of girls in modern pentathlon but that he expected difficulties with regard to women over 18 for whom the sport might be too time-demanding and exhausting.[75] In contrast, Rositha Kirsch was probably the best example of a woman balancing both professional and sporting careers. Besides her work as an elementary school teacher, she undertook regular modern pentathlon training for 'about three hours a day' during the week and 'all weekend long'.[76] Following her model, the number of active women modern pentathletes slowly increased and also widened their experiences by taking part in international competitions.[77]

A year after a test event (designed to find the best women) was organised in Warendorf, Hiltrud Anna Maria Reder (née Mohr) became involved. The DVMF asked her for support in connection with the further development of women's modern pentathlon and she agreed.[78] At that time the DVMF was not willing to give more rights to women but rather wished to limit such initiatives. However, the women and girls profited by this choice and had found in Hiltrud Reder a competent and understanding tutor. From that point on, the training of female athletes moved from single local activities to a systematic nationwide programme. While Henze was fighting for the recognition of ladies' modern pentathlon at an organisational level, Reder was working with the same enthusiasm for the establishment of frequent training and competitions for women at the grass-roots level. Her focus was not the outcome of real choice but rather resulted from the fact that in the 1970s women could hardly be found in sports federation bodies, which, as in the case of modern pentathlon, were ruled exclusively by men. However, it was clear that Reder's only chance to support the emancipation development lay in 'bottom-up' work, partly following and partly accompanying Henze's achievements.

Fighting for female emancipation seems to be more obviously part of a woman's biography than that of a man. However, knowing key points of Reder's life provides the background to her never-ending enthusiasm for a sport that she had never practised herself but to which she nevertheless dedicated all her leisure time without receiving any financial compensation. Born in Bensheim on 10 October 1939, Hiltrud Reder followed the example of her father and brother in practising sport. Even though her mother and the convent school she attended taught her according to traditional gender roles, she began early to fight against personally perceived inequality. For instance, as class representative, she advocated the concerns of her peers for nine years, even, if necessary, against the authorities. When she became an adult, she quickly escaped the traditional patriarchal structures and implemented equality in her own partnership.[79] Despite battling against the bonds of her education, she had perfect conditions from which to start a sports career. Her grandfather owned several horses, and she had taken part in horse-riding and athletics competitions for nine years and emerged as a nationally and internationally recognized fencer.[80] Like Henze, she had taken part in most of modern pentathlon's single sports but never in their combined form.

Even though during her active sports career modern pentathlon was out of question for women, she had always been fascinated by this all-round test.[81] Some assume that this adoration of the complete athlete might have also led to her marriage with Karsten Reder, a successful modern pentathlete of that time.[82] Besides frequently watching modern pentathlon in practice while her husband was an active competitor, she also took part in training sessions in fencing with modern pentathletes. It was not until 1977 that she gave up her sports career and competed for the last time in the German fencing championships, finishing in third place.[83]

Reder was aware of the difficulties involved in fighting against male dominance and retrospectively concluded: 'If you are a woman you anyway need to do everything perfect'.[84] Being a perfectionist,[85] this suited her well. Several other aspects of her life made Hiltrud Reder an excellent 'champion' of women's modern pentathlon. As a high-school teacher in sport, geography and social policy she had the background to build up systematic modern pentathlon training for women. As a sportswoman she had experienced the requirements of high-level athletes. With her support, the city developed to be one of the main German centres of women's modern pentathlon in the 1970s. The local sports club and the opportunity to use the facilities of the Bundeswehr provided good conditions for a smooth start.

Even though the UIPMB had planned the World Championships for 1977,[86] they did not take place, rather the first German Ladies' Modern Pentathlon Champion-ships were held in Leverkusen-Opladen.[87] Internationally experienced Imke Schmitz came out as winner and was thus the first female German champion. In the same year the Modern Pentathlon Association of Great Britain also transformed their Ladies' Tetrathlon Championships into the first British Ladies' Modern Pentathlon Championships and in doing so provided another chance for the German team to collect international experience. The exchange between Great Britain and Germany was quite active in those days, so that the British organisers predicted a positive future to women's modern pentathlon: 'It is no exaggeration to say that the standards the Ladies now achieve in the sport world have seemed incredible to those first intrepid pioneers of ladies' pentathlon over a decade ago. A friendly but highly competitive event is certain – the first of many.'[88] Later in October, in addition to British competitors, Imke Schmitz and Rositha Kirsch from Germany took part in a special competition for women on the occasion of the men's World Championships in San Antonio, USA.[89]

There seemed no end to the surge of new competitions. In 1978 the first 'World Cup Series' was decided upon at the UIPMB congress in Jönköping, Sweden. The travel schedule for the teams to reach Zielona Góra/Grünberg (Poland), Jönköping (Sweden) and London (Great Britain) were full of difficulties, as they had neither a professional service team nor a bus sufficient in size.[90] Reder continued working in an honorary capacity as coach and official representative of Germany. At a time when neither the federation nor the government supported the emancipation movement, Hiltrud and Karsten Reder offered the athletes accommodation and meals free of charge.[91]

Furthermore there was no position on the DVMF with a responsibility to coordinate training and travel. Thus, Hiltrud Reder organised training camps in her home town, looked for sponsors who could subsidise the cost of trips and material and contacted young athletes in their schools.[92] However, this passion to support ladies' issues was not appreciated by everybody and discrimination against women competing in modern pentathlon remained. For instance, during the 1979 World Cup in Warendorf, Hiltrud Reder remembers how DVMF members commented on the physical appearance of her athletes: 'Look, what a broodmare with such an expended pelvis!'[93] Surprisingly enough, sometimes women themselves also supported men's prejudices against female sport.[94]

Despite personal accusations and insults, Reder continued her work with the athletes and became a member of the Committee for Women and Girls in Modern Pentathlon in 1978.[95] Her attitude was that she 'preferred being inconvenient instead of inconspicuous'.[96] Nevertheless the absence of two competitions from its calendar, the World Championships and the Olympic Games, still distinguished women's from men's modern pentathlon. Whereas the IOC remained hostile with regard to including women's competitions, the establishment of World Championships seemed to be a rather realistic middle-term goal. Thus, at a UIPMB session in Ruhpolding, FRG, on 27 January 1979, the creation of Ladies' World Championships was taken to be considered once a minimum of ten federations would be able to participate in them. However, this was a hard precondition, which could not be satisfied easily.

In the meantime, men were becoming aware of women's progress with regard to sports participation. For instance, in equestrian sports in 1976 seven of the nine medals in the military team event were gained by women.[97] Accordingly, in modern pentathlon men's objections and fears increased and were reflected in the German press. Die Welt, for instance, illustrated the remaining hostile mentality of male sports colleagues against female emancipation in two articles, both published in 1977. The director of the Bundesausschuss Leistungssport (Federal Board of Competitive Sport), Helmut Meyer, stated in an interview with Sport-Illustrierte: 'They [the women] destroy the balance sheet.'[98] On the suggestion that the pentathlon federation should deal with women in the same manner as with men, he commented that 'these are, however, the problems that we have'.[99] Also Hiltrud Reder remembers meeting him during the German Championships in Sindelfingen, when he responded to her claims: 'You cannot equally compare women to men.'[100]

Another example was Axel Stratmann, a contemporary athlete, who addressed a statement to Rositha Kirsch at the Men's World Championships in San Antonio: 'Now you also want to conquer the only male bastion and this just because you crazy women need to emancipate yourselves. But with us you are not achieving this.'[101] What he had imagined in his worst dreams had finally come true: Rositha Kirsch indeed had overtaken him by finishing in third place, whereas Stratmann finished in only 18th place. The author described Kirsch's success as follows: 'Mrs. Kirsch stood her ground in a sport which the former Hungarian world champion Andras Balc[z]o[102] named as "five filters in which only real man get caught".'[103]

So even when women practised modern pentathlon it was still regarded as the 'man in them' who achieved it. Accordingly, the German federation did not change its attitude in terms of focussing on men's events. As a result, financial and organisational difficulties remained and hindered a real breakthrough of women's modern pentathlon. But due to the never-ending enthusiasm and dedication of Henze and Reder, Germany became one of the most active countries. Thus, the World Cup for Women had its German debut in Warendorf, a city that in 1979 had been the men's modern pentathlon capital.[104]

The years between 1977 and 1980 were marked by progress in ladies' modern pentathlon in Germany, as Henze still tried to put his protective hand over the development that took place without any major disruptions or interferences. At the same time, the issue of 'greater participation by women in sport' was frequently broached by responsible European politicians.[105] Concerning participation in sport, Germany benefited from well-off women who could pay for material, coaching and travel costs privately. It seemed also that the German girls were lucky and talented enough to achieve good results even without a perfect organisational structure.[106]

According to an estimate by Germany's national (men's) coach Herbert Rieden in 1978, almost as many women and female pupils were active in modern pentathlon as men.[107] Rieden called the fact that ladies entered his sport 'a phenomenon'[108] and wished also that the men were as ambitious. Although this first statement sounds one of admiration, he gave a rather different impression when it came to financial issues: 'It would be a waste if a profiled pentathlon coach was appointed for the ladies, because as a not supported and not recognised discipline no effectiveness is expected from the women's pentathlon.'[109] At that time he probably spoke as many of his colleagues and modern pentathlon delegates actually felt in their hearts.

The financial support for women's modern pentathlon was still missing in 1980 when it was affirmed by the DVMF that there was no possibility for 'finance on a national level international competitions and seminars'[110] for women. Insufficient work at the base level and scarce performances were put forward as excuses.[111] Apparently unimpressed by the DVMF's attitude or possibly even in opposition to it, Hiltrud and Karsten Reder founded in the very same year the modern pentathlon section in the local sports club SSG Bensheim and thereby provided even better training conditions for future male and female athletes.[112]

To stay abreast of the ongoing changes with regard to the emancipation movement, the national federation had to make some contributions. Thus, at a meeting of the DVMF executive committee on 4 November 1978, the foundation of a so-called *Ausschuß für Modernen Fünfkampf für Frauen und Mädchen* (Commission for Modern Pentathlon for Women and Girls) was decided upon and quickly implemented around a month later.[113] At its first meeting, held on 19 January 1979, in Bensheim, the members, among them Hiltrud Reder,[114] agreed that due to the increasing activities of German women in modern pentathlon the need of a *Frauenfachwart* (women's professional attendant) on the DVMF executive board had arisen. The requirement was underlined by the recommendations of the German

Sport Federation (DSB) as well as the national sports associations (LSBs).[115] However, for the next two years this issue remained unchanged.

In 1981 Martina Goedicke, who was already ranked number two in the World Cup Series a year before, won the German Championships organised in Warendorf.[116] In 1982 female modern pentathletes received for the first time a small sum from the German *Sporthilfe* (Sport Aid Foundation).[117] Due to the increasing success and recognition of women, the DVMF was once more urged to give more room for ladies on its board. Gerhard Wien, the chairman of the Women's Modern Pentathlon Commission – significantly this position was again held by a man – suggested a change of regulations at the DVMF meeting in Hannover in 1981 so that one chair would be permanently assigned to a woman. This proposal was refused. Nevertheless, as a gesture of goodwill the federation declared all positions in the executive board as being 'generally open for all women'[118] and elected Hiltrud Reder as first woman onto the DVMF *Leistungsausschuss*, a performance committee dealing with training, finances and competitions.[119] At first glance, it seemed as if ladies' modern pentathlon in Germany had taken a big leap forward; however, it was likely that the DVMF aimed to object to a decision that allowed a woman to hold a seat on a more important board. There was, however, neither at the national nor the international level still any special position assigned to dealing with women's issues.[120] Thus Reder was indeed the first female DVMF executive board member, but ladies' modern pentathlon was still the province of the *Sportwart* (sports officer) and the female youth came under the control of the *Jugendwart* (youth officer).

Finally, President Grein admitted that there was not yet any real awareness of women's modern pentathlon, so that lamentations were indeed legitimate. He promised that the efforts to achieve progresses on that point would be continued in case the DVMF could find sufficient time and opportunity to prove it.[121] The request for a special women's award, the *Länderkampfnadel*, was also postponed by the president: 'We must rethink this still.'[122] For the moment, however, Grein did not see any possibility for financial support in a domain that was not fully recognised: 'We are not able to bring the expenditures for women justifiable to account because they are not counting as eligible. We as a federation only have the possibility to divide something off our donations revenue.'[123] Thus funding the ladies meant having less money left for the men and this was unthinkable.

As a consequence, even the female elite athletes had to pay for training, the seminars and participation in international competitions themselves.[124] Hiltrud Reder described her desperate situation as follows: 'We [cannot] send the best, but only those who have the money.'[125] While the German delegates still asked for time, the women did not have such moments of recreation, as the next competitions took place right on the doorstep. So the 'female couriers of the Federal Republic … went without state support to the war which was meanwhile directed into more peaceful paths'.[126]

Following the decision at its congress in Lahti, Finland, on 17 February 1981, the UIPMB finally staged the first Women's World Championships six months later (18–22 August) in London and thereby gave women's modern pentathlon a legitimate international base.[127] Great Britain, the United States and Sweden had the most successful teams. The German squad (Figure 1) was composed of four athletes, Ute Schiffmann accompanied the team but had not qualified. The three best of the four athletes came in the standings (Krapf: 2, Wiehn: 10, Kirsch: 19, Goedicke: 27) and the three best athletes came in the standings (Krapf: 2, Wiehn: 10, Kirsch: 19) and

Figure 1. German Women's Modern Pentathlon Team, London 1981.
Source: Hiltrud Reder private archives.

achieved fourth place in the team competition.[128] In the individual competition Sabine Krapf took second place. Her success is even more remarkable, as her mother had begged Hiltrud Reder to ensure that Sabine did not strain herself too much.[129]

Even though 1981 marked a big step towards women's emancipation internationally, ladies' events were not yet fully integrated in the modern pentathlon movement. As an exterior sign of the interior separation, the men organised their own World Championships in Zielona Góra, Poland, 769 kilometres from London.

Conclusion

When finally in 1981 after 14 years of persistence, the first World Championships were held in London, this provided an international base for the growth of women's modern pentathlon. The fact that in the very same year the Women's Federal Soccer Cup and the unofficial Female Soccer World Championships were also organised for the first time proves that modern pentathlon had not been the last bastion of men's resistance.[130] As in 1981 the first female IOC members were also elected,[131] the early 1980s generally marked a further step towards gender equality in Europe and underlined how modern pentathlon depended upon the wider female emancipation movement. So is the emancipation of female modern pentathlon simply one aspect of those general achievements or does the history of modern pentathlon also contain something particular which differentiates it from other emancipation movements in sport?

The combination of military and aristocratic heritage in modern pentathlon makes its long male dominance traceable. However, it does not explain why gender equality did not come along with the rule-changes of its single cavalry disciplines, fencing, shooting and horse-riding, which took place several decades earlier. There are two additional factors which made women's entrance into modern pentathlon especially difficult. First, preparation for modern pentathlon required training in five different sports and was thus considered too time-consuming and too exhausting for ladies. Comparing the development of female participation in other multidisciplinary events that also required 'masculine attributes' such as strength, aggressiveness and endurance,[132] this argument loses strength.

While continuing the search for reasons why modern pentathlon excluded female athletes for such a long time, a second point seems to be worth mentioning; namely that no other sport was so long and so exclusively connected to the IOC. Whereas the foundation of independent single sport federations happened during the early twentieth century,[133] modern pentathlon did not achieve organisational independence until 1948. Thus the development of men's modern pentathlon was for the first 36 years exclusively connected to the Olympic domain. The female movement, in contrast, primarily gained ground through localised activities in the second half of the twentieth century. The delay in the men's branch of the sport freeing itself from Olympic 'exclusivity' might indicate why the development of the women's branch was held back in comparison to other sports that had established non-Olympic competitions much earlier. Furthermore, modern pentathlon might have been so carefully protected from female intrusion as it was seen as the last remaining field for male virility in the 1970s.

Whatever the real reason, the sex barriers women had to break down in order to be granted admittance were numerous and considerable. Facing the male and military constitution of the UIPMB as the international decision-maker, a top-down development seemed unlikely. Delegates rather had to be confronted with a fait accompli, which is why, in the course of the 1970s, women began to practise the sport in single European nations. Germany was among these pioneer countries, as it had both an influential man ready to convince his male colleagues and a rigid woman willing to strengthen women's activities; both of whom became leading personalities. The woman, Hiltrud Reder, was named as 'mother of the female modern pentathlon'[134] and likewise called her fellow-combatant Henze the 'father of women's pentathlon'.[135] The man, Peter-Wilhelm Henze, once more thanked the 90-year old for her 'excellent and so successful dedication to women's pentathlon'.[136] Whereas Henze concentrated on the organisational level, Reder focused on the practical requirements of the female athletes. Of course they are only two people who contributed to the growth of ladies' modern pentathlon in Germany. Without the engagement of several small German communities and the Bavarian and the North Rhine-Westphalia Modern Pentathlon Association[137] progress would not have been achieved, especially during the long period when the German federation DVMF did not consider women's modern pentathlon to be credible.

Thus, the history of women's emancipation in modern pentathlon has been a struggle for participation but also a fight for the recognition of female athletes. Whereas participation was achieved, discrimination against female modern pentathletes continued into the 1980s. For instance, at the Women's World Championships in Bensheim, make-up courses were offered to the attending teams.[138] Along with a press which even contributed to spreading traditional patriarchal stereotypes, such incidents proved that although women had indeed entered the sport, in male heads traditional gender roles remained. Accordingly, women's World Championships remained locally and temporally separated from those of men until 1986.[139] Another 14 years passed until the struggle towards equal participation finally ended in September 2000, when for the first time women competed in the Olympic modern pentathlon competition in Sydney. Reder commented that the Olympic inclusion was a great success: 'Working 30 years for women's modern pentathlon was worth it. Now our goal is 100% achieved.'[140]

Notes on Contributor

Sandra Heck is a PhD candidate in the Faculty of Sport Science, Ruhr-University Bochum, Germany. Her work currently focuses on military sport history, the Olympic Games and French-German sport relations.

Notes

1. During the nineteenth and early twentieth century a first wave of feminism took place in the United Kingdom and the United States, so the developments in the 1960s and 1970s were named as a second wave. Whereas the first wave of feminism focused on legal issues, the second wave of feminism dealt with several unofficial inequalities (sexuality, family, workplace etc.).
2. Title IX is a law enacted on 23 June 1972. The law states: 'No person in the United States shall, on the basis of sex, be excluded from participation in, be denied the benefits of, or be subjected to discrimination under any education program or activity receiving Federal financial assistance': Simon, *Sporting Equality*.
3. The MLF was founded in 1968 and followed by further French associations such as *Choisir* and *La Cause des Femmes* in 1971.
4. Trappe, *Emanzipation oder Zwang?*, 215.
5. Pfister, 'Sport for Women', 167.
6. Heck, 'Modern Pentathlon and the First World War'.
7. Heck, 'Modern Pentathlon and Symbolic Violence'.
8. Email-correspondence with Jürgen Höfner, business manager of the OSC Potsdam and vice-president of the LV Brandenburg for modern pentathlon, dated 1 March 2010; Heckert, 'Sport komplett'.
9. Ute Engels's article in the *Festschrift* on occasion of Henze's 90th birthday marks an exception. International research rather focused to date on women's entrance into other sports, for instance rowing or football. See for instance Schweinbenz, 'Paddling against the Current', or Pfister, 'Must Women Play Football?'.
10. Besides analysing historical documents of the private archives of Hiltrud Reder in Bensheim/Germany, oral history is used to explore this neglected aspect of women's sport history. As the meeting minutes of the German Modern Pentathlon Federation are unfortunately not public, the author would especially like to thank Hiltrud Reder and Walter Grein for the courtesy of providing access to their private archive material and for being available for interview. Hiltrud Reder was interviewed by the author on 7 December 2009 in Bensheim; Walter Grein on 12 April 2010.
11. With regard to the topic of this paper, the present chapter only includes those aspects of Henze's biography that were connected to the investigated research topic. For a more detailed biography, see Krüger and Wedemeyer, *Aus Biographien Sportgeschichte lernen*, esp. 18–46.
12. Krapf, *Der moderne Fünfkampf*, 47 (author's translation from German); Engels, 'Now the Problem', 47–66.
13. Engels, 'Now the Problem', 64.
14. UIPMB, 'Modern Pentathlon, Biathlon and Olympism', 696.
15. When the *Bundeswehr*, the German armed forces, was founded in 1955, women remained excluded from every military issue. The Basic Constitution Law underlined this behaviour by determining that 'they [women] by no means are allowed to provide a service with the weapon'. Not before 1975 was an exception made that allowed women to work as sanitary officers in the army. See Campbell, 'Women in Combat'.
16. Besides his military career, he was a former Olympic modern pentathlete, reaching the fifth place in 1928. He was especially talented in the military disciplines of shooting and horse-riding which made him afterwards successfully compete in Olympic shooting

competitions. At the Olympic Games in 1932 as well as in 1936 Hax took the silver medal in shooting with the rapid fire pistol.

17. Compare Hargreaves, *Sporting Females*, 125.
18. Engels, 'Now the Problem', 50.
19. Henze, 'Das Fecht- und Duellwesen an der Universität Göttingen'.
20. Interview by Ute Engels with Wilhelm Henze, 2 Dec. 1999, quoted in Engels, 'Now the Problem', 51.
21. Ibid., quotation translated from the German.
22. Wilhelm Henze in a thank-you letter to Hiltrud Reder on occasion of his 90th birthday, without date (approximately 2000), private archives Hiltrud Reder, translated from the German.
23. The author was informed about these rumours in a talk with a citizen from Göttingen, March 2010.
24. Interview by Ute Engels with Wilhelm Henze, dated 17 Dec. 1999, quoted in Engels, 'Now the Problem', 64, quotation translated from the German.
25. Engels, 'Now the Problem', 50.
26. Hartmann-Tews and Luetkens, 'The Inclusion of Women into the German Sport System', 65.
27. Ibid.
28. The UIPM was re-named as UIPMB (B for Biathlon) in 1968. Compare for the institutional history of modern pentathlon: Heck, 'L'institutionnalisation d'une idée'.
29. Engels, 'Now the Problem', 65, quotation translated from the German.
30. Krapf, *Der moderne Fünfkampf*, 47.
31. Henze, *Modern Pentathlon for Women*, private archives Hiltrud Reder.
32. Ibid.
33. Horse-riding for men was first included in the 1900 Olympics and reappeared in 1912. Originally only commissioned officers were allowed to compete. Cross-country riding was included in the so-called eventing that embraced in total three horse-riding events and was introduced for men in 1912.
34. Women took generally part in athletics since 1928 when the competitions embraced the 100m and high jump.
35. Interview by Ute Engels with Wilhelm Henze, 2 Dec. 1999, quoted in: Engels, 'Now the Problem', 51.
36. Henze, 'Zur Entwicklung des Modernen Fünfkampfes für Frauen', 33, quoted in Engels, 'Now the Problem', 54.
37. Besides Henze (Germany), Jarrot (France), Larkas (Finland) and Ziegler (Switzerland) were part of this commission; ibid.
38. Lyberg, 'Women's Participation in the Olympic Games', 51.
39. Reder, *Die Entwicklung des Frauenfünfkampfes in Deutschland*, 1; Krapf, *Der moderne Fünfkampf*, 49.
40. Hiltrud Reder in an interview with the author, Bensheim, 7 Dec. 2009.
41. Pfister, 'Must Women Play Football?', 48.
42. DVMF, *Mitteilungen*, Dec. 1972, 10, 34, 36.
43. Henze, *Bericht über die Entwicklung des Modernen Fünfkampfes*, 1.
44. Among these ten countries were Australia, Finland, Hungary, Italy, Japan, Poland, Sweden, Switzerland, Soviet Union and USA: ibid. 3.
45. Namely Italy, Japan, Poland, Hungary, Finland, Soviet Union, Australia and USA.
46. Assuming that among the countries that did not answer at all, no interest and thus no practice in female modern pentathlon existed.
47. Henze, *Bericht über die Entwicklung des Modernen Fünfkampfes*, 5.
48. Ibid.
49. UIPMB, 'Modern Pentathlon, Biathlon and Olympism', 697.
50. Wilhelm Henze in a thank-you letter to Hiltrud Reder on occasion of his 90th birthday, without date (approximately 2000), private archives Hiltrud Reder.
51. Ibid.
52. Henze in a letter to the National Associations of the DVMF, dated 18 Oct. 1976, quoted by Engels, 'Now the Problem', 53.

53. Dechavanne, 'Women, Sport and Europe', 288.
54. Henze, *Zur Entwicklung des modernen Fünfkampfes*, 33, quoted in Engels, 'Now the Problem', 54.
55. Translated from the German. Wilhelm Henze in a thank-you letter to Hiltrud Reder on occasion of his 90th birthday, without date (approximately 2000), private archives Hiltrud Reder.
56. 'DVMF president to the administrative council', DVMF, Mitteilungen, January, 1974, 3.
57. Reder, Die Entwicklung des Frauenfünfkampfes in Deutschland und der UIPMB, without pages.
58. Wilhelm Henze in a thank-you letter to Hiltrud Reder on occasion of his 90th birthday, without date (approximately 2000), private archives Hiltrud Reder.
59. Ibid., quotation translated from the German.
60. Wolfgang Goedicke was German modern pentathlon champion in 1962. Internally he competed, too, but with moderate success. At the World Championships in Stockholm in 1957 he was 8th; 18th in Aldershot in 1958; 31st in Harrisburg in 1959; 20th in Moscow 1961; 14th in Mexico in 1962; 12th in Magglingen in 1963. With regard to the Olympics he was 28th at the Olympic Games in Rome 1960 and 12th in Tokyo 1964, Krapf, *Der moderne Fünfkampf*, 117, 122–4.
61. Letter of the DVMF addressed to the National Associations, 'Moderner Fünfkampf für Mädchen und Frauen', dated 24 March 1975, private archives Hiltrud Reder.
62. Letter by Henze addressed to the DVMF's National Associations, dated 18 Oct. 1976; 'Report of the Frauenwartin Hiltrud Reder about the meeting of the BLMF', dated 10 Dec. 1976, private archives Hiltrud Reder.
63. Hiltrud Reder in an interview with the author, Bensheim, 7 Dec. 2009.
64. Wolgang Goedicke won for instance the German Championships in 1962. DFMF, *Mitteilungen*, Dec. 1971.
65. Ibid., quotation translated from the German.
66. Krapf, *Der moderne Fünfkampf*, 49.
67. Pupils' Championships were organised from 8 to 11 June 1973 in Berlin: DVMF, *Mitteilungen*, June 1973.
68. For instance, in Munich in 1973 Manueal Nigro, Helene Urban, Marina Nigro and Martina Wunderer competed: DVMF, *Mitteilungen*, Nov. 1973.
69. The German championships were for the first time organised in 1974 on occasion of the NRW-championships in Leverkusen-Opladen. In the same year Bavaria and North Rhine-Westphalia participated in their first foreign competitions in Hungary. DVMF, *Mitteilungen*, May 1972; Reder, *Die Entwicklung des Frauenfünfkampfes in Deutschland*, 1.
70. Imke Schmitz comparably competed better than the men: 'Imke Schmitz war die Beste', no. 31 (6 Feb. 1973), private archives Hiltrud Reder.
71. DVMF, *Mitteilungen*, Feb. 1974, 12.
72. For instance, at the international youth championships, organised in Neustadt, Germany, 3–5 Sept. 1976 (certificate of attendance), private archives Hiltrud Reder.
73. Reder, *Die Entwicklung des Frauenfünfkampfes in Deutschland*, 1.
74. Engels, 'Now the Problem', 53.
75. The youth officer of the BLMF in a letter addressed to Henze, 2 April 1975, private archives Hiltrud Reder.
76. Interview with Rositha Kirsch, in Elaine Noll: 'S.A. heat saps West Germany pentathlon', private archives Hiltrud Reder.
77. Imken Schmitz, for instance, successfully competed in South Africa in 1976. See Martina Gassen, 'Zum Fünfkampf in den Schwarzen Kontinent'', unknown newspaper, no. 67, March 1976, private archives Hiltrud Reder.
78. 'Antrieb: Recht der Frau auf Gleichberechtigung im Sport – Hiltrud Reder hilft Modernem Fünfkampf nach oben', Bergsträßer Anzeige (daily newspaper), 2 April 1987, private archives Hiltrud Reder.
79. Hiltrud Reder in an interview with the author, Bensheim, 7 Dec. 2009.
80. Curriculum vitae, private archives Hiltrud Reder.
81. 'Eine Frau verändert den "Offizierssport"', *Bergsträsser Anzeiger*, private archives Hiltrud Reder.

82. From 1966 to 1976 Karsten Reder was a member of the national team and in 1969 and 1970 a participant in the World Championships in Budapest and Warendorf. He twice won the bronze medal with the team, was three times German champion, and was bronze medallist four times. See 'Bei so etwas verlier' ich jedes Mal fünf, sechs Kilo', unknown newspaper, private archives Hiltrud Reder.

83. 'Verfechterin des Modernen Fünfkampfes', *Bergsträsser Anzeige*, 11 Jan. 1984, private archives Hiltrud Reder.

84. Katrin Hoffmann, 'Bensheimerin lernt in China das Neinsagen', *Bergsträsser Anzeiger*, 13 Aug. 2008, private archives Hiltrud Reder, quotation translated from the German.

85. Hiltrud Reder in an interview with the author, Bensheim, 7 Dec. 2009.

86. See note 42.

87. Reder, *Die Entwicklung des Frauenfünfkampfes in Deutschland*.

88. 'Ladies' Modern Pentathlon: The Background', without year/author, private archives Hiltrud Reder.

89. DFMF, *Mitteilungen*, Dec. 1971, in: Reder, *Die Entwicklung des Frauenfünfkampfes*, VII: Weltmeisterschaft Moderner Fünfkampf – Frauen, Bensheim an der Bergstraße, 2–8 Aug, 1987.

90. H. Reder, 'Ein Bericht über die ersten Welt-Cups im Frauenfünfkampf 1978', private archives Hiltrud Reder.

91. Reder, *Die Entwicklung des Frauenfünfkampfes in Deutschland*, 2.

92. Hiltrud Reder in an interview with the author, Bensheim, 7 Dec. 2009.

93. Ibid., quotation translated from the German.

94. Ibid.

95. Curriculum vitae, private archives Hiltrud Reder.

96. 'Hiltrud Reder, die Vorreiterin – Für die Mädchen den Männern lästig werden', *FAZ* 277 (7 Dec. 1984), 61.

97. Among the equestrian events, the military is considered 'the most gruelling of all equestrian events': Lyberg, 'Women's Participation in the Olympic Games', 48.

98. 'Merken die Sportfrauen tatsächlich nicht, daß sie an den falschen Fronten kämpfen und Scheinsiege bejubeln? – Männerargumente zu einem vieldiskutierten Thema', in Reder, *Die Entwicklung des Frauenfünfkampfes in Deutschland*, no page numbers, quotation translated from the German. For the demonstration of women in the German yellow press, see Klein and Pfister, *Goldmädel, Rennmiezen und Turnküken:*.

99. Reder, *Die Entwicklung des Frauenfünfkampfes in Deutschland*, quotation translated from the German.

100. Hiltrud Reder in an interview with the author, Bensheim, 7 De. 2009, quotation translated from the German..

101. 'Merken die Sportfrauen tatsächlich nicht, daß sie an den falschen Fronten kämpfen und Scheinsiege bejubeln? – Männerargumente zu einem vieldiskutierten Thema', private archives Hiltrud Reder.

102. Andras Balczo was a successful modern pentathlete in the 1960s.

103. See Blume, 'Frauen haben letzte Bastion gestürmt', *Die Welt*, 1977, private archives Hiltrud Reder, quotation translated from the German.

104. Reder, *Die Entwicklung des Frauenfünfkampfes in Deutschland*.

105. Dechavanne, 'Women, Sport and Europe', 286.

106. Ulrich Fey, 'Einigkeit macht deutsche Mannschaft stark – Fünfkämpferinnen in Harmonie führend', *FAZ*, 7 Aug. 1987, 38, private archives Hiltrud Reder.

107. 'Der Moderne Fünfkampf wird zum Sechskampf', *FAZ*, 16 Feb. 1978, private archives Hiltrud Reder.

108. Ibid, quotation translated from the German.

109. Lore Knoll, 'Die Mädchen können sich die Peitsche sparen', *Die Welt*, 1978, private archives Hiltrud Reder, quotation translated from the German.

110. Protocol of the meeting of the DVMF *Frauenausschuss* (women's committee) in Bensheim on 18 April 1980, dated 20 April 1980, quoted in: Engels, 'Now the Problem', 56.

111. Ibid., 57. The mentioned cases were in conflict with the achievements of women in modern pentathlon. In October 1977 Rositha Kirsch reached an excellent third rank at a frame competition on the occasion of the World Championships in San Antonio. The female German team took 4th place at the World Cup in 1979; one year later 3rd; in the

individual rivalries, places between 7 and 13. See for the German women's success also a letter of Gerhard Wiehn addressed to Hiltrud Reder, dated 25 Jan. 1980 and Michael Wedegärtner, 'Pionierin mit "kleinen Schritten"', unknown journal, 5 Aug. 1983, private archives Hiltrud Reder.

112. Curriculum vitae, private archives Hiltrud Reder.

113. Invitation to a preparing meeting in Frankfurt/Main on 2 Dec. 1978. See letter of the president Walter Grein addressed to the national associations, 14 Nov. 1978, private archives Hiltrud Reder.

114. The commission was composed of five persons: Sigrid Bartholomäi, Peter Kroner, Hiltrud Reder, Helene Urban and Gerhard Wiehn. Besides them a spokesperson for the active athletes, Ute Schiffmann and a coach, Elmar Frings, were nominated. See the protocol dated 6 Dec. 1978, private archives Hiltrud Reder.

115. Protocol of the first session of the DVMF women's committee which took place on 19 Jan. 1979 in Bensheim, dated 21 Jan. 1979, private archives Hiltrud Reder.

116. Martina Goedicke followed Ute Schiffmann, who won in Munich in 1978, Rosita Kirsch, who won in Neuss in 1979 as well as in Heidenheim in 1980. One year later, in 1982, Goedicke proved her ability and was again German champion in Darmstadt: Krapf, *Der Moderne Fünfkampf*, 143–4.

117. Reder, *Die Entwicklung des Frauenfünfkampfes in Deutschland*, 2.

118. See 'Verbandstag 1981 in Hannover' (report), without source and date, private archives Hiltrud Reder, quotation translated from the German.

119. Besides Hiltrud Reder, her husband Karsten Reder as well as Rudi Trost and Walter Esser were members of the *Leistungsausschuss*. See Reder, *Die Entwicklung des Frauenfünfkampfes in Deutschland*, 2.

120. 'Women in the World Sports Organizations', 401.

121. 'Verbandstag 1981 in Hannover' (report), without source and date, private archives Hiltrud Reder.

122. Ibid., quotation translated from the German.

123. Holger Dieckmann, 'Die Forderung nach Förderung bleibt unerfüllt, doch die Athletinnen sind unverdrossen vom Pioniergeist beseelt', *Die Glocke*, 1981, private archives Hiltrud Reder, quotation translated from the German.

124. Protocol of the meeting of the *Frauenausschuss* on 24 Jan. 1981, dated 1 Feb. 1981 and its subsequent entry dated 23 Feb. 1981, private archives Hiltrud Reder.

125. Jürgen Paul, 'Noch viele Etappen auf dem Weg der Gleichstellung', *FAZ*, 7 April 1981, private archives Hiltrud Reder, quotation translated from the German.

126. Stefan Lazar, 'Die Ladies greifen an', unknown newspaper, private archives of Hiltrud Reder, quotation translated from the German.

127. UIPMB, 'Modern Pentathlon, Biathlon and Olympism', 699.

128. Krapf, *Der Moderne Fünfkampf*, 141; Hiltrud Reder in a personal E-mail on January 31, 2012.

129. Hiltrud Reder in an interview with the author, Bensheim, December 7, 2009.

130. Pfister, 'Must Women Play Football?', 48–50.

131. Lyberg, 'Women's Participation in the Olympic Games', 48. Pirjo Haggman of Finland and Flor Isava-Fonseca of Venezuela were the first female IOC members.

132. Dechavanne, 'Women, Sport and Europe', 287.

133. The Fédération Internationale de Natation (FINA) was created in 1908, for instance, and the Fédération Internationale d'Escrime (FIE) five years later in 1913. In 1922 all single sports of which the modern pentathlon was composed already possessed their own federative boards. Heck, 'L'institutionnalisation d'une idée'.

134. Engels, 'Now the Problem', 55, quotation translated from the German.

135. Reder, *Die Entwicklung des Frauenfünfkampfes in Deutschland*, 1, quotation translated from the German.

136. Wilhelm Henze in a letter addressed to Hiltrud Reder on occasion of a thank-you letter to his 90th birthday, approximately 2000, private archives Hiltrud Reder, quotation translated from the German.

137. The Urban family from Bavaria and the Wiehn family from North Rhine-Westphalia were especially active: Krapf, *Der moderne Fünfkampf*, 50; Reder, *Die Entwicklung des Frauenfünfkampfes in Deutschland*, 2.

138. 'Schminkkurs für Sportlerinnen', newspaper article, without date, approximately published in 1987, when Bensheim hosted the women's World Championships, private archives Hiltrud Reder.

139. Afterwards both events were separated again until 1993 when for two years the both sexes shared the same location. Finally, from 1997 onwards men's and women's World Championships took place at the same location and time for long term.

140. Hiltrud Reder in an interview with the author, Bensheim, 7 Dec. 2009, quotation translated from the German.

References

Campbell, D'A. 'Women in Combat: The World War Two Experience in the United States, Great Britain, Germany, and the Soviet Union'. *Journal of Military History* 57 (April 1993): 301–23.

Dechavanne, N. 'Women, Sport and Europe'. *Olympic Review*, no. 284 (June 1991): 286–91.

DVMF (German Modern Pentathlon Federation), Mitteilungen (various numbers between 1971 and 1974).

Engels, U. 'Now the Problem: Modern Pentathlon for Ladies – zur Rolle Prof. Dr. Peter-Wilhelm Henzes bei der Entwicklung des Modernen Frauenfünfkampfes', in *Aus Biographien Sportgeschichte lernen: Festschrift zum 90. Geburtstag von Prof. Dr. Wilhelm Henze*, eds. A. Krüger and B. Wedemeyer. Hoya: NISH [Niedersächsisches Institut für Sportgeschichte], 2000, 47–66.

Hargreaves, J. *Sporting Females: Critical Issues in the History and Sociology of Women's Sports*. London: Routledge, 1997.

Hartmann-Tews, I. and Luetkens, S.A. 'The Inclusion of Women into the German Sport System', in *Sport and Women – Social Issues in International Perspective*, eds. I. Hartmann-Tews and G. Pfister. London and New York: Routledge, 2003, 53–69.

Heck, S. 'Modern Pentathlon and Symbolic Violence – A History of Female Exclusion from Stockholm 1912 to Paris 1924'. *International Review on Sport and Violence* no. 4 (Oct. 2010): 1–14.

Heck, S. 'Modern Pentathlon and the First World War – When Athletes and Soldiers Met to Practise Martial Manliness'. *The International Journal of the History of Sport* 28, nos. 3–4 (March 2011): 410–28.

Heck, S. 'L'institutionnalisation d'une idée. Le pentathlon moderne du programme olympique à une fédération internationale', in *Histoire(s) de la performance du sportif de haut niveau*, eds. T. Bauer and D. Gomet. Paris: INSEP, 2011, 229–41.

Heckert, K. (Red.). 'Sport komplett: Historie. Moderner Fünfkampf – DDR – Meisterschaften (Herren – Einzel)'. Available online at http://www.sport-komplett.de/sport-komplett/sportarten/m/moderner_fuenfkampf/hst/26.html

Henze, W. *Bericht über die Entwicklung des Modernen Fünfkampfes für Frauen und Mädchen von Juli 1976.* [no location or publisher], 1976.

Henze, W. 'Das Fecht- und Duellwesen an der Universität Göttingen (1734–1940)'. PhD diss., Georg-August-Universität Göttingen, 1942.

Klein, M.-L. and Pfister, G. *Goldmädel, Rennmiezen und Turnküken: Die Frau in der Sportberichterstattung der Bild-Zeitung* (Sportsoziologische Arbeiten. vol. 9). Berlin: Bartels & Wernitz, 1985.

Krapf, S. *Der moderne Fünfkampf.* Neuhausen: Weber-Söhnen, 1987.

Krüger, A. 'Forgotten Decisions: The IOC and the Eve of World War I'. *Olympika – The International Journal of Olympic Studies* VI (1997): 85–98.

Krüger, A. and Wedemeyer, B., eds. *Aus Biographien Sportgeschichte lernen: Festschrift zum 90. Geburtstag von Prof. Dr. Wilhelm Henze.* Hoya: NISH [Niedersächsisches Institut für Sportgeschichte], 2000.

Lyberg, W. 'Women's Participation in the Olympic Games'. *Olympic Review* (Feb.–March 2000), 46–53.

Mallon, B. and Widlund, T. *The 1912 Olympic Games: Results for All Competitors in All Events* (Results of the Early Modern Olympics, vol. 6). Jefferson NC: McFarland & Co, 2002.

Mitchell, S. 'Women's Participation in the Olympic Games 1900–1926'. *Journal of Sport History* 4, no. 2 (1977): 208–28.

Pfister, G. 'Must Women play Football? Women's Football in Germany, Past and Present'. *Football Studies* 4. no. 2 (Oct. 2001): 41–57.

Pfister, G. 'Sport For Women', in *Sport and Physical Education in Germany*, eds. R. Naul and K. Hardman. London: Routledge, 2002, 165–90.

Reder, H. *Die Entwicklung des Frauenfünfkampfes in Deutschland und der UIPMB*. Bensheim: [no publisher], 1996.

Schweinbenz, A.N. 'Paddling against the Current: An Analysis of Women's Entrance into the 1954 European Rowing Championships'. *Journal of Sport History* 33. no. 3 (Fall 2006), 253–72.

Simon, R.J. *Sporting Equality: Title IX Thirty Years Later*. Piscataway, NJ: Transaction Publishers, 2005.

Tiedemann, C. 'Alliierte Rechtsbestimmungen zum Sport in Deutschland 1944–1950', in *Die erstrittene Einheit, Von der ADS zum DSB (1948–1950)*. Bericht der 2. Hoyaer Tagung zur Entwicklung des Nachkriegssports in Deutschland, ed. L. Peiffer. Schriftenreihe der NISH e.V. vol. 7. Duderstadt: Mecke, 1989, 87–150.

Trappe, H. *Emanzipation oder Zwang?: Frauen in der DDR zwischen Beruf, Familie und Sozialpolitik*. Berlin: Akademia-Verlag, 1995 (also diss., Freie Universität Berlin, 1994).

UIPMB (Union Internationale de Pentathlon Moderne et Biathlon). 'Modern Pentathlon, Biathlon and Olympism'. *Olympic Review 192* (Oct. 1983): 688–724.

'Women in the World Sports Organizations – First Part: The International Sports Federations' [author not named]. *Olympic Review 82–3* (Sept.–Oct. 1974): 401–14.

Women's Sport in Portugal from 1974 (the 'Carnation Revolution') to 2000

Maria Claudia Pinheiro

Instituto Superior de Maia, Portugal

The transition from the 'New State' regime in Portugal (which lasted approximately 40 years) to the democratic period brought important changes to women's lives. Women began to enter university courses traditionally considered masculine ones, entered the labour market in greater numbers, entered professional careers that once had been closed to them, became more involved in women's groups fighting for changes in their situation and began to be more involved in the political life of the country. The legal and social changes that occurred in relation to women, as well as the sports policies that were followed after the revolution, contributed to a faster increase in the numbers of women taking part in sport generally, and also in traditionally male-appropriate sports. However, this does not mean that women did not face any resistance. This paper seeks to examine women's participation in sport and the resistance they faced in relation to their participation in certain sports.

Introduction

From 25 April 1974 until the establishment of the first constitutional government in 1976, Portugal went through a period of great political instability. This instability is evident in the fact that, over a period of two years, Portugal had six provisional governments. The various provisional governments, all of which had a very strong presence of left-wing parties, including the Communist Party, attempted to secure their political position and to deal with the economic and social problems facing the country. However, they had to take into account the actions of other groups that also sought to control the political and economic activity of the country. The interests of one group often collided with those of other groups, leading to the emergence of several tensions among the different groups involved in the struggle for power. But none of the groups involved in this struggle for power was sufficiently powerful to be able to control the unstable economic and social situation in Portugal. While the *Movimento das Forças Armadas* (MFA – Armed Forces Movement) and left-wing parties were quarrelling among themselves, other emergent political parties such as the *Partido Popular Democrático* (PPD – Popular Democratic Party), *Centro Democrático Social* (CDS – Social Democratic Centre), *União Democrática Popular* (UDP – Popular Democratic Union), *Movimento de*

Esquerda Socialista (MES – Socialist Left Wing Movement), *Partido Popular Monárquico* (PPM – Popular Monarchic Party) and *Movimento Democrático Português* (MDP – Portuguese Democratic Movement) were setting down their roots within civil society.[1] Though they were less powerful, they organised demonstrations and congresses where they attempted to present themselves as alternatives to the existing political power.

Besides the political instability, this period was also marked by a corresponding social instability. There were strikes involving different sectors of the population, houses were occupied, factories and land began to be put under popular control, some companies were taken over by workers and others were abandoned by their owners. This period was also marked by a number of nationalisations and land expropriations. Banks were nationalised as well as other sectors: petrochemical, cement, fertiliser, tobacco, iron and steel companies, the major breweries, the large shipping lines, most public transport, two of the three principal shipyards, the radio and television networks and important companies in the glass, mining, fishing and agricultural sectors. When the process of expropriation of certain rural estates was regulated, several farms were delivered to rural workers who formed themselves into cooperatives of agricultural production or another form of collective company, called collective unity of production.[2]

On 2 April 1976, the Portuguese Constitution was approved and on 25 April the first elections for the Portuguese National Parliament were held. With these elections a democratic and parliamentary regime was founded. For the first time 'a political system was ... based on fundamental civic and parliamentary rights including universal suffrage and freedom of political activity'.[3] With these elections Portugal was entering a period in which political exile, prisoners of conscience or the concept of political crime ceased to exist.

The period between 1976 and the mid-1980s, was marked by some government instability. Most of the governments in this period 'were mainly of a coalition type and never ended their terms'.[4] From the second half of the 1980s onwards there was greater government stability. From 1985 to 1995 the governments were social democrats and from 1995 to 2000 there was a socialist government. In spite of the political orientation of the governments, they all shared a common concern with the political stability of the country, the resolution of the economic problems and the development of the Portuguese economy. This period was marked by an increase in inflation, which was not accompanied by an increase in terms of salaries, by a decrease in terms of private consumption and investment and by an increase of unemployment.[5] In order to deal with these economic problems, the government twice requested the assistance of the International Monetary Fund (IMF). However, the IMF imposed several conditions that implied severe austerity measures.[6] These measures were unpopular with certain sectors of the Portuguese population, especially the working classes who were already at or near poverty level. In 1986, Portugal became a full member of the EEC and from 1987 onwards the European Funds that were transferred to Portugal were used to develop various infrastructures, to improve the means of transportation and to modernise Portuguese industry.

Women

With the revolution of 1974, the legal and social position of women changed considerably. Within the family, husband and wife were given equal legal rights and duties. The figure of 'head of the family' disappeared and the family structure and size changed.[7] Divorce became legal due to changes in the XXIV article of the Concordat.[8] Advances in household technology gave women more possibilities to engage in activities other than housekeeping and childcare.[9]

The end of censorship and the disappearance of the political police, two important instruments of repression, allowed a freedom of expression practically unknown until then. Newspapers and writers that had had their articles and books censored during the 'New State' were now publishing without any restrictions. Individuals from different sectors of the population who before had been followed closely and sometimes arrested by the political police for expressing opposition to the regime were now free to organise opposition social groups without fearing the intervention of the political police. It was in this context that women were able to take part in unions, working committees, public demonstrations and other organisations to campaign for greater rights. For the first time, women not only showed, in public, their discontent but also demanded changes in their situation, particularly in terms of their civic rights, employment opportunities and health care.

The freedom of expression allowed after April 1974 permitted a more open and free discussion of issues once considered as taboo, such as abortion, sexuality and contraception. Most of this discussion was carried out through the women's groups that were formed after the revolution.[10] These groups, through the debate of such issues, were giving voice to women's interests and concerns particularly in relation to unwanted pregnancies and clandestine abortion.

The restrictions concerning access to professional occupations disappeared and women began to enter the labour market in greater numbers than before. After the revolution of 1974, women were able to be appointed for the first time to positions in areas once regarded as male preserves, such as diplomatic careers and the judiciary.[11] However, in spite of an increase in the economically active female population and despite legislation designed to create equality of opportunities between men and women in the labour market and in employment, women's unemployment has remained significantly higher than that of men and women's employment rate has been lower than that of men.[12] As low wages failed to keep pace with inflation, this also had an impact upon employed women, who had wages lower than those of employed men. This situation pushed women to a position of greater financial dependency on men within the family, whether fathers or husbands.

In terms of education one of the major changes that occurred after 1974 and impacted upon women was the establishment of co-education, which made possible a more democratic education for both boys and girls together.[13] For some of the Portuguese feminists of the democratic period, co-education was seen as a means to promote equality between boys and girls. It was argued that, if males and females were used to living together in other social spaces, the school should not be different. Boys and girls had to learn how to live and learn together and women would learn how to be independent.[14]

Women's involvement in the political life of the country has also increased since 1974. But in spite of greater participation, women's participation in the political life has always been quite limited. For example, in 1976, 1995 and 1999, of the total number of deputies in the National Parliament, 5%, 12% and 20%, respectively, were women. For the same years and in relation to government (including ministers, secretaries of state and sub-secretaries), of the total number of government positions, 5,5%, 8,6% and 12%, respectively, were women.[15]

Since women continued to be under-represented in the government and national Parliament, in 1999 the government created, for the first time, the position of Minister for Equality. Ten months after its creation this ministry was closed down without explanation.[16] The establishment of this minister can be regarded as the outcome of a process that had started in 1970 with the establishment of the *Grupo de Trabalho sobre a Participação das Mulheres na Vida Económica e Social* (Working Group on the Participation of Women in Economic and Social Life). This group was later replaced by the *Comissão para a Política Social relativamente às Mulheres* (Commission on Social Policy for Women). In 1975 this commission changed its name to *Comissão da Condição Feminina* (Commission on the Status of Women). This commission acquired more importance and gained more credibility when in 1977 it was attached to the Prime Minister's office. It was the first governmental body totally devoted to women's issues. In 1979, with the publication of a decree-law specifying equality between men and women in the work sphere, the *Comissão para a Igualdade no Trabalho e no Emprego* (Commission for Equality in Work and Employment) was created.[17] In 1991, the Commission on the Status of Women was replaced by the *Comissão para a Igualdade e para os Direiros das Mulheres* (Commission for Equality and Women's Rights or CIDM).[18]

Despite setbacks and slow progress, improved education, the possibility of divorce and a greater participation in the labour market gave women more independence and power. The greater participation of women in the public sphere, the changes in the family size and structure, and the legislative changes with effects upon women, as well as wider changes in society at large, brought about a gradual change in the balance of power between men and women towards a greater equalisation.

Sport after the Revolution

The two years following the revolution were marked by a political orientation radically different from that during the 'New State' period. The socialist orientations of those in power had some impact upon sports policies in this two-year period. Their intention was to change the way sport was understood and to make it accessible to everyone. In this period, the various provisional governments tried to make sport accessible to everybody in the country. In the process of promoting sport all over the country, the state sports organisation *Direcção Geral dos Desportos* (DGD – General Directorate of Sports) was assisted by city councils and local sports organisations. During this period, the central government and local authorities took the major responsibility for the promotion of sport. Regional sports associations, big sports clubs and sports federations were not prioritised by government since it was believed by those in power that these organisations were more interested in promoting sport for an elite, rather than in promoting sport for all throughout the country.

With the nomination of the first constitutional government and the publication of the Portuguese Constitution, the sports policies and the forms of state intervention in sport began slowly to change. The various constitutional governments that were elected did not neglect the importance of sport for all, though they focused much more on competitive sport, and especially high-performance sport. Hence, during this period, sports policies became much more oriented towards elite sport.

State financial investment in sport also increased but, when compared to other developed countries, continued at a low level.[19] Most of this investment was directed towards competitive sport. With the transition from the New State regime to the democratic period, the state did not lose its central position as the main financial supporter of sport. However, there was a growing involvement of the private/ commercial sector in the financial support of sport and, especially of competitive and high-performance sport.

Women's Participation in Sporting Activities

After the revolution until more or less the mid-1980s, the sports policies followed by the government were directed primarily towards the democratisation of sport. In the attempt to make sport accessible to all, everybody was encouraged to take part in physical and sporting activities. Women were no exception. Some women's magazines, such as the monthly magazine *Mulheres*, began to devote a page specifically to women's sports.[20] This magazine presented, through articles and photographs, the achievements and the tenacity of Portuguese and foreign women athletes. The use of such examples attempted to show that many women, in spite of practical difficulties (lack of financial means, lack of support from the family and other relatives, not having a lot of free time due to their professional careers or domestic responsibilities, being married and having children) considered sport as an important part of their lives.

Still, in the context of persuading women to take part in sport, in 1978 an article was published in a sports medicine handbook in which it was noted that old prejudices regarding women's involvement in sport did not make any scientific sense. Sport did not masculinise women as had been popularly believed. On the contrary, as long as it was correctly guided, sport could enhance femininity. It was also pointed out that, in the period that followed menstruation, women could attain very good results since it was in that 'stage that they reach[ed] the maximum energy, skill and psychic balance'.[21] In order to encourage more women to take part in physical and sporting activities, in addition to the health benefits of such practice, the social and moral benefits were also highlighted:

'The time devoted to physical activities is not lost time, since with them is attained a true intellectual rest, a physical and psychic regularisation ... which is always useful, always creative.'[22]

However, caution was still recommended. Though involved in sporting activity, women should not forget their femininity; women had always to bear in mind their beauty, their grace and their responsibility for childbearing:

The concern for keeping their health condition, their strong youth and attractiveness, their natural graciousness and beauty, at last their femininity. ... The woman when dedicating herself to sport cannot forget that all her corporeal activity must be harmonious, adjusted, exact and appropriate to her condition of male companion and essential bearer of the important mission of the perpetuation of the human species.[23]

The kind of concern expressed here shows that the traditional ideology concerning women and their role and position in society remained strong. Images of women continued to be based on traditional stereotypes. Women continued to be regarded as the male's companion and as having the main responsibility for the perpetuation of the species. As had been advocated during the dictatorship, it was still held that women could take part in sport but should not put at risk their childbearing responsibilities. Women had to be careful in relation to the kind of sports in which they were involved in order to preserve their feminine qualities and to protect their reproductive organs. The focus continued, for many people, to be on women's biology.

In spite of such considerations, after the 1974 revolution and in comparison to the 1960s, women's participation in physical and sporting activities at the level of sports federations and Olympic Games has increased. For example, at the level of sports federations, in 1968/9 the number of women athletes registered was 8,097. This number rose to 30,162 athletes in 1979 and in 1998 to 45,742 athletes. As far as the Olympic Games are concerned, while in 1980 there was only one female athlete in the Portuguese delegation, in 1996 there were 26 female athletes.[24]

But women's participation in sport remained quite low. According to the two national studies carried out in Portugal, in 1988 and 1998, only 18% and 14% of Portuguese women respectively took part in some sort of physical and sporting activities.[25]

In order to understand the lower involvement of Portuguese women in sport, one has to take into account the ideals of femininity and sporting masculinity that prevailed within Portuguese society for decades. Women have, for generations, been discouraged from taking part in sport or at least in some sports, due to the strong association traditionally made between some sports and masculinity. Although these constraints can also be found in the history of other west European societies, it can be argued in relation to Portuguese society that, due to the influence of the Catholic Church and the politics followed during the dictatorship, these traditional constraints were much stronger in Portugal than in other European countries. The Catholic Church and the political ideology followed during the New State period praised motherhood, the importance of the family, a traditional ideal of femininity and gave little importance to women's involvement in sporting activities. According to the New State ideology, strongly supported by the Catholic Church, women could practise sport but only certain sports, in moderation and with respect to moral and Christian principles. While men were encouraged to take part in sport in order to become physically strong, healthy and energetic so they could serve and defend the nation, women were advised to practise sport only with moderation and not to be involved in certain sports that could threaten their femininity. By the end of the twentieth century most mothers and grandmothers, as well as fathers and grandfathers, had been educated in this context. As a result of their own socialisation into this strong tradition, many parents, even if they acknowledged the importance of undermining gender values, were unable 'to prevent their own subliminal responses'.[26] In the education of their children many parents still transmit gender values that reproduce traditional gender stereotypes.[27] That is, while some parents may wish for their girls a life different from the one they had, and many encourage them to have a better education, to have a professional career and to be more physically active, other parents have continued to transmit the values and the behaviour patterns that were dominant during their own youth.

Entry into Traditional 'Male' Sports

Before 1974 women were participating and competing in sports such as gymnastics, basketball, tennis, swimming and volleyball among others. But women's participation in sports traditionally considered 'as bastions of male identity and privilege', such as football, rugby, handball or judo, developed only in the years after the 1974 revolution.[28] For example, the first judo national competition for women took place in 1975. In handball the first women's national competition took place in 1975/6. The first national competition in roller hockey organised under the aegis of the federation took place only in 1991 and in women's cycling the first official competition took place in 1990. In rugby the first competition among women was organised under the aegis of the rugby federation only in 2000/1. However, the first women's rugby game took place in Coimbra in 1970, organised by the rugby section of the Associação Académica de Coimbra. In 1994/5, in order to promote rugby among men and women, the rugby federation organised several games for male and female teams. In 1995 the first Portuguese women's team, 'The Lusitanas' played against Germany and lost by 50 points to nil. From then until 2000/1, most of the female competitions have been promoted by juvenile rugby.[29] Due to an increasing interest in rugby on the part of girls and to an improvement in the quality of the games, in 2000/1 the first women's national competition was established.

In football, the first women's national competition organised under the aegis of the football federation, the women's national football cup, took place in 1985. However, women were involved in football long before that date (in the 1930s some women were already playing football). Moreover, in the latter 1970s, there were also some Portuguese women playing football and taking part in national and international competitions organised by clubs rather than by the national federation or sporting associations. In fact, at that time the main supporters of women's football were the sports clubs. The federation and associations were not involved in the promotion of women's football. In 1984/5 the first national championship for women was organised. This competition has continued to be held regularly since then and most of the female teams were, at the end of the twentieth century, not part of the larger and most well-known Portuguese clubs, but were found within quite small clubs. As far as the female national team is concerned, according to a former player, in 1981 Portugal took part in an international competition.[30] Those who organised this participation, due to the good performance by the players, became very enthusiastic and decided to register the team in the first women's football European championship. But after participation in this competition the national team ceased to exist, apparently due to a lack of financial means. The female national team was re-established once again in 1993. Since then, the team has participated in several international competitions, including qualifying games for the VI and VII European Championships and for the World Championship.[31]

It can be said that women's participation in sports traditionally considered a male preserve has increased since the revolution. Women's participation in football, five-a-side football, weightlifting, cycling, boxing and rugby are good examples of women's entrance into sports traditionally associated with men. For example, in 1977/8 there were no women registered in the football federation, but by 1990 there were 451 women football players. By 1996 this number had increased to 636 and in 1998 there were 2,439 female athletes registered with the football federation. In weightlifting, this increase is also evident. In 1977/8 there were no women registered in the federation but by 1998 women represented 13.4% of the total number of registered weightlifters. Similarly, in 1998 there were no women in the rugby federation, but by 2000 there were 76 registered women rugby players.

By the end of the twentieth century, although more women were involved in traditionally male activities, they still tended to be much more involved in sports traditionally regarded as female-appropriate, such as gymnastics, swimming and equestrian sports.[32]

Stereotyped Ideas Surrounding Women's Participation in Sports

At this time girls and women's football continued to face several problems, especially financial problems. According to a former female football player, the lion's share of finance went to men's football and only after that was female football considered.[33] This former player argued that sometimes the clubs questioned the maintenance of women's teams, allegedly due to a lack of financial resources, but they did not do the same in relation to men's teams. Apart from the financial problems of clubs, there was sometimes, as well, insufficient support from parents or other players' relatives. For example, as a former player and now coach put it: 'Sometimes there is a lack of support from the husband or boyfriend. They do not tell them not to play, but they do not show any interest in supporting.'[34]

The gradual growth of women's participation in sports traditionally considered as men's sports has not been straightforward. Some female Portuguese athletes, when they started practising such sports, were told that these sports were for tough people or they were called 'tomboys'. Their involvement in these sports was not taken as seriously as that of men. In spite of these difficulties, many of those girls and women did not give up and continued practising; thus challenging traditional ideas of femininity as well as those of masculinity.

Although more women were playing football their presence was, sometimes, criticised. After the revolution a climate of suspicion in relation to women's involvement in football continued to exist. Football continued to be viewed as a male activity and women's involvement in it continued to be regarded by many as unladylike. Moreover, due to the strong association traditionally made between football and masculinity, women who became involved in football have tended to be regarded as less feminine, and their femininity sometimes questioned. The femininity of women athletes involved in sports conventionally regarded as male-appropriate such as football, in addition to being compromised in the eyes of others, is also sometimes compromised in the eyes of the athletes themselves.[35] A former female football player who later became a coach in an interview with the magazine *Executiva*, said that when she started playing football, she 'was labelled tomboy just because she played football'.[36] Later, when she became a student and mentioned that she liked to play football, people looked at her with suspicion. Women who played football, or who were involved in sports traditionally considered as male-appropriate, faced the risk of being ostracised since they were involved in sports that did not conform to conventional ideas of femininity. The suspicion in relation to women's football can be seen through the words of, a former female football player who started playing in 1976.[37] Although she was highly supported by her family and friends, the club she represented, and which was a pioneer in terms of women's football, encouraged her parents to become more involved in order 'to see that it had a good ambience, ... that it was interesting and that it was an activity that could even help me in terms of self-confidence, discipline, etc'.[38] It appears that, because of the suspicion in relation to women's football, the club itself sought to reassure the parents that football did not constitute a threat to their daughters' femininity. She also mentioned that the club travelled frequently to different areas of the country to play matches. A lot of people attended those games because, as she said, it was something new. But she remembered hearing some less agreeable comments at the beginning of the games: 'Go home' or 'What is this? Women playing football? Go home. Sew the socks.'[39] But such comments were only at the beginning of the games because once the public had seen them playing they would change their comments to 'Eh, you wish you could play as well as they do'.[40] At the beginning there was, then, some suspicion in relation to their participation in football, but after watching them playing this distrust tended to diminish. Due to their technique, the quality of their games and their persistence, pre-conceived ideas tended to change:

> At first, the initial impact was sarcastic ... they went to the circus, not to a football field, they went to see the 'show' ... this is going to be fun! After, due to the quality of the game they became more sympathetic to women's football and found out that it was valid to be there to watch the game and not the girls.[41]

However, in 1999 it was still possible to find those who were critical of women's participation in football. For example the writer Alvaro Magalhães, in an article published in the newspaper *Jornal de Notícias*, said that the only 'real' football was male football.[42] Though formally acknowledging the necessity of promoting equality between women and men, he argued that this did not apply to football, since 'football is a specific and undoubtedly masculine activity'.[43] This comment illustrates the continuing hostility of some people to the fuller participation of women in sport.

Women's participation in those sports, in particular, has not been easy. Besides the derogatory comments they sometimes heard, they did not usually have the same financial support as male athletes, and clubs did not give the same attention and support to female and male athletes and teams. For example, in relation to women's involvement in football within some clubs, female teams have been disbanded. At the end of the twentieth century, a female football team, the national champions several times, was disbanded. In spite of their good results, the club decided to disband the female football team while keeping the male team, even though the men's team obtained less good results. The former female football player mentioned above (who was the coach of this team), mentioned that she went to several club assembly meetings in order to discuss this decision. In some of them she heard comments such as 'I am an associate of male football'.[44] These comments show the way some people understood football and the way they continue to regard women's involvement in football.

Women's Initiatives

Since 1974 women's participation in sport has not been a major topic of discussion. A limited number of studies have been carried out and a few articles published and there have been some master's and doctoral theses on this issue. Before 1996, almost no feminist-organised actions or initiatives were carried out to raise the issue of women and sport. Moreover, until 1998 there was not in Portugal any special action group to promote women's sports.

The first initiative carried out in Portugal to raise the issue of women and sport took place in 1991 in Coimbra, where the gynaecology service of the *Maternity Bissaya Barreto* organised the first symposium on women, health and sport.

In 1996 the *Movimento Democrático de Mulheres* (MDM – Women's Democratic Movement), with the support of the Lisbon City Council, organised the first conference on women and sport. This conference was the first step in Portugal towards implementing the Brighton Declaration.[45] For the first time women from all areas (current and former athletes, coaches, university teachers, women in leadership positions) got together to discuss the situation of women in sport. Because it was the first initiative of this kind, this conference received quite a lot of attention from the printed media. At the end of the conference it was decided that all efforts had to be developed in order to create a special action group on women's sport. In 1998, and following developments in other countries, the *Associação Portuguesa a Mulher e o Desporto* (Portuguese Association on Women and Sport) was established. The association has since promoted several initiatives. For example in March 1999, in order to celebrate the International Day of Women, the association organised games of five-a-side football among girls from Lisbon, and also promoted public debates. In 1999 it promoted another conference on women and sport. This was the first international conference organised by the association. In 2000 the association published a book on equity on physical education and sport in schools and in 2001 a special issue of the magazine *Ex-aequo* (edited by the *Associação Portuguesa da Estudos sobre as Mulheres* – Portuguese Association of Women's Studies) was devoted to women and sport.

It can be said that it was only in the 1990s that people became more aware of the issue of women and sport. Following broader social changes, particularly the greater awareness of women's issues in general, the 1990s marked the decade during which the issue of women and sport became more discussed, with more initiatives and more studies being carried out. This was, then, the period during which the issue of women and sport attained more visibility and more knowledge was produced.

In terms of governmental intervention, it can be said that little has been done to change the patterns of discrimination still visible in different areas of the sport figuration. In 1997 the First Global Plan for Equality of Opportunities included the first political statement on women and sport: 'To promote equality between women and men in sport politics.'[46]

Conclusion

Women's gradual and greater involvement in different types of sporting activities has not been a simple process. Apart from becoming involved in sporting activities that before 1974 were regarded as not suitable for women, women have also fought for changes in other areas of life, such as better education, equal opportunities to different types of jobs, changes in the civil code in order to bring changes in their social status and civil rights, and also for greater involvement in decision-making processes in general. Thus, since the revolution, women's involvement in sport has been a part of the larger movement for social transformation that has been taking place since 1974. Women have not been fighting simply for a greater participation in different areas of the sport figuration. They have been also involved in other struggles in order to change the position of women within society more generally. This growing women's involvement in sport, during the democratic period, can be considered as one part of a broader social process.

Notes on Contributor

Maria Claudia Pinheiro is a professor of sociology of education and sociology of leisure at the Maia Institute of Higher Education, and she is also a member of the Research Centre for Sports Sciences, Health and Human Development. Her research interests are gender and sport, health and sport, pain and injury in sport.

Notes

1. Lloyde-Jones, 'Portugal's History since 1974'.
2. Vieira, *Portugal Século XX*.
3. Barreto, *Mudança Social em Portugal*, 5.
4. Freire, *Second Order Elections and Electoral Cycles*.
5. Vieira, *Portugal Século XX*,
6. Some of the measures that were taken were: containment of public expenditures, reduction of investments, liberalisation and increase of prices, increase of some taxes, reduction of the real wages in the public secto.r See Leão, 'Das Transformações Revolucionárias à Dinâmica Europeia'.
7. Since the revolution the traditional model of the family has been changing. Family size began to reduce and to show an inverted triangle structure with the parents in the majority. Single-parent families have been increasing). See Rosa, 'O Envelhecimento da População Portuguesa'.
8. Partly due to this change the divorce rate has been increasing. For example, in 1971 there were registered 542 divorces. In 1985 this number rose to 8,988 and in 2000 to 19,302.
9. Many families were able to buy much more than in previous periods. They began to buy cars, houses, personal computers, telephones, cameras, radios and domestic appliances (washing machines, microwaves, vacuum cleaners, refrigerators and cookers in greater numbers.
10. Some of these women's groups were informed by a radical feminist perspective (MLM, IDM, GMP, GAMP, etc.), others by a Marxist/socialist perspective and others followed a more liberal feminist perspective (APME, IF, AMAP).
11. However, they have been continuously under-represented in these areas. For instance, in 1992, of the total number of people involved in the diplomatic service (405) 19.1% were women. As far as the magistracy is concerned, for this same year, of the total number of judicial magistrates (906) 29% were women. Though there was an increase in the number of women lawyers between 1976 and 1991, women continued to be under-represented in this area (1976: of the total number of lawyers – 2,969 – 7.8% were women; 1991: of the total number of lawyers – 9980 – 23.6% were women) See Comissão para a Igualdade e para os Direitos da Mulher, *Portugal*.
12. Act 392/79, 20 Sept., cited in Ferreira, 'Positive Action and Employment Segregation'. In percentage of the active population of each sex, in 1974 women's and men's unemployment rate was 3.5% and 2.5% respectively, in 1997 these percentages rose to 7.3% and 6% respectively. As far as employment rate is concerned, in percentage of the active population of each sex in 1974 women's and men's employment rate was 96.5% and 97.5% respectively and in 1997 it was 92,7% and 94% respectively. See Barreto and Preto, *A Situação Social em Portugal, 1960–1999: Desemprego (Sentido Restrito)*; Barreto and Preto, *A Situação Social em Portugal, 1960–1999: Desemprego Feminino (Sentido Restrito)*; Barreto and Preto, *A Situação Social em Portugal, 1960–1999: População Activa Feminina*; Barreto and Preto, *A Situação Social em Portugal, 1960–1999: População Empregada*.
13. Magalhães, *Movimento Feminista e Educação*.
14. The establishment of co-education did not prevent, however, the existence of a male social order that continues to persist in schools. The curriculum structures ensure that the activities carried out within schools and the relationships within schools reinforce a male social order. For a more detailed analysis of this issue see Magalhães, *Movimento Feminista e Educação*, ch. 4.
15. Viegas and Faria, *As Mulheres na Política;* Romão, 'European Database'.
16. González, 'Portuguese Report 2000 – Part 2'.
17. Decree-law no. 392/79 (20 Sept. 1979)

18. Datas e Factos na Evolução da Condição da Mulher em Portugal (2001), available at http://www.ongdm.org.pt/datas.htm; Romão, 'European Database'.
19. For example, according to data from the University of Limoges and the World Bank, in 1996 the financial support in Germany, Great Britain, Italy and Spain was of 3,463.4, 1,540.5, 1,463.4 and 7,666 million dollars respectively, while in Portugal this support was 244.3 million dollars: cited in Ferrari et al., 'Sport and the Welfare Policy in Italy'.
20. The magazine *Mulheres* began publication in May 1978 and from July onwards it began dedicating an entire page to women's sports. In those pages were presented the results of women's competitions, the achievements of some Portuguese and foreign athletes were also presented and given as examples to be followed. The examples from abroad focused mainly on athletes from Cuba and East Germany, thus showing the tendency to follow the programmes and type of sport practised in other countries and the sympathy that those in the sports sphere during the first years after the revolution had for countries such as Cuba, East Germany or even the then Soviet Union.
21. Barroco, 'A Mulher, as Actividades Físicas e o Desporto', 22.
22. Ibid, 30.
23. Ibid, 30, 31.
24. Instituto Nacional de Estatística, *Estatísticas da Cultura, Desporto e Recreio*; Ministério da Educação Nacional, *Carta Gimnodesportiva de Portugal Metropolitano (1965/66)*; Ministério da Educação Nacional, *Carta Gimnodesportiva (1968/69)*; Direcção Geral dos Desportos, *Elementos Estatísticos;* Direcção Geral dos Desportos, *Desporto Federado*; Estatísticas do Desporto Federado, cited in Almeida, 'A Mulher e o Desporto'.
25. Marivoet, *Hábitos Desportivos da População Portuguesa*; Marivoet, 'O Género e o Desporto'.
26. Hargreaves, *Sporting Females*, 148.
27. Greendorfer, cited in Kay, 'Sport and Gender'.
28. Hargreaves, *Sporting Females*, 27.
29. Federação Portuguesa de Rugby, *Pequeno Historial do Rugby Feminino*.
30. A. Silva, personal communication, 2005.
31. 'Os Primórdios do Futebol Feminino', available online at http://www.terravista.pt/guincho/1846/Primordiosfutfeminino.htm; Silva, 'Caracterização do Futebol Feminino Português'.
32. Almeida, 'A Mulher e o Desporto'; Direcção Geral dos Desportos, *A mulher e o desporto*.
33. Leirianet – 'Senhoras de Monte Real dão Contas no Futebol', available at http://www.leirianet.pt/leiria/noticia.php3?ind-3800.
34. Ibid, paragraph 7
35. Dunning, *Sport Matters*.
36. Cited in Miranda, 'Elas vão à Bola'.
37. A. Silva, personal communication, 2005. This female football player started playing football in 1976 at the age of 12. She represented several clubs and at the present time she is a women's football coach. She played several times for the national team.
38. Ibid.
39. Ibid.
40. Ibid.
41. Ibid.
42. A. Magalhães, 'Menina não Entra', *Jornal de Notícias*, 19 Nov. 1999, 86.
43. Ibid.
44. A. Silva, personal communication, 2005.
45. The Brighton Declaration emerged from the first international conference on women and sport that took place in Brighton in 1994. The delegates from all the countries representing governmental and non-governmental organisations that participated in such conference endorsed the declaration. This declaration 'provides the principles that should guide action intended to increase the involvement of women in sport at all levels and in all functions and roles'. The main purpose of this declaration 'is to develop a sporting culture that enables and values the full involvement of women in every aspect of sport'. See The Brighton Declaration on Women and Sport, available at http://www.iwg-gti.org/pdfs/brighton_e.pdf, paras. 1 and 2.

46. Resolução do Conselho de Ministros, 'Plano Global para a Igualdade de Oportunidades'.

References

Almeida, C.M. 'A Mulher e o Desporto'. *Desporto 9*, no. 12 (1999): 4–13.

Almeida, C.M. 'A Mulher nas Instâncias Federativas do Desporto'. *Desporto 3* (2000): 6–11.

Barreto, A. *Mudança Social em Portugal, 1960/2000*. Lisbon: University of Lisbon, Instituto de Ciências Sociais, 2002. Available at http://www.ics.ul.pt/publicacoes/workingpapers/wp2002/WP6-2002.pdf.

Barreto, A., and Preto, C.V. *A Situação Social em Portugal, 1960–1999: Desemprego (Sentido Restrito)*. Lisbon: University of Lisbon, Instituto de Ciências Sociais, 1999. Available at http://www.ics.ul.pt/investiga/projectos/sitsoc/cap/0410.htm

Barreto, A. and Preto, C.V. *A Situação Social em Portugal, 1960–1999: Desemprego Feminino (Sentido Restrito)*. Lisbon: University of Lisbon, Instituto de Ciências Sociais, 1999. Available at http://www.ics.ul.pt/investiga/projectos/sitsoc/cap/0411.htm

Barreto, A. and Preto, C.V. A Situação Social em Portugal, 1960–1999: População Activa Feminina. Lisbon: University of Lisbon, Instituto de Ciências Sociais, 1999. Available at http://www.ics.ul.pt/investiga/projectos/sitsoc/cap/0401.htm

Barreto, A. and Preto, C.V. *A Situação Social em Portugal, 1960–1999: População Empregada – Taxa de Emprego.*Lisbon: University of Lisbon, Instituto de Ciências Sociais, 1999. Available at http://www.ics.ul.pt/investiga/projectos/sitsoc/cap/0402.htm

Barroco, M. 'A Mulher, as Actividades Físicas e o Desporto'. *Cadernos de Medicina Desportiva* 4 (1978).

Comissão para a Igualdade e para os Direitos da Mulher. *Portugal – Situação das Mulheres*, 10th edn. Lisbon: Ministério do Emprego e da Segurança Social, 1992.

Direcção Geral dos Desportos. *Elementos Estatísticos*. Lisbon: Gabinete de Estatística, 1975.

Direcção Geral dos Desportos. *Desporto Federado*. Lisbon: Gabinete de Estatística, 1979.

Direcção Geral dos Desportos. *A Mulher e o Desporto*. Lisbon: Direcção Geral dos Desportos, 1980.

Dunning, E. *Sport Matters*. London and New York: Routledge, 1999.

Federação Portuguesa de Rugby, *Pequeno Historial do Rugby Feminino*. Available at http://www.fpr.pt/FPR_Textos_RugbyFeminino.asp [Accessed December 1, 2002].

Ferrari, F., N.Porro and P. Russo. 'Sport and the Welfare Policy in Italy', in *Sport and Welfare Policies – Six European Case Studies*, ed. K. Heinemann (Series Club of Cologne, vol. 3). Germany: Hofmann, 2003, 253–94.

Ferreira, V. 'Positive Action and Employment Segregation', in *Shifting Bonds, Shifting Bounds – Women, Mobility and Citizenship in Europe*, ed. V. Ferreira, T. Tavares and S. Portugal. Oeiras: Celta Editora, 1998, 271–80.

Freire, A. *Second Order Elections and Electoral Cycles in Democratic Portugal, 1975–2002*. Lisbon: University of Lisbon, Instituto de Ciências Sociais, 2003. Available at http://www.ics.ul.pt/publicacoes/workingpapers/wp2003/WP3-2003.pdf

González, M.P. 'Portuguese Report 2000 – Part 2. Gender Impact Assessment and the Employment Strategy. (2000)'. Available at http://www.mbs.ac.uk/research/centres/euroepan-employment/projects/gender-social-inclusion/documents/GIA_Portugal.pdf

Hargreaves, J. *Sporting Females – Critical Issues in the History and Sociology of Women's Sports*. London and New York: Routledge, 1994.

Instituto Nacional de Estatística. *Estatísticas da Cultura, Desporto e Recreio*. Lisbon: Instituto Nacional de Estatística, 1988.

Kay, T. 'Sport and Gender', in *Sport and Society*, ed. B. Houlihan. London: Sage Publications, 2003, 89–104.

Leão, E.R. 'Das Transformações Revolucionárias à Dinâmica Europeia', in *Portugal Contemporâneo*, vol. 3, ed. A. Reis. Lisbon: Seleções do Reader's Digest, S.A., Publicações, 1996, 557–608.

Lloyde-Jones, S. 'Portugal's History since 1974'. *CPHRC, Working Papers,* Series 2, no. 2 (2001). Available at http://www.cphrc.org.uk/essays/portugal-since-1974.pdf

Magalhães, M.J. *Movimento Feminista e Educação – Portugal Décadas de 70 e 80*. Oeiras: Celta Editora, 1998.

Marivoet, S. *Hábitos Desportivos da População Portuguesa*. Lisbon: Ministério da Juventude e do Desporto, Instituto Nacional de Formação e Estudos do Desporto, 2001.

Marivoet, S. 'O Género e o Desporto: Hábitos e Tendências'. *Ex-Aequo* 4 (2001): 115–32.

Ministério da Educação Nacional. *Carta Gimnodesportiva de Portugal Metropolitano (1965/66)*, Ano V, 17. Lisbon: Direcção Geral de Educação Física, Desportos e Saúde Escolar, 1969.

Ministério da Educação Nacional. *Carta gimnodesportiva (1968/69)*, VII, 2, no. 26. Lisbon: Direcção Geral de Educação Física, Desportos e Saúde Escolar, 1971.

Miranda, M. 'Elas vão à Bola'. *Executiva* 5. (2000). Available at http://www.centroatl.pt/edigest/edsuplem/edicoesup/abr2000/exe5vp-lazer.htm

Resolução do Conselho de Ministros. 'Plano Global para a Igualdade de Oportunidades' Diário da Républica – I série B no 70 (24 March): 1324–1326.

Romão, I. 'European Database – Women in Decision Making'. Report from Portugal by our Transnational Partner. Available at http://www.db-decision.de/Core/Portugal.htm.

Rosa, M.J.V. 'O Envelhecimento da População Portuguesa'. *Cadernos do Publico*, no. 3. Lisbon: Instituto de Ciências Sociais e Publico, 1996.

Silva, A. 'Caracterização do Futebol Feminino Português Enquadrado num Contexto Internacional'. *Proceedings of the Conference A Mulher e o Desporto*. Lisbon: Câmara Municipal de Lisboa – Pelouro do Desporto, 1998.

Viegas, J.M.L. and S. Faria. *As Mulheres na Política*. Oeiras: Celta Editora, 2001.

Vieira, J. *Século XX: Crónica em Imagens*, vols. 6–9. Lisbon: Círculo de Leitores, 1999–2001.

Sport as a Cultural Model: Italian Women's Soccer over the Past Ten Years

Ivana Matteucci

'Carlo Bo' University of Urbino, Italy

The paper presents sport as an important cultural model in modern Italian society, fully integrated into the logic of consumption, communication and spectacularisation. In this sense, sport emerges as a field in the Bourdieuan sense, or rather, 'a socially defined independent sphere with strong frameworks of sense and meaning'. Sport creates social and cultural capital, often objectified in the result (record), and it also reproduces and reinforces social distinction within each particular sport. An example is provided by the case study presented here on Italian women's soccer over the past ten years. The research, carried out on a representative sample of one hundred female players, shows that stereotypes and social prejudices associated with gender dominate the game. At the same time, it can be observed that the dynamics of communication and consumption, closely related to one another in the sphere of sports over the last ten years, reproduce and subsequently reinforce the separation of men and women in social relationships also found in society. For a long time the history of sport was characterised by a clear male predominance, and even today sports are marked by deep gender differences: men participate more in sports in general and at the same time male sports are more relevant economically and culturally.

Introduction: A New Cultural Model for Sport

As a product of modernity, sport has developed in such a way that it can now be considered a 'field' in the Bourdieuan sense, or in other words, 'a socially defined independent sphere with strong frameworks of sense and meaning'.[1] This sphere is regulated by a sense of time, parallel to that which marks ordinary social processes, a set of values and norms, which govern the world of sports just as they govern everyday life, as well as a set of symbolically and materially distinct practices. This change in the cultural model goes hand in hand with a new philosophy of free time[2] and corresponds to a whole range of needs that come to the fore with the emergence of different lifestyles. Lifestyles, viewed from a Bourdieuan perspective as different systems of attitudes, depend on the individual's position, his or her social capital and tastes.[3] Hence sport becomes a cultural object as well as an object of consumption of modernity.

Speaking of cultural capital, the economic development of modern sport can be divided into five stages, each of which marks a break from sport's original playful dimension while conferring a sense of cultural industry to the phenomenon.

The first stage of development can be defined as *spectacularisation* of sport,[4] i.e. the privileging of the characteristics of a phenomenon associated with the evocation of collective emotions. The idea of holding competitions within special areas (save for a few exceptions) was born out of the inclination to make pre-sport games into a show and the need for modern rational organisation. Over time such areas were equipped and access was progressively reserved to a paying public. The commercialisation of the relationship between the public and the sporting event led to the steady improvement in the quality of the competition, pushing it towards higher and higher technical, athletic and organisational levels. These changes regard three classes of actors: the athletes and coaches; the financial backers and organisers; and the audience.

The second stage in the growth of the cultural industry of modern sport was made possible by the effect of the mass media and its popular function. The *mediatisation* of sport[5] made it into a kind of folk-tale aimed at an audience, which was not limited to those attending the event in person. Furthermore, the advent of the electronic media (making live narration of the contest possible) thoroughly redefined the experience of the 'consumption' of the competition on the part of the spectator. Such an experience was differentiated into direct and mediated experience, with the latter becoming dominant, taking on the status of socially shared experience. Hence the second stage also involves actors in the mass media.

The third stage of development is marked by the recognition of the vast potential of the world of sport as an advertising vector and its subsequent *commercialisation*. The advent of advertising, favoured by the capillary diffusion of the mass media, led not only to the search for more effective communication channels to spread a company's message, but also to the search for favourable contexts for the diffusion of the message itself. Thanks to its symbolic emotional content, the world of sport became a privileged area for advertising campaigns, and the investments were not limited to the technical competitive dimension, but also targeted the single actors who were asked to lend their image to advertising campaigns. In short, the new emerging actor in this stage was industry itself.

The fourth stage began with the explosion of televised sport or the *televisation* of sport. As occurred in the field advertising, in the medium of television there was a transformative period in which sport became a strategic resource for the commercial development of television. The role of sport became even more important with the spread of pay-per-view TV, which, as a new medium that sets out to conquer the market already occupied by traditional TV, is able convince its viewer-clients to purchase programme packages only if they offer particularly attractive exclusive contents. The most important strategic elements in these packages are premiere films and live sporting events. In this stage, as in the one that follows, new actors did not come onto the scene, but there was a change in the equilibrium among already existing actors, as well as a change in their performance logic. The entrepreneurial organisers and a part of the media system made a mutually beneficial pact exchanging managerial and organisational resources. In some cases, the television networks themselves also filled the role of organisers.

The fifth and final stage encompasses the process of transformation of the sports fan into customer, or *customerisation*. This process occurred as resources were developed and optimised in search of new areas for commercial expansion. Within this new framework, the competitive dimension of sport is just one aspect of the business, and the relationship between the sports sphere and its audience is thoroughly commercialised. Moving beyond the phase in which this relationship is mainly based on passion and emotional engagement, the sporting audience is now viewed as a vast pool of potential customers. While in the previously described stages the commercial relationship between the audience and the sports sphere was based almost exclusively on paid access to the sporting event (ticket office sales, pay-per-view television etc.), in this new stage the search for customers spills over into other areas. The passion of the sporting audience becomes the target of marketing operations connected with the sale of various items as a way of fostering fan loyalty (credit cards bearing the team logo, invitations to take part in financing operations), not to mention the offer of a series of paid services (association and recreational activities). Hence this phase marks a sort of genetic mutation in the relationship between the sports fan and the object of his or her passion. The latter goes from being immediate to mediated, or rather filtered, by a commercial and cultural logic.

Sport and Gender: Differences between Men and Women regarding Participation and Importance

Social research on sport has been strongly influenced by idealistic concepts that tend to emphasise the gratuitous and playful nature of sporting activities. Hence these activities have been considered as a sphere of action in which the social actor enters freely, choosing any kind of activity and expressing himself/herself and his/her own desires and independence. The differences between male and female involvement in sport have been attributed to fundamental natural differences between men and women: the former seen as strong, competitive and active, the latter weak, submissive and passive. In other words, men have been viewed as athletic and women as sedentary. Thus if the view that sport is naturally male territory, given men's physical characteristics, is still widely held in our societies, biologic determinism has also long been dominant in the academic study of sport, and the ideology of the radical difference between the sexes was, and still is, borne out by sports medicine. Simply attributed to natural biological differences, different levels of male and female involvement in sport were long believed not to warrant thorough sociological analysis.

Even with the emergence of a whole series of critical approaches to sport showing how the consolidation of sport as a specific and relatively separate sphere of action coincides with the advance of modernity and the bureaucratisation of behaviours that were once spontaneous and playful,[6] little attention has been paid to the divisions and internal boundaries within sport itself, especially those that separate women and men. Despite their lack of focus on gender distinctions, these approaches nonetheless made it possible to show that sport has both an integrative function, (i.e. the reproduction of the social order) and a dialectic function, (i.e. the reproduction of conflicts, including latent conflicts between groups and categories of people and the symbolic boundaries that support those conflicts). From this standpoint, the consolidation of modern sport, the growing mediation of sport by forms of commercialisation, is linked to the need to include the lower classes in the capitalistic system, offering them amusements that reproduce and legitimise values such as competition and individualism.

However, in line with the general evolution of social thought, there has also been a change in the way we view sport, with our attention for boundaries and social distinctions progressively shifting away from social class towards more obvious differences that had been perceived as natural, such as gender. Hence today in the field of sports sociology, gender differences are considered among the power relationships that innervate sports and make them a sphere of social conflict.[7]

In sports studies there is a growing effort to show how 'natural differences' between men and women are actually ingrained in bodies through the practice of sports as well. This is accomplished, for example, by adopting different rules for female versions of more traditionally male sports and developing typically female sporting activities which aim to emphasise and reproduce physical characteristics more traditionally associated with femininity, such as grace, lightness, etc. Hence from works that dealt with the practice of sports in general, unaware that they were actually only considering male experiences, we moved on to works that recognised the role of women in sport and dedicated specific space to them, and to works that, often concentrating only on female sports, recognise that it is necessary to go beyond differences between men and women, and to deal instead with the power relationships that structure the very definitions of masculinity and femininity.[8]

Emphasising the constructed and relational nature of gender, even in sport, obviously does not mean that subjects can freely, effortlessly and indifferently act as a woman one moment and as a man the next, or that women competing against men in masculine activities would have the same chances of success.[9] It is not easy to violate cultural gender boundaries and, in particular, to challenge the hegemonic image of femininity and masculinity. In fact, the femininity of female athletes who pose the greatest challenge to symbolic gender boundaries by engaging in typically male activities requiring physiques that are particularly muscular, large, strong etc. – shot-putters for example – are often called into question. By the same token, male versions of sports such as synchronised swimming, which call for characteristics – grace and lightness – in antithesis to traditionally masculine qualities, have a hard time gaining popularity. However, in this case as well, we are dealing with distinctions that are as solid and rooted as they are social and conventional, linked to the specific history of sport in each country. This is well illustrated, for example, by the fact that a sport such as women's soccer can be very popular in one country, the USA, where there is a very limited men's soccer tradition, while in Europe, the cradle of the men's game where soccer and images of masculinity are closely associated, women's soccer struggles.

Hence today there is a strong awareness of the fact that sport spreads and reinforces the orientations and categories that culturally and practically define what is appropriate and natural for men and women. The social organisation of sport provides ideologies and structures through its images, a mechanism for maintaining and legitimising a particular organisation of the relationship between the sexes found in society tending to reinforce gender-based social stratification.[10] If for young men sports still constitute an almost obligatory rite of passage, epitomising idealised male characteristics such as competitiveness, aggressiveness and loyalty, traditionally, even after the Second World War, physical activity and sport were considered to be inimical to femininity. In the eyes of most Western populations, female athletes were long seen as a deviation from femininity, an abnormal masculinisation, so much so that even the correctness of the their sexual orientation was called into question. In fact, the negative stereotype of women athletes involves their sexuality, and the resulting homophobia appears to limit the possibilities of closeness among women athletes. The idea that doing sport can ruin and masculinise a woman's appearance, and therefore damage the proper relationship between the sexes, especially in the sexual sphere – promoting homosexual tendencies – certainly emerged as one of the main obstacles to the spread of women's sport. Indeed many female athletes must still often deal with such stereotypes.

However, today on the whole femininity is seen less and less as antithetical and alternative to physical and sporting activity. In part, this is due to the evolution of the sports universe. Undoubtedly, within the sports sphere, in the many organisations and clubs that organise competitive and non-competitive activities, sexism still lurks. Even in the United States, where so much has been done to promote female sports, still in the mid-1970s a famous soccer coach unabashedly dismissed the female sport as a harbinger of homosexuality to be resolutely opposed.[11] In the twentieth century, and above all after the Second World War, there was a growing 'feminisation' of sports, which entailed a growing female participation, a steady reduction in the sports reserved only for men, the development of women's sports on the Olympic level and so on. Nevertheless, there are very few sporting activities, such as sailing, in which there are not distinct gender categories, and male athletes and male sports are still at the top of the hierarchies that structure the sports universe. Even today, sport is an arena in which differences between men and women are reproduced and, often, emphasised. Indeed, every aspect of sporting activity, from its internal organisation to its medical- physiological aspects and representation in the media – is more and more frequently interpreted from a perspective that highlights gender differences.

Italian Women's Soccer: A Short History

Italian female soccer has a long history. The uphill struggle of the female soccer associations in the Italian sports scene was, until 1986, conducted outside the long-established FIGC (Italian Soccer Federation), but by no means was it lacking identity or ferment. The first reports of women's soccer in Italy date back to 1930 when the *Gruppo Femminile Calcistico* (Female Soccer Group) was founded at 12 Stoppani Street in Milan. Reports from the period describe the female players coming onto the field in skirts, unlike their German and English counterparts who had already been playing the sport since 1910.[12]

The early history of Italian women's soccer is rather sketchy, but we can retrace some of its fundamental stages. In 1946 two female teams, the Triestina and the Girls of San Giusto were founded in Trieste. The *Associazione Italiana Calcio Femminile* (AICF – Italian Association of Women's Soccer) was founded in Naples in 1950 and several clubs joined the association. In 1959 there was a game between Rome and Naples held in Messina, and this was the last event ever sponsored by the AICF. In 1965 a game between Bologna and Inter was held in Milan's Arena and the participating female athletes, who were all from Milan, ranged in age from 14 to 17. The coach of both eams, not to mention the game's referee, was Valeria Rocchi. In this same year the Genoa and Giovani Viola clubs were founded.

The founding of the *Federazione Italiana Calcio Femminile* (FICF – the Italian Women's Soccer Federation) in 1968 is commonly considered the real starting-point for women's soccer in Italy. The soccer season ran from May to September with two divisions (North and South), each with five teams. The first championship team was crowned in a final match between Genoa and Rome held in Pisa, which saw the

Ligurian team emerge victorious. Everything appeared to be proceeding well, but on 31 January 1970 in Rome, ten clubs abandoned the FICF and signed on with the *Federazione Femminile Gioco Calcio* (FFIGC – the Italian Female Soccer Sports Federation) under the presidency of Aleandro Franchi. For the first time there was talk of an A League with one division of 14 teams and a B League with four divisions and a total of 24 teams. Guidelines were established for league membership and the issue of compulsory medical visits was considered for the first time.

Hence there were two federations, the FICF and the FFIGC, organising two Italian leagues, with two league champions (Gomma Milano in the FFIGC and Real Torino in the FICF). The situation remained unchanged until 1972 when, thanks to the work of the Florentine attorney Giovanni Trabucco, the two separate leagues merged, forming the *Federazione Femminile Italia Unita Gioco Calcio* (FFIUGC – United Women's Soccer Sports Federation). Attorney Trabucco was elected president of the federation and remained at the helm until it entered the FIGC in 1986. The federation started out with 45 teams divided into four divisions.

Under Trabucco the league gained momentum. It was structured along the lines of the FIGC, with all the women's clubs viewed with a mix of reverential awe and curiosity. Over the years the federation developed its organisational structure with a president and two vice presidents, who also served as presidents of the national and regional leagues and federation advisers. National A and B leagues, inter-regional C leagues and regional D leagues were set up, as well as provincial activities and tournaments for young athletes.

The *Associazione Italiana Calciatrici* (the Italian Female Soccer Players' Association) was formed in Bergamo in 1980. The president of the association, Annamaria Cavarzan, became a member of the federation board, giving a voice to the needs of the female athletes. This association continued its activities until it broke up in 1989. In 1983 the female FIGC was recognised as part of the Italian National Olympic Committee (also receiving financial support from the committee) and began setting up regional and provincial committees responsible for promotional activities.

During these years, a group of referees worked within the women's FIGC. It was headed by the international referee Pieroni from Rome who enlisted the help of referees who had left the men's FIGC. In addition, training courses leading to a referee's licence valid in the female branch of the sport were organised. The soccer season ran from January to December with a 20-day break in August. The idea was to fill the summer gap left open by the male sport. The league, which lasted until 1985, split its calendar into two seasons: the first ran from January to August and the second from September to June in order to adapt to the FIGC.

The female branch of the sport was then absorbed into the framework of the LND (*Lega Nazionale Dilettanti* – National League of Amateurs) with the formation of the Female Soccer Committee. Starting in 1987, various committees for the study of ad hoc guidelines for the development of women's soccer were formed and in 1989 the first president, Maurizio Foroni, was nominated. Foroni moved forward following the guidelines set out by the committees into which the president of the women's soccer association was co-opted. Efforts were also made to give incentives to the sport on a regional level.

In 1991 Evelina Codacci Pisanelli was appointed president. She divided the national sport into an A League with 14 teams and a B League with two divisions, each containing 12 teams. She also began involving regional presidents, a policy which has been continued by the current president Natalina Ceraso Levati. While the clubs awaited the opportunity to elect their president directly, Marina Sbardella was appointed to fill the position of deputy president and organised the first youth tournament on regional and national levels for the 12 to 17 age group. In addition, she expanded the A League to 16 teams and divided the B League into three ten team divisions.[13]

On 1 May 1997, for the first time since entering the FIGC, the clubs in the national A and B leagues elected the president of the Female Soccer Division in the person of Natalina Ceraso Levati, in accordance with the new guidelines that called for a president's council composed of six members (three committee presidents and advisers chosen by the division president).[14]

The national female sport was thus organised: an A League with 16 teams in a single division, a B League with 14 teams divided into three divisions. The Super Cup was introduced, pitting the winner of the Italian Cup against the champion of the A League. In 1998, as it continued to grow and develop, the B League was divided into four 12-team divisions with play-offs to establish three winners to be promoted to the A League. The under-14 tournament was also established for regional representatives, with athletes taking part in junior, debutant and youth soccer tournaments to increase the number of girls practising the sport. Furthermore, a number of training camps were set up under the direction of the national team coaches in order to scout out athletes for the under-18 women's national team. In 1999 an eight-player soccer tournament was established in collaboration with the youth school division in order to encourage young female players. With growing interest in the sport and swelling memberships (9,667 registered members) and clubs (396), the female national team represented the tip of an iceberg and participation in the World Cup in the USA served as a platform to promote the sport. In the 2001/2 season the number of associations grew to 401, with almost 500 teams that compete in provincial, regional and national leagues.

But how has the situation evolved in the last few years? Table 1 displays the statistics provided by the *Lega Nazionale Dilettante* (National Amateur League) on 30 June 2007. Moreover, taking into consideration amateur and recreational soccer, the total number of registered members totals around 1,100,000.

Unfortunately, the statistics do not tell us the number of registered female players. However, a rough estimate can be made. Considering that among the 728 female teams there is a percentage of 5 vs 5 soccer (at least 15%), it can be hypothesised that:

n. 100 five-player teams x 10 players = 1,000

n. 628 11-player teams x 18 players = 11,304

We can therefore estimate that there are roughly 12,000 registered female players throughout Italy. Table 2 shows a regional breakdown of registered female players:

Table 1. Football club membership as of 30 June 2007.

	11-a-side men	5-a-side men	women	youth section	total
Associations	9876	1664	170	2661	14371
Teams	13061	3593	728	41422	58804
Members	470485			374427	844912

Source: *Lega Nazionale Dilettanti* (National Amateur League)

Table 2. Registered female football players in Italy, by region, 2007.

	Region	Associations	Teams	Female players
1.	Abruzzo	10	21	452
2.	Basilicata	15	23	341
3.	Calabria	16	31	366
4.	Campania	18	31	409
5.	Emilia Romagna	41	68	1275
6.	Friuli Venezia Giulia	14	28	302
7.	Latium	16	32	296
8.	Liguria	14	26	570
9.	Lombardy	57	88	1550
10.	Marche	25	24	380
11.	Molise	8	21	480
12.	Piedmont and Valle d'Aosta	29	71	1295
13.	Apulia	18	20	470
14.	Sardinia	29	47	1065
15.	Sicily	14	20	398
16.	Tuscany	28	48	674
17.	Trentino Alto Adige	18	18	398
18.	Umbria	14	19	205
19.	Veneto	47	92	992

Source: Lega Nazionale Dilettanti.

We must be aware that men and women experience sports in completely different ways. Indeed, some sports are decidedly female while in other sports men consistently outnumber women.

Table 3 contains data from 2000 and 2006 showing the number of practitioners of each sport broken down by gender.[15]

Gymnastics, aerobics and fitness class are more popular among women (39.5% compared to 15.3% of men) as well as swimming (26.6% compared to 16.9%), ballet and other forms of dance (13.5% to 1.4%) and volleyball (8% compared to 3%).

In all other sports, male practitioners consistently outnumber their female counterparts. Some sports are particularly male-dominated: among such sports is soccer (practised by 39.7% of men compared to a meagre 1.5% of women), cycling (9.6% compared to 2.9%) tennis (7.7% compared to 3.7%), hunting and fishing (practised exclusively by men).

Not much appears to have changed between 2000 and 2006: there is a slight increase in the number of males participating in gymnastics (13.5% compared to 15.3%) and women practising athletics (7.3% compared to 10.8%) and cycling (6.3% compared to 8.1%). We can observe that there is a small decrease in the number of men who play soccer (from 41% to 39.7%) with some increase in the number of men who play indoor soccer (from 7.3% to 12.4%). There is a slight increase in the percentage of women who play both soccer (from 1.4% to 1.5%) and indoor soccer (from 0.3% to 0.6%).

Women's Soccer: A Survey

The following questionnaire, which was distributed among a representative sample of 100 women who play soccer regularly, tries to show what obstacles block the development of the female sport and what motivates female athletes to continue

Table 3. Sport practitioners in Italy, 2000 and 2006.

Type of sport	Men Data in thousands		Men Out of 100 practitioners (a)		Women Data in thousands		Women Out of 100 practitioners (a)	
	2000	2006	2000	2006	2000	2006	2000	2006
Soccer, indoor soccer	4.197	4049	41.0	39.7	94	103	1.4	1.5
of which indoor soccer	747	1266	7.3	12.4	21	42	0.3	0.6
Gymnastics, aerobics, fitness	1.385	1561	13.5	15.3	2.866	2759	44.2	39.5
Water and underwater sports	1.718	1831	16.8	18	1.959	2083	30.2	29.9
of which swimming	1.606	1720	15.7	16.9	1.842	1856	28.4	26.6
Winter sports, on ice and other mountain sports	1.447	1157	14.1	11.4	839	780	12.9	11.2
of which downhill skiing	1.155	919	11.3	9	662	626	10.2	9
Bicycle	1.309	1445	12.8	14.2	407	566	6.3	8.1
of which cycling	1.042	979	10.2	9.6	230	202	3.6	2.9
Athletics, running, jogging	1.021	1196	10	11.7	475	751	7.3	10.8
of which Athletics	659	840	6.4	8.2	320	498	4.9	7.1
Racket sports	1.037	833	10.1	8.2	310	276	4.8	4
of which tennis	997	785	9.7	7.7	300	258	4.6	3.7
Ballet and other forms of dance	65	140	0.6	1.4	438	943	6.8	13.5
Volleyball	339	303	3.3	3	649	560	10	8
Martial arts, boxing	488	482	4.8	4.7	125	143	1.9	2.1
Basketball	491	512	4.8	5	114	99	1.8	1.4
Hunting	354	260	3.5	2.5	..	..	..	..
Fishing	314	324	3.1	3.2	9	4	0.1	0.1
Bocce, bowling, billiards	211	157	2.1	1.5	11	19	0.2	0.3
Boating	164	122	1.6	1.2	27	33	0.4	0.5
Other ball sports	140	140	1.4	1.4	41	47	0.6	0.7
Other sports	422	439	4.1	4.3	272	259	4.2	3.7

Source: ISTAT, Aspetti della vita quotidiana

playing the game. The socio-cultural situation, which is the backdrop for the poor diffusion of the women's game, was related to the almost *primordial* level of communication of this reality and the limited media coverage it receives. The sample group was selected by random sampling from a pool of all female players from the national B league. The questionnaire was distributed and collected personally by the author of the research who was able to verify that all the questionnaires were fully completed.

Questionnaire

(1) How long have you played soccer competitively?

(2) How long has your team been in existence?

(3) Are you compensated for your play?
  Yes   No

(4) If you are, what sort of compensation do you receive?
  Reimbursement for expenses
  Game bonuses
  Salary

(5) Does your team have a website?
  Yes   No

(6) If it does, who manages the website?

(7) Does your team have sponsors?
  Yes   No

(8) If it does, how many?

(9) If it does, who are they?

(10) Does your team sponsor any commercial products?
  Yes   No

(11) If it does, which ones?

(12) Do you watch television sports programmes on Saturday and Sunday?
  Yes   No

(13) If you do, which ones?

(14) Are you a pay-per-view TV subscriber?

(15) Have you ever been a guest on a nationally broadcast television sports program?
  Yes   No

(16) If you have, how many times?

(17) Do you think national television channels dedicate time to women's soccer?
  None
  Little
  Enough
  A lot

(18) Do you read national daily sports newspapers?

(19) If you do, which ones?

(20) Do you think the national daily sports newspapers dedicate space to women's soccer?
  None
  Little
  Enough
  A lot

(21) What motivates you to play soccer? (you can mark more than one answer)

Passion   Enjoyment
Health and well being   Competition
Economic compensation   Diversion
Personal pleasure   Group experience
Other (specify)

(22) Have you ever been discouraged from playing soccer?

Yes   No

(23) If you have, by whom?

(24) If you have, for what reasons?

(25) What goals would you like to reach in women's soccer? (you can mark more than one answer)

Fame   Success   Money   Profit
Records   Athletic achievements   Good health
Other (specify)

By processing the answers to the questionnaire and analysing the graphically represented results, one can draw many interesting conclusions that help us understand the underlying gender logic that governs society and sports, some sports in particular.

Q.1. Above all, it should be noted that women soccer players who completed the questionnaire have been involved in the sport for varying lengths of time. Most have been involved in the sport from five to 10 years, while cases of very long involvement – up to 26 years – are more rare, as are cases of recent involvement – minimum of two years (Figure 1). In any case, we can observe that on average, respondents have been involved in the sport for a significant length of time: 2% of the women have been involved in the sport for 2 years; 3% for 3 years; 10% for 5 years; 18% for 6 years; 15% for 8 years; 8% for 9 years; 16% for 10 years; 5% for 12 years; 6% for 14 years; 4% for 15 years; 5% for 18; 5% for 22 years; 3% for 26 years.

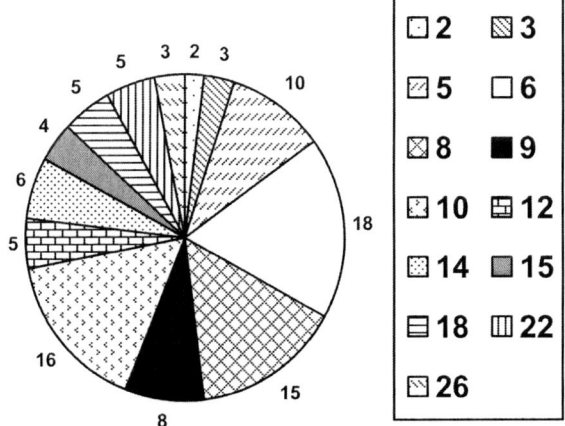

Figure 1.   Responses to Q.1 – How long have you played soccer?

Q.2. We note a marked lack of knowledge of the world of soccer in which they are directly involved: 30% of the women do not know the history of their own team, including how long it has existed. Other answers were: 'my team has been in existence for 40 years' (17%) or 'for 35 years' (18%) – see Figure 2.

Qs 3 and 4. Some female players (43%) receive compensation that is defined as occasional (reimbursement of personal expenses, game bonuses) – see Figures 3 and 4) This explains why the sport is rarely played professionally.

Qs 5 and 6. Regarding publicity, it was found that the majority of women's teams have a website, but it is managed by a one of the players on the team or by one of the

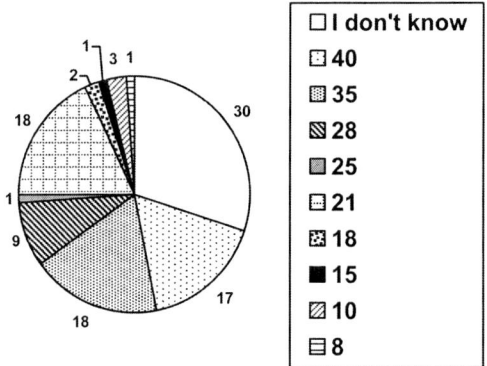

Figure 2.   Responses to Q.2 – How long has your team been in existence?

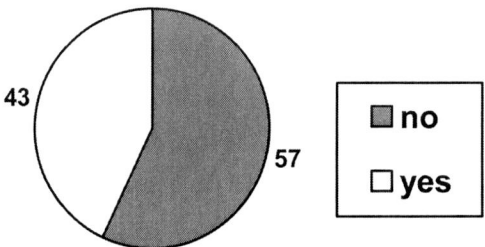

Figure 3.   Responses to Q.3 – Do you receive compensation for your play?

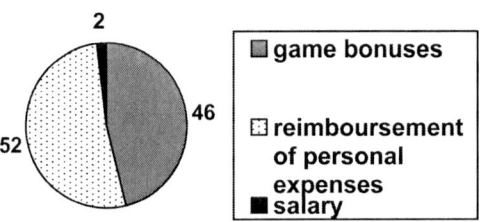

Figure 4.   Responses to Q.4 – What sort of compensation did you receive?

team managers. The presence of a press agent was found in only 2% of the cases (Figures 5 and 6)

Qs 7, 8 and 9. As is the case in the world of men's soccer, women's clubs are all financed by sponsors, but this situation, which appears similar on the surface, is actually quite different. Men's soccer teams have many different sponsors. On the contrary, women's teams, in most cases, have no more than ten, and the sponsors are cafés, restaurants, shops and local businesses that decide to do some 'profitable charity' by sponsoring women's teams (Figures 7, 8 and 9).
Q. 10. We can observe that almost no women's teams, even in the A League, sponsor commercial products (Figure 10).

Qs 11, 12 and 13. In any case, the female soccer players appear to be interested in sports-sponsored products, and generally there is not a lack of interest in media coverage of the world of sports (Figures 11, 12 and 13).

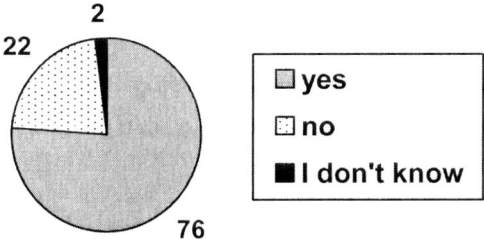

Figure 5.   Responses to Q5 – Does your team have a website?

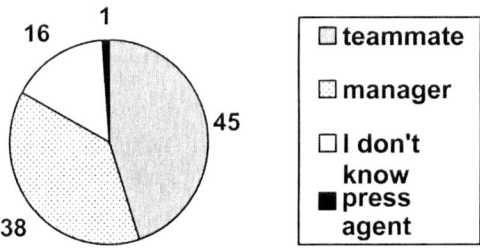

Figure 6.   Responses to Q.6 – Who manages your team's website?

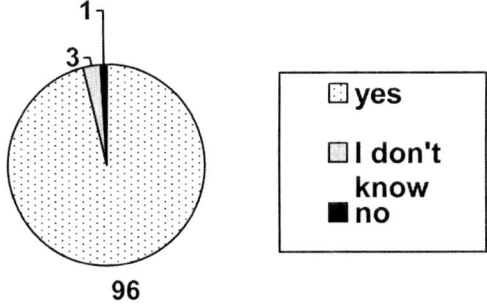

Figure 7.   Responses to Q.7 – Does your team have sponsors?

Qs 14 and 15. Only a quarter of all the female players have been guests on national television sports programmes, appearing just once in their entire careers on such programmes. This shows how very little space the media dedicate to the world of women's soccer (Figures 14 and 15).

Qs 16 to 19. Further analysis of the questionnaire shows that over half of the women consistently follow sports news both in national newspapers and on national television and some even on pay-per-view TV. Nevertheless, most of the respondents believed that the print media and television do not dedicate enough space to the world of women's soccer. On the contrary, they often dedicate no space whatsoever (Figures 16, 17, 18 and 19).

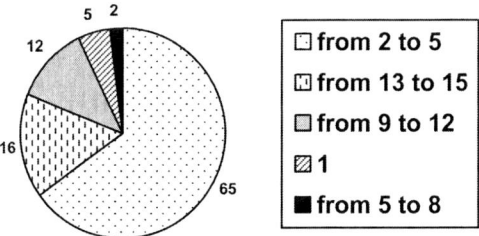

Figure 8.   Responses to Q.8 – How many sponsors does your team have?

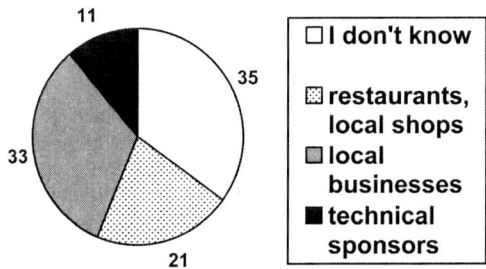

Figure 9.   Responses to Q.9 – Who are the sponsors?

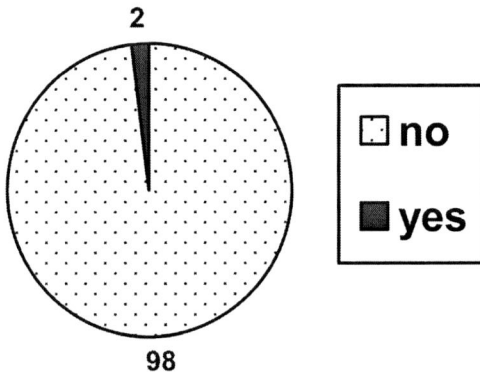

Figure 10.   Responses to Q.10 – Does your team sponsor a commercial product?

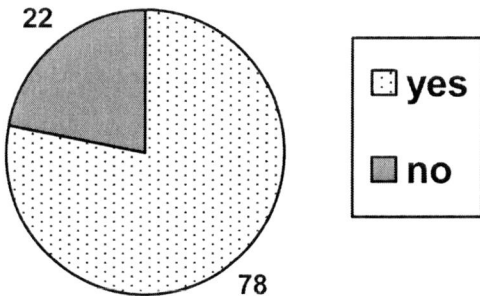

Figure 11.   Responses to Q.11 – Do you watch television sports programmes?

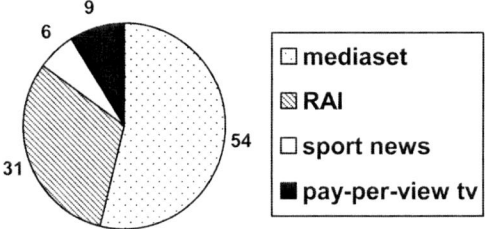

Figure 12.   Responses to Q.12 – Which ones?

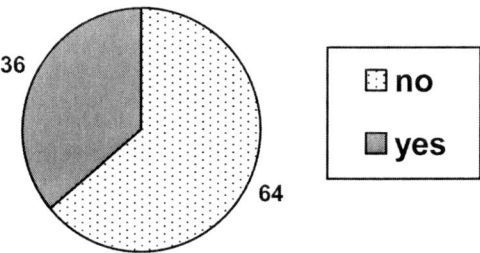

Figure 13.   Responses to Q.13 – Are you a pay-per-view TV subscriber?

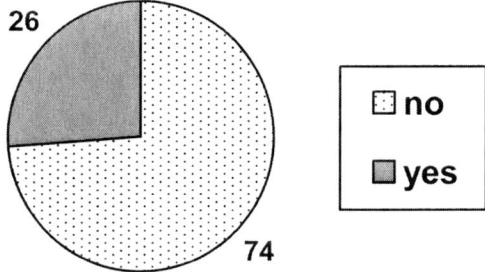

Figure 14.   Responses to Q.14 – Have you ever been a guest on a national sports television programme?

Given the results of the questionnaire, one aspect that warrants further investigation is the reason why respondents play soccer. As can be seen in the first figures, only a very small percentage of respondents earn a salary as professional players. All the other female players are often not even reimbursed for travelling expenses, and sometimes the only compensation they receive is a symbolic game bonus for league victories (Figures 3 and 4). Even those who play in the A League certainly cannot afford a house in the centre of the cities where they play, nor can they afford a luxury car to drive to practice or any of the other things that male soccer stars display on television or in the newspapers.

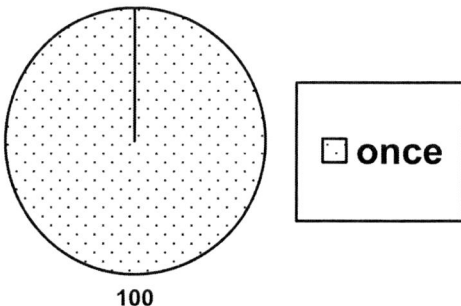

Figure 15. Responses to Q.15 – How many times have you been a guest on a national TV programme?

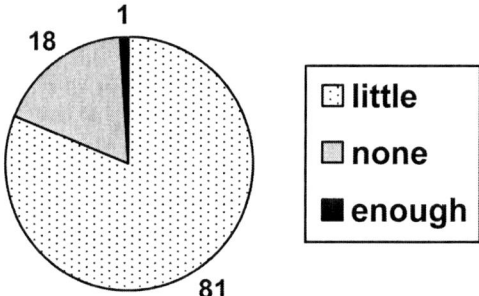

Figure 16. Responses to Q.16 – How much space does national television dedicate to women's soccer?

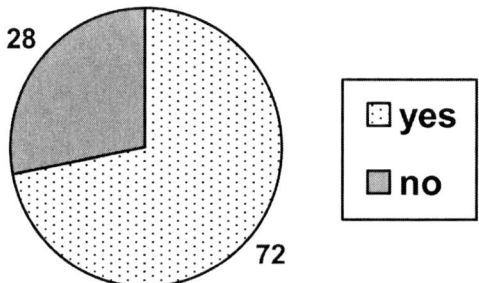

Figure 17. Responses to Q.17 – Do you read national daily sports newspapers?

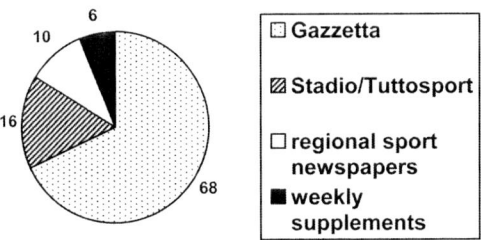

Figure 18. Responses to Q.18 – Which daily papers do you read?

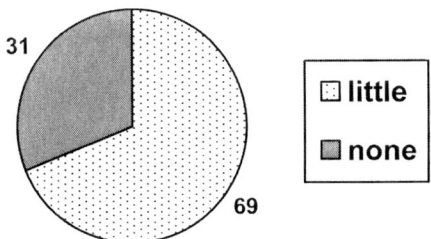

Figure 19. Responses to Q.19 – How much space do the daily papers dedicate to women's soccer?

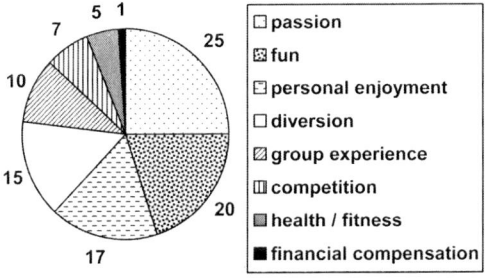

Figure 20. Responses to Q.20 – What motivates you to play soccer?

So what motivates the thousands of young women who play soccer? At the top of the list we find passion for the sport and the enjoyment they get out of playing. Many of them have been repeatedly discouraged from playing the game by parents, relatives and friends for different reasons, but above all, because women's soccer is not comparable to the men's game. Many women play for simple personal pleasure and use the sport as a diversion to get a break from the repetition of everyday life. As one might expect, the percentage of those who play soccer only for financial compensation is very low.

Qs 20 to 24. Finally, we can observe that the goals that female players strive for in the game are not the same as those of their male counterparts. They do not play the game for a living or for fame and fortune; they just play for fun, to spend time together with their teammates and for pure personal satisfaction (Figures 20, 21, 22, 23 and 24).

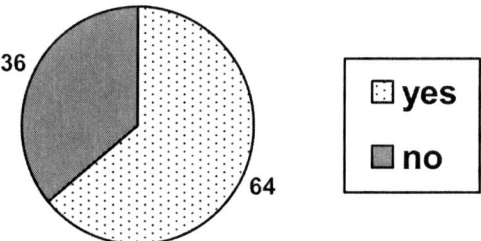

Figure 21. Responses to Q.21 – Have you ever been discouraged from playing the game?

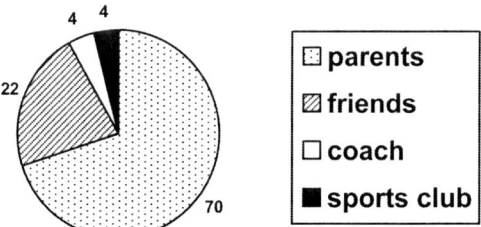

Figure 22. Responses to Q.22 – By whom have you been discouraged?

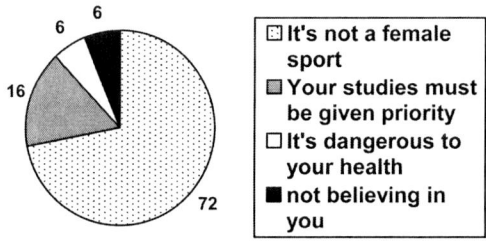

Figure 23. Q.23 – For what reasons?

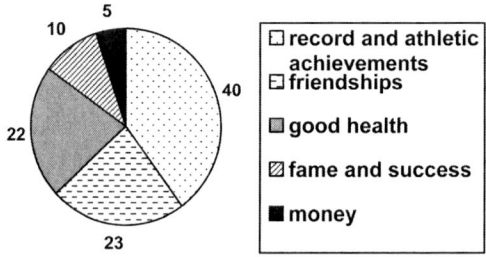

Figure 24. Responses to Q.24 – What goals would you like to reach in women's soccer?

Conclusions. What is the Future of Women's Soccer?

In line with what emerged from the questionnaire, an analysis of television programming schedules or the contents of the print media reveals little interest in women's soccer. For example, last summer, when the under-19 national women's team won the European Championship, the national daily paper par excellence, the *Gazzetta dello Sport*, only dedicated a short article to the story that took up less than half of a page. Every week the same paper dedicates no more than 20 lines to the results and standings in the Women's A League. The day after Bardolino played in the Champions League quarter-finals, the *Gazzetta's* coverage of the event did not include a single photo of a Bardolino player and only carried a photo of Bontegodi stadium in Verona (well-known because Verona's professional men's team plays there). The website of the same paper dedicates just one page to women's soccer, reporting scores and A League standings.

Television is certainly no less parsimonious than the print media in its coverage of the sport. In the numerous television sports programmes broadcast every day on the RAI state television channels and the private Mediaset channels, women's soccer is completely ignored, with neither of the networks even bothering to report scores or standings on Monday after Sunday's games. It is rare to see people from the world of women's soccer on the numerous programmes dedicated to in-depth coverage of the sport. Such programmes do not even carry short reports on women's games. The only way to see some women's games is to subscribe to SKY pay TV, which occasionally shows some the national team's games, as well as World Cup and European Cup matches.

Regarding the Internet, it should be mentioned that the Women's Soccer Division (*Divisione Calcio Femminile*) set up a website completely dedicated to the sport just two years ago. The site is rather simple, and limits itself to reporting essential news, or rather final scores and standings for the national A, A2 and B leagues and any interruptions in league play. There is no information on trades or player sales, no gossip surrounding female players, no news of coach firings or new acquisitions for the upcoming season.

In conclusion, gender differences accompanied by prejudice and stereotypes rooted in our culture, which are still very much alive and require time and effort before they to begin to fade from society's consciousness, are reflected in the media. Indeed, just as we can say that there is a gender-biased society, we can also say that there is a gender-biased media. Nevertheless, in postmodern culture, the Internet and new media represent and opportunity for the democratisation of society guaranteeing free flexible access, and paving the way for possible changes and the recognition of different cultures.[16] The web can be the ideal tool for circulating ideas, changing behaviours and smoothing the rough edges that block a dialogue among cultures, and for the promotion and recognition of and respect for diversity, including gender diversity.[17]

Notes on Contributor

Ivana Matteucci is professor of the sociology of sport in the Faculty of Motor Sciences, and director of the Laboratory for the Scientific Communication on Health and Wellness at the University of Urbino, Italy. She has published on the communication of sport, with a focus on gender and cultural stereotypes.

Notes

1. Bourdieu, *La Distinction*, 229. In his analysis of differential systems in our societies, Bourdieu claims that a 'field' is a space of preferences characterised by specific expressive modalities, particular stylistic codes and a precise lifestyle.
2. In the modern era, sport channels the need of the working class for leisure activities. Cf. Lo Verde, *Sociologia del tempo libero*, 45–51.
3. Bourdieu, *La distinction*, 267ff.
4. According to Frederic Jameson, spectacularisation, i.e. the new culture of the image and the simulacrum, with a weakening of historicity and the depth of reality, is the most critical result of postmodern culture; see Jameson, *Postmodernism*. Guy Debord, at the dawn of the advent of television, had understood that society would transform itself into images, and he describes the spectacular spread of consumerism in *La société du Spectacle*.
5. See Martelli, *Lo Sport mediato*, 35–90.
6. On the fundamental aspects of modern sport see Guttman, *From Ritual to Record*. On the playful nature of sport see Huizinga, *Homo Ludens*.
7. Sugden and Tomlinson, *Power Games*.
8. Mangan, *Making European Masculinities*.
9. As the French sociologist Pierre Bourdieu wrote, gender cannot be reduced to a volunteer act since it is grounded in both material facts – bearing, manner, size etc. – and symbols – classifications and categories – which tell us about the subject: Bourdieu, *La domination masculine*.
10. Murphy, 'Sport and Gender', 272.
11. Schinabargar, 'Sexism and Sport'. According to the author, the ideology of distinct roles for the two sexes creates a certain social gender structure on the basis of which unequal opportunities and compensation for women who practice sport are legitimised. Cf. 46.
12. Bonizzoni, *Il calcio femminile*, 78–94.
13. Evelina Codacci Pisanelli was the first female president of the women's division of *Federcalcio* between 1991 and 1992. Natalina Cervaso Levati was a member of the UEFA Commission for Women's Soccer from 1998 to 2006. As the first president elected by the clubs, she was confirmed for two terms: 2001–4 and 2004–8. Marina Sbardella was the head team manager of the national women's soccer team and member of the FIFA Commission for women's soccer.
14. For additional information on the history of Italian women's soccer, see Leali and Risaliti, *Il calcio al femminile*. Also see Caroli, *La donna nel pallone*, 46–79.
15. The source for the table is the study by ISTAT (Italian state entity that compiles statistics), *Aspetti della vita quotidiana*.
16. Formenti, *Cyberspazio*, 23–54. In this work Formenti, an expert on problems connected to the advent of new forms of media, deals with the social, political and ideological aspects of cyberspace, which is developing more and more into a public space. It is public because it is the place where people meet and compare views, the perfect forum to express ideas, interests, opinions and beliefs.
17. The debate over opportunities for the democratisation of society offered by the new media is raging more than ever. Not everyone has the same view regarding such opportunities, and there are those who denounce the advent of new inequalities in web access. We find ourselves before an old conflict of the 'apocalyptics' and 'integrated' which caused so much debate among intellectual media scholars in the 1960s: Eco, *Apocalittici e Integrati*. Today, we have Chomsky, *Necessary Illusions*.

References

Bonizzoni, C. *Il calcio femminile*. Rome: Società Stampa Sportiva 1988.

Bourdieu, P. *La distinction*. Paris: Les édition de minuit, 1979.

Bourdieu, P. *La domination masculine*. Paris: Édition du Seuil, 1998.

Caroli, A. *La donna nel pallone* [*Women in Soccer*]. Turin: Graphot, 2000.

Chomsky, N. *Necessary Illusions. Thought Control in Democratic Societies*. Cambridge, MA: South End Press 1989.

Debord, J. *La société du Spectacle*, Paris: Gallimard 1992.

Dunning, E. Sport As a Male Preserve: Notes on the Social Sources of Masculine Identity and Its Transformations, *Theory, Culture and Society*. 3: 1(1986): 79–90.

Eco, U. *Apocalittici e Integrati*, Milan: Bompiani 1964.

Formenti, C. *Cyberspazio. Utopie postdemocratiche e nuovi media*, Milan: Cortina 2008.

Guttman, A. *From Ritual to Record. The Nature of Modern Sports.* New York: Columbia University Press, 1978.

Huizinga, J. *Homo Ludens.* Turin: Einaudi, 1972.

ISTAT. *Aspetti della vita quotidiana.* Rome: ISTAT, 2006.

Jameson, F. *Postmodernism, or the Cultural Logic of Late Capitalism.* 1/146, July–August 1984, London: New Left Review, 1984.

Leali, G. and M. Risaliti. *Il calcio al femminile.* Rome: Società Stampa Sportiva, 1996.

Lo Verde, F.M. *Sociologia del tempo libero.* Bari: Laterza, 2009.

Mangan, J.A., ed. *Making European Masculinities. Sport, Europe and Gender.* London: Frank Cass, 2000.

Martelli, S., ed. *Lo Sport mediato. Le audience televisive di Olimpiadi, Paraolimpiadi e campionati europei di calcio (2000–2008).* Milan: Angeli, 2009.

Matteucci, I., 'The Gendered World of Sport: an Analysis of the Influences on Italian Society and Communication', in *Sport and Gender Matters in Western Countries: Old Borders and New Challenges*, ed. G. Gori. Sankt Augustin: Academia, 2008.

Murphy, P. 'Sport and Gender', in *A Sociological Perspective of Sport*, ed. W. Marcellus Leonard. London: Macmillan, 1988.

Schinabargar, N. 'Sexism and Sport. A Feminist Critique'. *Concilium* 5, no. 205 (1989): 44–53.

Sugden, J. and A. Tomlinson, eds. *Power Games. A Critical Sociology of Sport.* London: Routledge, 2002.

Epilogue: Heritage, Progression, Regression and Advance!

J.A. Mangan

Formerly Strathclyde University, Glasgow, United Kingdom, Now Retired

The gender ocean still has hidden depths[1]

Heritage

The distinguished Professor Roberta Park recently recalled:

> In 1984 J.A. Mangan, then the first Chair of the British Society of Sports History which he co-founded, invited me to contribute to the BSSH Second Annual Conference. My topic was 'Sport Gender and Society in a Transatlantic Victorian Perspective' ... after the conference [he] suggested that we co-edit *From 'Fair Sex' to Feminism: Sport and the Socialisation of Women in the Industrial and Pre-Industrial Eras.*[2]

It was published by the visionary Frank Cass in 1987 with a striking cover which includes a detail from the exquisite painting by Sir John Lavery; eye-catching covers were a Cass hallmark!

'Fair Sex' to Feminism by common agreement blazed a trail! There followed further Cass/Mangan publications on the relationship between female emancipation and modern sport with equally compelling covers including *Freeing the Female Body: Inspirational Icons:*[3] another stunning cover, a reproduction of Picasso's dramatic and symbolic *The Race.* Then came the publication *Soccer, Women and Sexual Liberation: Kicking off a New Era.*[4] The blazed trail became a broader path. And recently there appeared *Sport, Women and Society: Further Reflections – Reaffirming Mary Wollstonecraft,*[5] and the biannual *IJHS* issue commissioned in 2010[6] on *Women, Sport, Society*; and now, arising out of the *IJHS* Conference Workshop[7] at the University of Urbino impressively organised by Professor Gigliola Gori there is *Sport and the Emancipation of European Women: The Struggle for Self-fulfilment.* The path has become broader. *Sport and the Emancipation of European Women* walks in step along the path with Professor Gori's own publication, *Sport and Gender Matters in Western Countries: Old Borders and New Challenges.*[8]

These seminal publications, a seriated corpus, explore the contributions and achievements of women in a variety of historical and geographical contexts and seek to broaden understanding 'about the background, motivations and achievements of dedicated women ... in a variety of different areas and for different purposes'.[9] Furthermore, all represent women who are the direct outcome of, to quote the magisterial Roy Porter, 'the Enlightenment's secular value system ... which upholds the unity of mankind and basic personal freedoms and the world of tolerance, knowledge, education and opportunity'.[10] In pursuit of these laudable aims with right on their side and passion in their prose, these feminists have rightly challenged convention.

Progression

These studies represent 'a continuous contextualised commentary' on modern women and their striving for self-realisation through the powerful medium of modern sport, a modern global obsession and thus a vehicle for self-publicity, gender celebrity, national adulation and individual assertion. *Sport and the Emancipation of European Women* records the pulling down of barriers to the realisation of ability and release of talent clearing out of the way crushing inhibitions, inexcusable irrationality, intolerable prejudice and denial of opportunity to European women. No barriers came down without struggle.

'*Plus ça change*' ... is a neat aphorism but in the instance of European women and modern sport, it is inaccurate. Much has changed – if not everything– and mostly for the better. Reservations will be aired later. The break away from 'cloying custom' clearly evidenced in *Sport and the Emancipation of European Women* may be summarised as follows:

> The 'incompatibility with reason and reality' of the Victorian ideal of 'True Womanhood', by the twentieth century, produced by way of reaction the idea of the New Woman. It was a product of biological, psychological, sociological, educational and economic confrontation. An elite of middle class women resisted theories of disability, disposition and destiny. Physical activity was the centre of subsequent conflict, compromise, controversy and change. This situation was assured by the biological basis ascribed to social constructs of femininity.[11]

This is well recorded in *Sport and the Emancipation of European Women*. Nevertheless, throughout Europe, progress towards emancipation via modern sport as in other aspects of life, was *uneven*:

> Assimilation within prevailing gender definitions rather than accommodation to new concepts was the reality, and women's social inequality continued to be reinforced by theories and practices in sport implying inferiority well into this century. And there is a further point of significance. It was not all a process of successful change and assertion albeit cautiously circumscribed. Change came from pressure applied and itself applied pressure. In a sometimes bewilderingly transformed world some middle-class women responded positively and some negatively. On the one hand there was the stability of asserted physical release, on the other there was the lethargy of drug and alcohol dependency. Care must be taken to describe reality rather then to -establish [sanguine] stereotypes.[12]

Even in the middle class, the mover of change, there remained paradox, inconsistency and confusion throughout the early years of confrontation with custom, as the contributors to *Sport and the Emancipation of European Women* make abundantly clear. Cultural 'taxes' remained levied on female freedom. Be that as it may, involvement of upper- and middle-class women in the sport of the new industrialised, urbanised European culture was part of the general movement for female emancipation; in time a centrifugal force that threw off anachronism. By the end of the nineteenth century, in the cause of equality, progress had been achieved;

more was eventually achieved. Ratiocination up to a point had triumphed. To quote one comment referring to England but with wider applicability:

> While the circumstances of the Victorian period differed markedly from those at present, then, as now, … in counteracting the stereotype of female frailty, sportswomen reflected feminist hopes of diminishing the significance of (social) sex differences, providing women with every opportunity to develop all their powers, and enabling them to gain control over their own lives and bodies.[13]

Hope led to partial realisation.

Among the middle-class women of late Victorian and Edwardian England there was *no* uniformity of adoption of feminist's beliefs. The philosopher's stone was not transformed into pure gold. The 'sonority 'was not all supportive. Historical colour not monochrome is required. If nuance is to be pursued this must be recognised.

> Paradox conjoined with marked changes in society (economic, technological, scientific and demographic), and with philosophical shifts in human aspirations towards self-fulfilment, mobility and independence 'spawned a women's movement that raised questions about women's abilities and constricted place in society and sought a partial redefinition of sex roles', and stimulated the admission of women into spheres previously dominated by men. With the result … that 'one of the most vivid images of female emancipation at the turn of the century – one that recurred there in the illustrated journals and lodged itself in the popular mind was that of the New Woman engaging in sport'.[14]

It was much the same in the rest of Western Europe. Nonetheless, in England, to press home the point,

> The emerging model of the 'New Woman' … co-existed with the traditional image of the 'True Woman', yet seldom harmoniously and frequently contentiously. The reactionary Arabella Kenealy, for example, in a splendid surge of romantic retrospection condemned games-playing schoolgirls, calling their newly acquired musculature 'stigmata of abnormal sex-transformation' and labelled their enthusiasm as 'the cult of Mannishness'. The source of this condemnation was a widespread medical suspicion of education for women which hinged on the principle of 'the conservation of energy' – the body contained only a limited and fixed amount of energy. Its expenditure in one part denied another. At puberty, so the argument went, a girl's energy should be reserved for the development of the reproductive organs – the essence of her womanhood. Cerebral effort at this time would produce nervousness, feebleness and even sterility. And worse, she should bear sickly and neurotic children capable only of producing degenerate versions of themselves. In short, racial soundness was not consistent with advanced female schooling: brain and ovary could not develop simultaneously.[15]

Promulgated by canonical physicians, this theory held sway for years. And no wonder: the powerful force of medical orthodoxy was behind it. Its 'logicality' was dense with illogicality. No matter, it controlled both vertical and horizontal lines of authority. Paradoxically, however, there was hope for radicals. Medical opinion was on the side of mild exercise as a prophylactic against academic strain.[16] Matters in Western Europe as a whole were little different. The European forces of controlling convention ironically had chinks in their armour. They were effectively wounded by their ambiguity: some exercise but how much exercise? Liberal educationalists, as recorded in *Sport and the Emancipation of European Women*, took on medical orthodoxy and its cautious control and its arrogant conceits – and eventually largely won! They wove a strong thread that led the way out of the blocked pathways of the gender maze.

The struggle for freedom, however, is, as noted elsewhere, 'fraught with ambiguity' and perhaps there is too little ambiguity at times in *Sport and the Emancipation of European Women*. The reason is straightforward: a preoccupation with liberalisation. From the late nineteenth century onwards, of course, there was feminist forward momentum – and this is recorded carefully, interestingly and informatively. It was, however, not *all* forward momentum. This was especially true for working-class women then and arguably today. The thrust for the emancipation of the female body in Europe was by the middle class and largely benefited the middle class. To a degree is this still true today? No better illustration of unequal access to, and participation in, sport is to be found than in modern Britain: the disparities in access to facilities, the availability of coaching, the encouragement to participate in contemporary class – polarised education activities – symbolised by the extensive provision of playing fields in private schools – is increasingly class-defined. What of the rest of Europe? What past legacies associated with wealth impact on girls' sport for better as well as for worse? And what contemporary options in the form of popular culture, peer pressure and commercial sexualisation dictate alternative forms of recreation, life-styles and personal preoccupations? Is it the case that the new millennium is witnessing the pursuit of post-feminist hedonism rather than health resulting in regression rather than progression? *Sport and the Emancipation of European Women*, while covering some ground well, barely covers other ground at all as the past slips into present. Struggle is never over; conflict re-creates itself in each generation. Mutation is its forte. Reform can end in exhaustion, boredom and complacency; it can be considered itself a restriction. Are new images of 'free' femininity shouldering aside the old; is sport passé – and sex, drugs and alcohol the new freedoms? Is there a new cultural equation: liberty equals licence? More on this later.

To shift the focus and peer into the past. Are there gaps in historical evidence and analysis unfilled by academics? It could be argued with justification that attention on women emancipation and sport has wandered some distance from working-class women, repression, inhibition and release. Analysis that skirts this issue is incomplete. It was observed in *Fair Sex to Feminism* over two decades ago that emphasis had been invariably on the middle and upper class. The *cri de coeur* continued: 'Little or no attention has been directed to the pastimes of working class women ... little has been done as yet to present a comprehensive picture which cuts across class lines.'[17]

Has there been much change in Europe as a whole? Nigel Jones in *The Sunday Telegraph* recently commented on the approach of Juliet Nicholson in her *The Great Silence 1918–1920: Living in the Shadows of the Great War*. He remarked that ordinary people appear 'as props' connected to the upper classes by service.[18] To what extent is this true for studies of women, sport and emancipation with regard to working-class women? Is class failure to achieve reform due to circumstance insufficiently interesting? Have the complexities – successes *and* failures of emancipatory effort – been adequately considered?

A further point of substance: there should always be an awareness of the

complexity of the relationships between modern sport, female emancipation and power. One danger in any discussion of this triadic relationship is to fall prey to the weaknesses of a rigid dichotomous approach involving, for example, women as victims and men as oppressors. Clearly simplistic and too pervasive stereotyping of this kind is to be avoided in the interests of reality. Another danger is the tendency for men to recede into the background and become '*monolithic* supporting players' in women-centred studies. The dangers of such simplification are obvious: naïve male stereotyping, reduction of complex realities and inter-relationships and the failure, calculated or careless, to fully assess women's actual power, covert and overt, in male and female relationships whatever the *ostensible* formal, institutional, cultural and political frameworks.[19]

Yet a further point of substance: 'There is the risk that in attempting to understand ... cultural rules, insufficient attention has been given to the material constraints which determined the lives of the vast majority of people, both women *and* men. In recorded history most of both sexes have been oppressed.'[20] How far does the oppression of one sex impinge on the oppression of the other?

These cautious caveats apply throughout Europe as elsewhere. Furthermore, 'women, like men, have never comprised a single monolithic and homogeneous group. Thus women should always be compared, not only with men, but with other women.'[21] There was dissent, disagreement and disassociation within the 'sisterhood'; a point made earlier and made again here to ensure its notice. Has this been adequately considered? History is a totality or it is nothing. More on this below.

> *Freeing the Female Body* [revealed] that, whilst its women were often very different in their individual lives, circumstance and experiences, interestingly they mostly appear to have had certain things in common. These iconic inspirationalists were mostly middle class and mostly possessed the invaluable asset of *strong family support* [emphasis added]. In a real sense often their family – parent or parents and on occasion siblings – made them.[22]

There is scope here for further and deeper inquiry into sport, women and emancipation.

Are there further lacunae to be penetrated and filled in? To return to an earlier point to ensure it has required emphasis, how much of the confrontation *between* women over emancipatory demands for involvement in modern sport has been recorded? To ensure a comprehensive history of the thrust for female emancipation in modern sport, it would be valuable to have studies of conservative women with reservations about the outcome and need for emancipation. Does their conservatism have merit, or at least, some merit? It has been observed interestingly of Victorian conservatism, female education and activists that those

> who were publicly or privately critical of the suffrage involvement, and of the more insidious challenges to conventional gender roles ... have been neglected or sometimes misrepresented as bizarre and paradoxical: rather than being portrayed as polar opposites, feminism and anti-feminism need to be understood as *connected* [emphasis added] across an extended spectrum of areas.[23]

This comment applies with equal force to all European studies of women and modern sport.

Regression

Caveat:

> We are all spectators of the, sometimes attractive and sometimes unattractive, 'ceaseless gavotte of continuity and change'. There is always an abacus of human gain and loss, a calculation of the negative and positive. The proselytizer's understandable inclination is to suck on an empirical comfort blanket of bright colours. It is a constant temptation.[24]

However, to ensure analytical thoroughness, calculations of gain *and* loss should be made. In 'Retrospectus' the matter was raised of the rejection of sport by many modern young women. The arguments may be summed up as follows:

> Many social movements carry within themselves the seeds of their own destruction: it is as well also to be aware of the fact that freedom is not an inexorable linear progression. At the present time when young women drink alcohol increasingly free from social inhibition or restriction – a fact that is causing medical concern due to the associated rise in female alcoholism – the comment of the French diarist Henri Misson on women in London in the eighteenth century to the effect that they held their own with men in drinking bouts is both interesting, illuminating and topical. Pop-alcohol versus putting the shot is no contest![25]

And again,

> [S]ome consider that one subject begging for fuller enquiry is the sexualisation of the young female in western cultures, urged through a plethora of modern media means to be sensually 'hot' rather than physically fit, a point Natasha Walker, in her recent *Living Dolls*, which ponders the conundrum that at a time when feminism ought to be home and dry girls just want to look like tarts, makes with both force and fear. Despairing observers lament that too many girls want to look and act like binge-inclined, plastically enhanced Jordans, rather than self-disciplined, gold-achieving Amy Thompsons.[26]

And yet again,

> For some like the well-named Cassandra Jardine, borrowing a savage expression of Martin Amis, has argued that sometimes we seem to be worshipping 'two bags of silicone'. She too is of the view that Natasha Walker's 'backward progress' from *The New Feminism to Living Dolls* reveals optimism replaced by pessimism and she is at one with Dorica Shields who cannot comprehend why so many young women wish to emulate surgically enhanced celebrities and why they should want to look like Jordan rather than yearn for the dignity of Meryl Streep and why young girls should make others miserable by endlessly criticising each other for failing to match up to plasticised shapes and air-brushed images in magazines and on screen. It all seems a long way for many from the hoped for feminist prelapsarian Eden. For them the pressing issue is one of demeaning sexual exhibitionism born out of a preoccupation not with health but with a louche self-indulgent preoccupation with appearance which blocks the path to healthy dignity and pleasure through sport. For them obliquity appears to be the debased fashion. Are such critics misguided in their concern?[27]

Is this an evolving mutant of emancipation beyond freedom to enjoy sport with a by-product: 'The concealed pockets of the psyche contain undesirable and unlooked for change, one being the freedom of the woman-object to strip, to sell the object commodity at any price however, demeaning.'[28] Are we entering the new post emancipatory world beyond sport: a post-feminism pornographic projection period? More than a few women appear to think so. Is there a looming social incubus: the sexualisation of the very young with future repercussions including the increasing rejection of sport? This possibility has occasioned despairing comment in recent times both in British tabloids and broadsheets following up on various research studies. Is there a comparable anxiety elsewhere in Europe? Is there evidence of 'moving on' from an interest in sports performance to a greater interest in sexual projection? Is this something that proponents of equal sport for women should be concerned about? Has preoccupation with sexuality elbowed performance in sport off the 'track' and could there be deleterious consequences for modern young women? The Duchess of Cornwall has recently stated in the popular British *Daily Mail*: 'The link between young girls, eating disorders and osteoporosis is a ticking time-bomb.'[29] Clearly discerning a youthful preoccupation with sexual not sporting images, she advised the young: 'You can eat sensibly, *exercise* [emphasis added] and stay trim. You do not have to starve yourself and risk damaging your health irrevocably.'[30] Concern with the sexualised attitudes of young women are illustrated in Natasha Walter's *Living Dolls: The Return of Sexism*. In *The Big Fat Bitch Book for Girls*, Eva Figes 'dissected the destructive effects of the pursuit of stereotyped perfection [too often airbrushed] on young women'.[31] A recent post-feminist issue in Britain that drew heavy fire was the commercial exploitation of 'Lolita Looks' symbolised by padded bras for seven-year-olds available from shopping-mall stores. This provoked a report by a government alarmed by the sexualisation of young children. The television presenter Fiona Bruce got in on the act. She declared that the sexualisation of young girls is her 'biggest concern resulting *inter alia* in the "pornification" of society'.[32] The British tabloid *The Sun*, in April 2010, trumpeted a 'Sun Exclusive: PAEDO Bikini Primark [clothing store] selling padded bras for 7-yr-olds'![33] Is this sexualisation an overlooked dimension of personal female freedom and to what extent does it have an adverse impact on participation in sport? Is the phenomenon a justifiable cause for concern among those who have promoted the cause of girls and women's full participation in sport?

Advance

Future inquiries building on *Sport and the Emancipation of European Women* and similar studies as evidence and argument accrue over time will acquire increasing nuance:

> Studies going beyond a concern with the challenge modern women have rightly issued to past cultural traditions of the female body as essentially reproductive ... need now to be supplemented by a sophisticated Berlinesque pluralism dealing with cultural differences and similarities and involving inquiry into challenge – but also accommodation, adoption and compliance and embracing cultural, class and racial 'specificities', both historical and contemporary. Perhaps even more to the point, studies concerned with the *political* role of the female body, past and present, are called for. One obvious need, for example, is a long-overdue exploration of Chinese women, their physical exertions, courage and stamina in the famous Communist Long March and the impact on their subsequent image and later political resonances for the Peoples' Republic of China[34]

Recall Mao's reminder on achieving power: 'Women hold up half the sky'!

The point is made again without apology and with an eye to future enriched enquiries, that to build in something of the extraordinary complexities of human relations, societies and cultures is needed:

> If a political, cultural and psychological pluralism born of democracy and its inherent respect for the individual and individuality gains ground in at least some new places, and indeed some old places, in the twenty-first century, so a feminist, sometimes exaggerated, frequently negative and simplistically dichotomous preoccupation with men and women and associated concepts of patriarchy, exploitation, victimization and oppression associated with the female body (and mind and emotions) will be, and should be, augmented by more complete and sophisticated studies of the female body (and mind and emotions) in society and more realistic inquiries as to the nature of women's power and powerlessness, *through and beyond* [emphasis added] their bodies. The crucial point to be made is that nuanced inquiries into such power are most certainly overdue, and should include a conjunction with studies of women, their bodies and modern sport. In short, there should be in the future, fuller attempts to listen to a

proliferation of voices [and] take account of a plurality of perspectives and thus to ask 'new kinds of questions and seek different kinds of answers'.[35]

A question concerning the concrete world of reality as distinct from the arcane world of polemics: is it now time that this reality attracted more attention in feminist studies being crucial to a complete consideration of power in communities – in sport and beyond sport?

Is there merit in reflecting on the remarks of Joan Shilling that polemical generalisation always needs to be challenged in the interests of accuracy. She faced up the need: '[U]npalatable as it is to admit, for every frustrated female bitterly serving out her domestic sentence there are plenty of others: intelligent, thoughtful women, as well-qualified as their go-getting husbands, who have found an unambiguous satisfaction in the confining roles of housekeeper and nursery maid.'[36] She added an unrelated but interesting rider: '[P]assivity is not to be confused with *powerlessness* [emphasis added] ... the weapons of the martyr and victim are just as potent in their way as those of more visible transgressors.'[37] Is it reasonable to explore illustrations of women's power – constructive and destructive in sport, to ensure more complete studies of power in sport and in society. The bottom line is that reality often eschews simplification and shies away from generalities – and polemics. If this is done, the exploratory pathway of those seeking understanding of the relationship between women, society and modern sport is inexorably widened and lengthened – and that is all to the good.

And beyond studies in power? There is emphatically a need for more *fully contextual* biographies of European women whose convictions, efforts and determination influenced change – for the better. These creators of change should be set convincingly in political, economic, cultural and social circumstances. There is a similar need for more studies of men who advanced the emancipation of women in and through sport. And with regard to biographies, it is interesting to ponder on the observations of Patricia Ranft in her *Women in Intellectual Culture 600–1500* that women 'rarely approached intellectual matters with the same manner as men did'.[38] If this is true of women, more biographies by women of women in modern sport could add a richness of insight to be welcomed.

Nothing that has been set out immediately above in the interests of the integrity of scholarship denies past and present powerless, abuse and victimisation of women in the evolution of modern sport – the evidence is overwhelming:

'Women's advance in modern sport has been too frequently characterized by condescension and confrontation, denial and defiance, proscription and persistence, and too often, by necessary forced entry and grudging accommodation.' And the fullest praise should be showered on those who have 'demonstrated and to a degree determined through their determination ... that, despite historical belief, assertion and demand, women are not to be 'relegated' primarily or predominantly to reproduction, nor to subscription to the uterine tradition that defines women's bodies according to their reproductive potential'.[39]

Nevertheless, is there an obligation on scholars to seek, record and analyse the full story of the struggle for female fulfilment through modern sport? Thus a final reflection from the past with reference to the invaluable *Sport and the Emancipation of European Women*:

This set of essays repairs omissions but only to a limited extent. Certainly it deals with sport as a source of social tension, as a means of both sexual antagonism and conciliation, as an illustration of both continuity and change in social life. Furthermore it demonstrates ... that the history of sport is as much political as it is social. Power is frequently a central issue. But, of course, the work remains exploratory, tentative and incomplete. The topic is too large and the subject matter still too neglected to permit even an attempt at comprehensiveness. A great deal remains to be done. There is much still to learn about the relationship of women, sport, recreation and leisure not merely to political, social and cultural ideologies but to urban development, evolving work patterns, changing educational opportunities, public health improvements and social class fashions. ... The status of women, relationships between the sexes, attitudes to child-bearing, are mirrored in the recreational, leisure and sporting opportunities available to women in society, past and present.[40]

Therefore, with regard to *Sport and the Emancipation of European Women* qualified congratulations are in order. Inquiry into women's struggle for self-fulfilment by means of modern sport – in Europe and elsewhere, remains *work in progress*.

Coda

Obligation: every effort should always be made to ensure that knowledge triumphs over ignorance. And there is reason to be optimistic when the heritage of quintet of studies of sport and the emancipation of women associated with *IJHS* and *Sport in the Global Society* are piled high on the scholar's desk. They answer another obligation: 'Ability should always be encouraged and talent should be assisted – in both women and men in sport and beyond sport. In short: "All of us do not have equal talent, but all of us should have the equal opportunity to develop our talents."'[41]

Notes on Contributor

J.A. Mangan, Emeritus Professor, University of Strathclyde, Fellow of the Royal Historical Society and Fellow of the Royal Anthropological Institute, and Doctor of Letters (Dunelm), is the author of the internationally acclaimed *Athleticism in the Victorian and Edwardian Public School* (1981) and *The Games Ethic and Imperialism* (1986). He founded *The International Journal of the History of Sport* and several other journals and the series *Sport in the Global Society*. He has published many books, lectured all over the world and held Visiting Fellowships (or their equivalents) in America (Berkeley), England (Oxford and Cambridge), South Africa and Australasia. His latest publication 'Manufactured' Masculinity' has attracted exceptional praise in America, Asia, Australasia and Europe.

Notes

1. Unpublished doctoral programme lectures delivered at my research centre, Sport, Socialisation and Society, University of Strathclyde, in the 1990s.
2. Formal Tribute to J.A. Mangan – a statement for the celebratory conference at Jesus College, Cambridge, 13 and 14 Sept. 2011, 'Manufacturing Masculinity: the Mangan Oeuvre – Present into Future: Global Reflections', 1. And see Mangan and Park, *From 'Fair Sex' to Feminism*.
3. See Mangan and Fan Hong, *Freeing the Female Body*.
4. See Fan Hong and Mangan, *Soccer, Women, Sexual Liberation*.
5. Park and Vertinsky, *Sport, Women and Society*.
6. 'Women, Sport Society', *IJHS* biannual issue commissioned in 2010 by J.A. Mangan, then executive academic editor. This issue was edited by Susan S. Bandy, Dong Jinxia and Gigliola Gori.

7. The *IJHS* Conference Workshop held at the University of Urbino, Italy in 2010 entitled 'Sport and the Emancipation of European Women: The Struggle for Self-fulfilment', commissioned by the then executive academic editor of *IJHS*, J.A. Mangan, and part of the global network of *IJHS* conference workshops he initiated in 2008.
8. Gori, *Sport and Gender Matters*.
9. J.A. Mangan, Series Editor's Foreword, in Mangan and Fan Hong, *Freeing the Female Body*, 3, in the series *Sport in the Global Society*, created by J.A. Mangan in 1997.
10. Porter, *Enlightenment: Britain and the Creation of the Modern World* quoted in the Series Editor's Foreword; Mangan and Fan, *Freeing the Female Body: Inspirational Icons*, ix.
11. Mangan, 'The Social Construction of Victorian Femininity'.
12. Ibid.
13. Ibid., 7.
14. Ibid., 4.
15. Ibid.
16. Ibid.
17. 'Introduction', in Mangan and Park, *From 'Fair Sex' to Feminism*, 3.
18. Paul Jones in a review of Juliet Nicolson's T*he Great Silence 1918–1920*, in *The Sunday Telegraph*, 11 Sept. 2011, 29.
19. J.A. Mangan, 'Epilogue Retrospectus', in Park and Vertinsky, *Women, Sport, Society*, 196.
20. J.A. Mangan, 'Epilogue: Prospects for the New Millennium: Women, Emancipation and The Body', in Mangan and Fan Hong, *Freeing the Female Body*, 239.
21. Ibid., 238.
22. Mangan and Fan Hong, *Freeing the Female Body*.
23. Mangan, 'Epilogue Retrospectus', 195.
24. Ibid., 197.
25. Ibid.
26. Ibid.
27. Ibid., 198.
28. Ibid.
29. See the Duchess of Cornwall quoted in the *Daily Mail*, 27 Oct. 2011, front page and 26–7.
30. Ibid.
31. See Mangan, 'Epilogue Retrospectus', 195, for a brief but fuller discussion of Walter, Figes and others with similar views.
32. Laura Roberts, 'Young GIrls are Being Sexualised, says Fiona Bruce', *Daily Telegraph*, 16 March 2010, 16.
33. Jane Hamilton, 'Paedo-Bikini', *The Sun*, 14 April 2010, front page.
34. Mangan, 'Epilogue: Prospects for the New Year Millennium', 246.
35. Ibid., 246–47.
36. Quoted in Mangan, 'Prospects for the New Year Millennium', 242.
37. Ibid.
38. Karras, Review of Ranft, *Women in Western Intellectual Culture*.
39. J.A. Mangan, 'Prologue: Managing Monsters', in Fan Hong and Mangan, *Soccer, Women, Sexual Liberation*, 1.
40. Mangan, 'Epilogue: Prospects for the New Year Millennium', 237.
41. 'Introduction', in Mangan and Park, *From 'Fair Sex' to Feminism*, 8–9.

References

Fan Hong and J.A. Mangan, eds. *Soccer, Women, Sexual Liberation*. London: Frank Cass, 2006.

Figes, E. *The Big Fat Bitch Book for Girls*. London: Virago, 2009.

Gori, G. *Sport and Gender Matters in Western Countries: Old Borders and New Challenges*. Sankt Augustin: Academia, 2008.

Karras, Ruth Mazo. Review of *Women in Western Intellectual Culture 600–1500*, by Patricia Ranft. *History of Education* 34, no. 2 (March 2005): 207.

Mangan, J.A. 'The Social Construction of Victorian Femininity: Emancipation, Education and Exercise'. *The International Journal of the History of Sport* 6, no. 1 (May 1989).

Mangan, J.A. 'Prospects for the New Year Millennium: Women, Emancipation and the Body'. In *Freeing the Female Body: Inspirational Icons*. London: Frank Cass, 2001.

Mangan, J.A. and Fan Hong, eds. *Freeing the Female Body: Inspirational Icons*. London: Frank Cass, 2001.

Mangan, J.A. and Roberta J. Park, eds. *From 'Fair Sex' to Feminism*. London: Frank Cass, 1987.

Nicolson, Juliet. *The Great Silence 1918–1920: Living in the Shadow of the Great War*. London: John Murray, 2009.

Park, Roberta J. and Patricia Vertinsky, eds. *Sport, Women and Society: Further Reflections – Reaffirming Mary Wollstonecraft*. Conference in Celebration of J.A Mangan, Jesus College, Cambridge, September 2011. London: Routledge, 2011.

Porter, Roy. *Enlightenment: Britain and the Creation of the Modern World*. London: Allen Lane, 2001.

Ranft, Patricia. *Women in Intellectual Culture 600–1500*. London: Palgrave MacMillan, 2004.

Walter, Natasha. *Living Dolls: The Return of Sexism*. London: Virago, 2010.

'Women, Sport, Society'. Special issue of *The International Journal of the History of Sport*, biannual issue commissioned by J.A. Mangan when Executive Academic Editor, forthcoming.

Index

press see media
private and public sphere, separation between 100, 111
Proctor, Jo 77
professions, access by women to 139
progression 1, 11–14, 19, 21, 50, 125–7, 173–7
promotion of sport 140–1
prostitution 12
pseudo-science 38, 40
psycho-aesthetics 26, 37
public health and hygiene 10–14, 16, 59
publications 172–3 see also media
publicity 162, 173 see also media

quality 86, 88, 90, 121, 143, 145, 152
Qiu, Jin 1

race 14, 102–4
Ranft, Patricia 179
ratiocination 174
rational gymnastics 37
Ratjen, Dora 76
Récamier, Joseph 77–8
Reder, Hiltrud Anna Maria 123–9
Reder, Karsten 124–6
regression 176–8
Reichel, Franz 87
religion 7, 58–9, 61–2, 64–7, 142
repression 8, 109, 139, 175
reproduction 14, 22, 47, 73, 105, 142, 174, 179
resemblance feminism 26, 37, 39
resistance and opposition: fencing 85–96; Italian scouting movement 58, 59–60, 62, 66–7; Italian women's soccer 158, 160, 168; modern pentathlon in Germany 116–25; Olympics 70–4; Portugal 141–5; ski jumping 47–8, 51–3
respectability 17–18, 20, 105–8, 110–12
revolutionary socialism 14
Rieden, Herbert 126
Rocchi, Valeria 155
Roch, René 93–5
Rogge, Jacques 94
Rome Olympics 1960 74, 90
Rossi, Mary 57
rugby 143
Ruggi, Agostino 61, 63–4
Russia 11–12, 14, 19, 22, 95, 106–7

Sagen, Anette 53
Salle, Murielle 78
Saltin, B 28
Sars, Eva 45–6
Sbardella, Marina 157
Schantz, P 29
Schäper, Ute 92

Schiffmann, Ute 127–8
Schlik, Franz 49
Schmitz, Imke 124
Schneider, Max 46
'scientific' female gymnastics, creation of 26–40: Denmark 26–40; gender division 27, 31–6, 39; gender movement, new modes of 32–6; gender-specific exercises 31–2; homosexuality 30–2, 35, 39; Ling gymnastics 27, 29, 31, 33–4, 36, 38–40; masculinity 27–30, 39; pedagogy 26–40; perfect women 26–8; theory of gymnastics 27–40
Scott, Joan W 101–2
scouting see Italian scouting movement
Secher, Knud 39
'Second Wave' of feminism 1–2, 116
Second World War 1, 90, 118
Seligman, Edgar 87
self-control 18, 21, 34, 39, 102
self-fulfilment 2, 4–7, 52, 174, 180
self-perception 6, 28
self-promotion 6, 7, 62, 173
Semenya, Caster 75–6, 79–80
semiotics 2
Seoul Olympics 1988 93
separation of men and women 7, 8, 27, 31–6, 39, 74, 95, 104, 119, 128
sex and sexuality: 'free love' 14; homosexuality 7, 30–2, 35, 39, 74–5, 80, 104, 154–5; hygiene 14; morality 20; sexual satisfaction from sport 21–2; sexualisation 8, 109, 175, 177–8 see also sexual categorisation process, history of
sexual categorisation process, history of 75–81: anatomic examinations 77–8; appearance-prescription logic 80; Barr corpuscle test 78–9; bi-categorisation 70, 77–80; cheating 78–9; chromosomal test 78; femininity testing 7, 70, 77–9; gender verification test 75–6, 79; hermaphrodites, exclusion of 75–8, 80; intersexuality 78, 80; marathon 74, 76–7; medical certificates 77–8; morality 20, 77, 80; Olympics 75–81; sex testing 79; social construction of gender 78, 80; terminology 79; transsexualism 78–80
Shields, Dorica 177
Shilling, Joan 179
Simonsen, Julie 86
skating 19–22, 46, 48, 74
Skeggs, Beverly 105
ski-flying 53
ski jumping 45–53: class 51–2; competitive sports 45–51; dress 48, 50–1; early years 45–6; equality 6, 53; media 50; medical arguments 47, 51, 52–3; morality 45–6, 47, 51–3; 'New Woman', ski jumpers as 50–2;

Norwegian women 46–7, 49–52; number of participants 46, 48, 51; resistance and opposition 47–8, 51–3; trousers, wearing 51
skirts 18, 48, 87, 89, 144
Smith-Rosenberg, Carroll 2
soccer *see* football
social acceptability 95–6
social capital 151
social class see class
social construction 78, 80, 102
social conventions 4, 39
social instability 138
social necessity and facts 110
Söderqvist, Thomas 28, 40
Soundarajan, Santhi 76, 79–80
South Korea 93
Spain 31, 93
spectacularisation of sport 151–2
sponsors 125, 155, 160, 163–4
'Sporting the Nation' 101–3, 110
Stabenow, Gerhard 118
stand-at-ease position 37
standing to attention 33–5
Stang, Hilda 46
Stanton, Elizabeth Cady 1
Stephen, JF 22
Stephens, Helen 76
stereotyping: femininity 104, 110; fencing 85; homosexuality 154–5; Italian women's soccer 8, 169; media 129; modern pentathlon in Germany 129; Portugal 141–2, 144–5; sexualisation 178
Stockholm Olympics 1912 19, 71, 117, 119
Stratmann, Axel 125–6
Sweden 7, 100–12: class 100–1, 105, 107, 110–12; Cold War 100–1, 105–7, 112; Communist countries, women from 7, 105–7, 110, 112; culture 7, 100–5, 107, 109–12; dress 108; feminine Swedish girls and muscular Communist women 105–7; femininity 104–12; heterofemininity 106–7, 112; hobby, sport as a 108–9, 111; Ling gymnastics 27, 29, 31, 33–4, 36, 38–40; magazines 101–11; masculinisation 109, 111; masculinity and sport 102–4, 111–12; media 7, 100–12; medical arguments 105; national identity 102–3, 110; Olympics 7, 100–12; 'people's home' (folkhemmet) 100–1, 111–12; poster girl of the Olympics, idea of 107–8, 111; 'Sporting the Nation' 101–3, 110; women first, females second 7, 108–9
Switzer, Kathy 74, 76–8
Switzerland 89, 92–3, 118–20
Sydney Olympics 2000 74, 117, 129–30
symbolism 7, 28, 31, 71–2, 90, 101, 105, 111

symptomatic reading 27, 29, 35
synchronised swimming, gendering of 74, 154

taste 28, 35, 40, 151
televisation of sport 152
Terret, Thierry 7
Tervo, Mervi 105
Thofelt, Sven 119, 122
Thomsen, Else 39
thoracograph 34
Tokyo Olympics 1964 103
Tolvhed, Helena 7
touching and class 35–6
Trabucco, Giovanni 156
traditional attitudes 59–67, 104, 124, 141–2
Trangbæk, E 28
transsexualism 78–80
trivialising women's sport 108–9, 111
trousers 18, 51, 89, 90

United Kingdom 85–8, 90–1, 121, 124–5, 173–5
United States 46–7, 92–3, 105, 116, 154–5, 157

Van, Lindsay 53
Van Rossen, George 87–8
venereal disease 12
Vertinsky, Patricia 5–6
Vestby, Ingrid Olsdatter 46
Victorian period 173–4
Vigarello, Georges 71
violence 28, 96
virilism process 80
vital energy theory (VET) 47
Vogler, Walter 53
von der Lippe, Gerd 5, 46
vote, right to 1, 11, 51, 62

walking 20, 34–6, 86
Walter, Natasha 177–8
Western femininity, construction of 107–9
Wiehn, Suzanne 127–8
Wien, Gerhard 127
Wold, Anita 50
Wollstonecraft, Mary 1
'women first, females second' 7, 108–9
women's movements 1, 5, 11, 50–1, 116–17, 119, 128, 139, 174 *see also* feminism

Yuval-Davies, Nira 101

Žižek, Slavoj 27

Women, Sport, Society
Further Reflections, Reaffirming Mary Wollstonecraft

Edited by Roberta Park and Patricia Vertinsky

This book seeks to broaden our understandings about the backgrounds, motivations and achievements of dedicated women who have historically contributed to physical education, dance and sport in ways that go far beyond being teachers, athletes and coaches.

It was published as a special issue of the *International Journal of the History of Sport*.

Roberta J. Park is based at the Department of Integrative Biology, University of California, Berkeley, USA.

Patricia Vertinsky is based at the University of British Columbia, Canada.

December 2010: 246 x 174: 224pp
Hb: 978-0-415-59738-8
£85 / $135

Related titles from Routledge

Olympic Aspirations
Realised and Unrealised
Edited by J. A. Mangan and Mark Dyreson

Olympic Aspirations is a companion volume to the well-received *Olympic Legacies: Intended and Unintended* and draws on expertise from academics in all parts of the world. Both volumes have a similar purpose: to record Olympic ideals achieved but more importantly, to stimulate reflection on those as yet unachieved. Both are constructive in approach, positive in tone and optimistic in attitude. *Olympic Aspirations* offers original and insightful arguments that address the actions the Olympic Movement has taken to improve the Games. It argues that these actions are as yet incomplete. In concert with *Olympic Legacies*, it presents two sides of the same coin minted to advance the purity of the Olympic 'coinage'.

This book was originally published as a special issue of the *International Journal of the History of Sport.*

J.A. Mangan is Emeritus Professor, University of Strathclyde, UK, FRHS, FRAI, D. Litt.(Durham) and Founding Editor of the *International Journal of the History of Sport* and the book series *Sport in the Global Society*.

Mark Dyreson is Professor of Kinesiology and History at the Pennsylvania State University, USA, and is a former president of the North American Society for Sport History.

May 2012: 246 x 174: 432pp
Hb: 978-0-415-52586-2
£95 / $160